ULTIMATE MIND
CONTROL

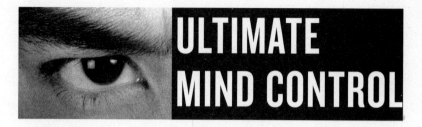

ULTIMATE MIND CONTROL

ASIAN ARTS of Mental Domination

DR. HAHA LUNG

with Christopher B. Prowant

CITADEL PRESS
Kensington Publishing Corp.
www.kensingtonbooks.com

CITADEL PRESS BOOKS are published by

Kensington Publishing Corp.
119 West 40th Street
New York, NY 10018

All Kensington titles, imprints, and distributed lines are available at special quantity discounts for bulk purchases for sales promotions, premiums, fund-raising, educational, or institutional use. Special book excerpts or customized printings can also be created to fit specific needs. For details, write or phone the office of the Kensington special sales manager: Kensington Publishing Corp., 119 West 40th Street, New York, NY 10018, attn: Special Sales Department; phone 1-800-221-2647.

First printing: March 2011

10 9 8 7 6 5 4 3

Printed in the United States of America

Library of Congress Control Number: 2010931895

ISBN-13: 978-0-8065-3201-1
ISBN-10: 0-8065-3201-7

To Robert D. Baughman, for his invaluable help and friendship

DISCLAIMER

"The information contained herein is meant to be used for *informational* and *educational* purposes only." . . . They made us say that. Of course, if you diligently study the "informational" part of this presentation you will be in a much better position to give your enemies a little "educational" comeuppance the next time they dare raise their hand against you or your loved ones!

Oh, and they also made us say "Don't try this at home." . . . (Instead try these techniques at work with your A-hole boss, and the next time you're trapped at the DMV with that *bee-atch* who you know is deliberately "slow-walking" you, and the next time you need to outsmart some would-be car-jackin', pants saggin', "economically underprivileged" street punk who can quote you the stats, birthday, and the jock-strap size of every player on his favorite B-ball team but who can't seem to sit still long enough to get his GED!

We heartily *disclaim* all such people!

CONTENTS

"What Is Ultimate Control— and How Can I Get Me Some of That?"

The problem of power is really the fundamental problem of our time and will remain the basic problem of all future history.
—*Power and Human Destiny* by Herbert Rosinski, 1965

"ULTIMATE CONTROL" is all about power and, in today's namby-pamby politically correct world "power" is not only a scary word (it's always been a scary word to some people) but power has also become a taboo word—if only because someone else is usually holding it over our heads, swinging it around like a bludgeon.

Why can't we be the ones exercising "power" for a change?

But in this day and age to even let on like we'd like to have a little more power in our lives is to put ourselves into competition with others—perhaps those others more *ruthless* than we know how to be? "Others" definitely more *dangerous*.

Best instead to just keep a "low profile," not stir up too much dust, not challenge the status quo—lest "they" (those with *real* power—perhaps "Ultimate Power") come for us in the middle of the night or, worse yet, freeze our bank accounts!

Nietzsche taught that each of us has within us "The Will to Power," an innate urge carved into our DNA that drives us towards our full potential as human beings, making us "push against our walls." Of course, "society" does its best to breed—and when necessary *beat*—this innate urge out of us.

Thus, if Nietzsche is to be believed, and that vague sense of dissatisfaction and longing you feel in the back of your mind (or perhaps in your gut) is to be listened to:

1. You have "power" you don't know you have, power to effect positive change in yourself and those around you. (And maybe even those assholes in Washington!)
2. Even if you suspect (or accept) that you do indeed have hidden reserves of untapped potential and power at your beck and call . . . you're probably *too afraid* to exercise that power. Am I right?

What would the world be like today if Moses, Caesar, Napoleon, Einstein, or General George S. Patton had refused to acknowledge the power pumping through their veins?

And, yes, before we go down that road, the world might have been better off had Attila the Hun, Hitler and Osama bin Laden NOT one day realized the innate—Nature given and God approved!—power surging through *their* veins.

But then, had there been no Hitler, there may have been no General George S. Patton. Had there been no Osama bin Laden there may have not been the heroes of 9/11, and the brave souls even today holding the line against chaos.

The power within you is a lot like the power to vote—use it or lose it. Because, sure as shootin', if you don't exercise your power to vote, somebody else will. Likewise, you might not be "interested" in gaining "power" but, rest assured (or, rather, rest uneasy—*very* uneasy!) there are many out there *actively* seeking power—power over you, power over your loved ones. Ultimate Power.

It therefore behooves us to develop and learn to fully use the power we possess within, ideally to protect ourselves and better safeguard those we love from others ruthlessly wielding power for their own dark desires, their own sick and twisted designs.

Commanding "Ultimate Control" over your life, with the power to influence all those around you, is kinda like owning a gun. Just because you own a gun it doesn't mean you're gonna go all "Dirty Harry" postal one day. But, Heaven help you when the wolves (both the four-legged and the two-legged kind!) are barking at your door and all you have is a baseball bat to beat back those beasts.

Or perhaps you prefer a more "civilized" example? Think of acquiring "Ultimate Control" as being like getting your college degree. If you have a college degree, it opens doors. Whether you choose to go through those open doors is up to you. It's always nice to have options . . .

And *survival* is always the nicest option to have!

So how do you go about gaining "Ultimate Power"?

You study those in days gone by who successfully—and, yes, often ruthlessly!—gained power, first over self then over others. You study their lives, and you listen to their words: Hannibal the Conqueror, Machiavelli the Advisor, Sun Tzu the strategist, Stalin the Merciless—Masters East and West, some honorable, some not—all successful!

Napoleon rightly observed "There are two powers in the world, the sword and the mind. In the long run the sword is always beaten by the mind."

If we accept this as so, it certainly evens out the playing field. Whereas, because of being born in the wrong place at the wrong time, possibly in the wrong skin color and *sans* a penis, we find that we cannot exercise "the sword" (i.e. blatant, perhaps bullying power), then we are left to move ahead through life by our wile and wit, our cunning and craft—our mind.

The good news is, if you accept Napoleon's assessment[1] the meek might not survive long enough to inherit the Earth but, in the end, the *mind* is going to beat out the *sword*.

"Ultimate Control" comes from first gaining control of yourself. Control of self not only gives you the focus needed but also inspires others to follow your lead.

Ultimate Control is simply "The Three Knows"—Know yourself, Know your enemy, Know your environment—taken to the next level:

> Knowing Yourself *gives you* Control over self.
> Knowing Your Enemy *grants you* Control over others.

---

1. And what did he ever do? Like how about conquering and ruling only a fair-sized hunk of the world, dude!

Knowing Your Environment *paves the way for* Control over:
1. Your surroundings and situation[2]
2. Current trends (aka Circumstance and Flux)

Ultimately, "Ultimate Control" is all about who has the power . . . and who's not afraid to use it.

Ultimate power = Ultimate Control, and Ultimate Control consists of your possessing or being (and not being afraid to exercise):

1. Overwhelming, unquestioned influence. This depends on the source of your power—whether true power of pretend power.[3]
2. Who has the power, who's in control when the smoke clears—the last man standing, usually determined by who's willing to (ruthlessly?) use the power available to them.

Within this work, you will not only learn how to awaken and wield the power latent within you—power that will give you "Ultimate Control" over any situation; you will also glean from the past masters of Ultimate Control—both those bright and those bloody, those who walked in the light as well as those who were all too adept at ruthlessly snuffing out the light:

- How they rose to power, gaining Ultimate Control.
- How they held on to power, maintaining and commanding Ultimate Control.

And most importantly,

- How they fell from power (so you don't make the same mistake).

What's that you say, you're not a "competitor," not interested in "personal power," let alone wanting or—God forbid!—ever wielding "Ultimate Power"?

On the one hand, assuming you're a "lone wolf," that's an "oh-so-

---

2. The extent to which you "know" (i.e., influence) your surroundings varies from person to person, measured by the degree of personal influence we exercise. For example, a king will exercise more influence over a greater field of endeavor than a peasant. It's good to be King!

3. See "The Five Types of Power" in Section I (p. 28).

noble," even humble attitude for you to have. On the other hand, if you're a family man (or woman)—or if there just happens to be another single person in this universe you give the least damn about!—then saying all high-and-mighty, "I'm not interested in power" just shows how selfish and *uncaring* you truly are.

If nothing else, we study these things so as to better protect *our loved ones.*

In any given situation, career, or crisis, ask yourself, "Who's got the power?"

If your answer isn't a resounding *"Me! I've got the power to do something, to make a difference!"* then someone else holds power—perhaps "Ultimate Power"—over you . . . and over your loved ones.

Maybe it's time you got a little of that "Ultimate Control" for yourself after all?

I.
Gaining
Ultimate
Control

There are two powers in the world, the sword and the mind. In the long run the sword is always beaten by the mind.
—Napoleon

BEFORE WE CAN even begin to consider being able to influence others, let alone exercise total, ultimate control over the thoughts and actions of others, we must first gain some semblance of control over ourselves—both physically and mentally. This will then, in turn, prepare us for then exerting our influence and ultimate control over others. In Asia, they often say that "the journey of a thousand miles begins with but a single step." Well, in the task at hand, our journey towards Ultimate Control—first over self, then over others—begins with *six* steps.

I.

The Six Steps to Ultimate Control

THE FIRST THREE STEPS are more concerned with *appreciation,* as they involve realistically assessing yourself and your surroundings: knowing ourselves, knowing our enemy (challenges in general, people in particular), and knowing our environment, i.e. recognizing a once-in-a-lifetime genuine opportunity, or else recognizing that the worm has turned and it's time to hightail it outta Dodge!

The remaining three steps to ultimate control involve hands-on *application*, putting what you've learned about yourself, your enemy, and your environment to practical—and profitable!—use.

THE THREE KNOWS

These are *"Know yourself," "Know your enemy,"* and *"Know your environment."* Lacking insufficient intelligence (both the innate kind you're born with and the espionage-gathered variety you take pains to diligently acquire) on any of these three "knows" limits our options in (1) responding to life effectively, (2) avoiding death indefinitely and, when the time does finally come, (3) shuffling off this mortal coil with *all* your marbles!

THE THREE KNOWS

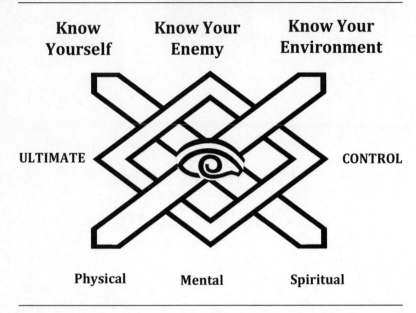

Figure 1.

Know Yourself

Knowing your strengths and weaknesses, knowing—and accepting—your limitations.

"Knowing yourself" first and foremost means *testing yourself*—constantly and consistently.

Life is nothing without challenge. Challenge is how Mother Nature separates the wheat from the chaff, the quick from the dead. Nietzsche constantly entreated us to "push against your walls." Likewise, in his "Ninety-nine Truths," Hannibal the Conqueror tells us: "Test yourself with fire and ice, sand and sea, bile and blood, before your enemies do."[4]

Thus, martial-arts students practice throwing solid kicks high to an opponent's head, not because they actually intend to throw such high kicks

---

4. Truth LXXIII. See all of Hannibal's "Ninety-Nine Truths" in Section III: *Commanding Ultimate Control* (p. 215).

during actual combat but, rather, because they realize if they can successfully throw a kick to the level of an opponent's head *everything below the head
belongs to them.*

"Knowing yourself" also involves realizing how you consciously (and
subconsciously) relate to others.

According to the ancient Chinese philosophy *pakua* (pronounced "ba-
kwa") there are "Nine Roles" we assume when dealing with others:

1. Father (i.e., authority figure)
2. Son
3. Husband
4. Wife
5. Older Sibling
6. Younger Sibling
7. Master (aka Mentor/Teacher)
8. Disciple (sometimes called "Servant")
9. Friend

With the exception of a true "friend-to-friend" relationship (a balanced
relationship), in any of these pairings we play either a dominant or a sub-
missive role.

Whenever you consciously or subconsciously assume one of these roles,
the person you are interacting with also consciously or subconsciously
assumes a corresponding role, a role either complimenting or opposing in
nature. This in turn creates what the Chinese call "The Five Relationships":

- Father to son
- Husband to wife
- Older sibling to younger
- Master to disciple
- Friend to friend

For example, in an interaction where one person has clear authority
over you (your boss for instance), you can assume the role of either the
authority figure "father" or the respectful and obedient "son." This basic interpersonal dynamic can be further broken down into sub-roles and sub-scripts,
e.g., obedient son versus obstinate son, a benevolent father versus a totalitarian one.

But just because you acknowledge another's authority, doesn't mean you don't control the interaction.

Say for example you find yourself in a confrontation where someone is questioning something you did. You can consciously assume the "role" of the Father, instantly turning the tables on the questioner by forcing them into a "father-to-son" scenario where, when a "disrespectful" son *dares* question his father's actions, the stern father immediately "asserts his authority" (trumping the upstart with his obvious age and wisdom), turning the table on the son. Instead of having to explain himself to "a child" he instead puts the son "in his place" (i.e., on the defensive) by changing the subject to something the son has done wrong.

Whereas the other person may have *consciously* come into the confrontation with the intention of asserting his or her authority (i.e. attempting to play the "father" role), your boldly seizing the higher ground (by first and firmly taking on the "father-authority" role) forces them, often without their realizing it (that's right, *subconsciously!*) into the subservient role of "son."

Master manipulators learn to recognize these roles in others and become adept at adopting these roles when necessary, always taking on the roles that will allow them to best control and manipulate the situation. Thus, manipulators do not always assume the "dominant" (e.g., father) role in an interaction. For example, for the out-gunned guerilla, there are times to pretend fear and play a subservient role in order to get his enemy (authority) to drop his guard, and/or in order to draw that enemy into an ambush.

Master manipulators deliberately choose words and symbols that allow them (and their agent-propagandists) to use both the Nine Roles and Five Relationships—all trusted *archetype* figures to our *subconscious*, no matter how suspicious our *conscious* mind remains. This explains the use and appeal of such titles as "Holy Father," calls to fight and die for the "Fatherland" or the "Motherland," and why your "*Uncle Sam wants you*"!

The more we understand about the use of such symbolic and surrogate relationships, and just how easily such relationships—real and symbolic—can be used to manipulate us, whether by Madison Avenue or a Charlie Manson, the better for our overall self-defense, both physical and mental. The first step to accomplishing this is "knowing ourselves" well enough to (1) accept that everyone—including us—are susceptible to these symbolic and surrogate relationships and (2) admitting (to ourselves) which of these interactions holds special meaning to us because of what these roles represent to our subconscious.

Psych 101: If we have a problem with "authority" it may stem from unresolved conflict we have (from childhood) with our father. A wily enemy, realizing this before we do ourselves, can then use such psychological "wounds," re-opening them at the worst time (for us), bleeding us even more.

Know Your Enemy

Penetrate inwards into men's leading principles, and thou will see what judges thou art afraid of, and what kind of judges they are themselves.
—**Marcus Aurelius**

"Political correctness" and "Judge not lest ye be judged" aside, the truth is we still judge people by first impressions. Before we even give them a chance to open their mouth we've already made several conclusions—true or false—about them based on:

- **Their height:** Tall or short? Studies have shown that women do prefer taller men. Men are just as guilty, just as shallow, judging taller women as more intelligent, assertive, and ambitious. Conversely, men see shorter women as more nurturing and considerate.[5]
- **Their age:** Everybody knows old people are senile, or at the very least stubborn and stuck in their ways. Young people on the other hand are brain-dead and irresponsible. And the rest of us, stuck somewhere in the middle, are probably already knee-deep in a "mid-life crisis."
- **Their hair color:** Blondes are dumb[6] and redheads are quick to anger.
- **Their size and shape:** Everyone "knows" fat people lack self-control, are lazy, and have more health problems. "Muscle-bound" men are all stuck on themselves and secretly insecure. And what was it Randy Newman said about "short people"?

---

5. *Psychology Today* Sept./Oct. 2005:32.
6. If you didn't know this, odds are *you're* a blonde!

- **Their race and apparent ethnicity:** "Those people" are all drunks. "Those other people" are all lazy . . . but for some reason, they make crackerjack gardeners and maids? Will "*that*" kind of person get along with my other workers? Aren't "*those people*" all terrorists? I heard "*his kind*" has trouble taking orders from women.
- **How they're dressed:** Isn't her dress cut kinda low? Aren't his pants a little too tight? What's that funny religious hat he's wearing? Nerds all wear glasses and pocket protectors.
- **How they stand or sit:** "Good girls" don't sit like *that*! Look how he puts his hands on his hips . . .

We often respond to another's body language without our being consciously aware of it. Body language 101: They're standing or sitting by themselves: Must be anti-social. Laughing in the middle of a crowd: Do they need to be the center of attention or are they just suckin' up? He's leaning against the wall: Drunk, or just lazy? Arms and legs crossed: He's closed off—he must not like my idea or offer?

- **The company they keep:** Beer buddies or the martini crowd? Your friends are a reflection of you, or at least of what you're willing to put up with. Hanging around the office cooler with your coworkers shooting the breeze or huddled down in your cubicle shooting the boss a snitch-memo ratting out all your coworkers who are hanging around the water-cooler shooting the breeze?

Are we ever wrong in our "first impressions"? Sure. But we're also *right* often enough to keep us doing this. Stop feeling all "politically correct" guilty about giving strangers the once-over. There's a reason "stranger" rhymes with "danger." This *instinctive* defense mechanism has its roots in a xenophobic survival instinct inherited from our more ape-like ancestors: Turning the corner and running smack dab into another caveman hunter, our ancestor needed to instantly "size-up" the other fellow as friend or foe just in case that other hunter had a hankerin' for dinosaur burger . . . but was willing to settle for the other white meat—*you*! Your being able to "read" him ASAP often spelled the difference between your starving little cave-kids left wondering why Og-daddy was late for dinner . . . while that other hunter and his cave-mates were having you for dinner!

Yeah, this is kinda like sizing up that stranger walking towards you at night in that deserted parking garage. For safety's sake, always keep in mind that that whole "evolution" thing didn't take with everybody. Quite a few Neanderthals seem to have made the cut!

So, beyond just our ability to accurately access "first impressions," what else do we need to know about our enemy (be they a romantic rival, a corporate raider, or simply the "other guy" come for the same job interview you have)? What are some of the other things we can look for?

We can look at how he deals with the world in general, either an extrovert facing life head on, or else an introvert retreating from life. Then we can delve into his needs and wants—often two very different things. Finally we can try to discern his agenda, the "ends" he expects out of life and the extent he's willing to go to achieve them.

First, is he an introvert or an extrovert?

Extroverts work the crowd, gossiping with coworkers, moving from clique to clique at a party.

They talk a lot. And when they talk, they put their whole body into the conversation—leaning in close to people, touching others. They use their hands to enliven their many tales of adventure.

And they get bored quickly, moving on to their next conquest or performance.

Extroverts fall into the "doer-feeler" category. They often act on their emotions (for example, initial enthusiasm for a project) without thinking things completely through—"We'll cross that bridge when we come to it!"

Extroverts *need* to keep moving. They need to be doing something at all times. If your ally is an extrovert—keep him busy.

If your enemy is an extrovert—keep him busy too, but keep him busy chasing after shadows. Or, you can frustrate him by making him spin his wheels, stifling his forward momentum.

Introverts, on the other hand, are quieter. They're in the "thinker-planner" category. They listen more. They watch—and see—everything.

They like to hold a drink or something in their hand (masking their nervousness). And, besides, they don't need their hands free to tell stories like the extrovert. Introverts don't tell stories—they relate facts, they recite statistics, they crunch the numbers.

Introverts speak more slowly, because they think about their answers before answering.

Because they take longer to answer, introverts are often *misjudged* as being less of a threat. Actually, some introverts can actually be *more* of a threat since—as listeners—they "hear" and "see" things an extrovert might miss.

Also, while all eyes are on the extrovert's antics (literally and figuratively), the introvert can be working diligently—behind the scenes, under radar—accomplishing quite a lot. Example: While the extrovert is busy entertaining the crowd, including his and the introvert's boss, the introvert is standing next to the boss. The boss is laughing *at* the extrovert. But he's laughing *with* the introvert; *sharing* a pleasurable experience with the boss. It's called "bonding."

When the introvert is your ally or worker, use this unassuming personality to accomplish projects and negotiations "behind the scene" where a more flamboyant extrovert might draw undue or untimely attention.

If your enemy is an introvert *don't underestimate* him. Still waters run deep.

Pull the enemy introvert out of his shell by forcing him into the limelight, where he'll sputter and stumble.

Second, what does he need and what does he want? (aka "What would Maslow do?")

Buddha taught that wanting things we don't need is the beginning of all suffering. Yet all of us have things we need in order to survive.

Psychologist Abraham Maslow (1908–1970) is famous for summing up a basic list of human needs and priorities in what has become known simply as "Maslow's Pyramid."

At the most basic level all of us have physical needs (food, sleep, sex) and safety needs (protection, freedom from fear, a need for familiar and reassuring structure in our lives).

Once these basic physical and safety needs are satisfied, we turn our attention to the second tier of the pyramid, needs for love and a sense of belonging.

Self-esteem needs (a need to feel vital and valued) and self-actualization needs (the need to explore one's full potential) top off Maslow's Pyramid.

Where a person focuses on this pyramid of needs determines their priorities. Determining a person's priorities then enables the mind-slayer to either encourage that person's negative priorities, or stifle his positive priorities. Finding out what an enemy needs, and more importantly, what he

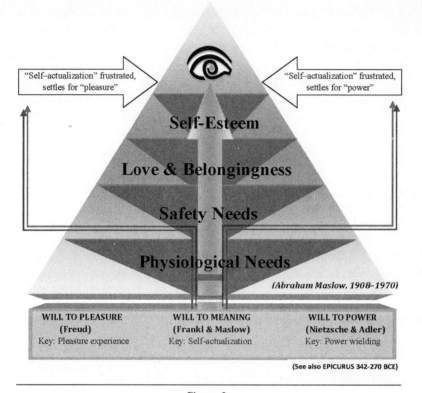

Figure 2.

wants, opens the doors to our either offering him those things ("Carrot Power") or else denying him those needs and wants ("Stick Power").

This sounds daunting until you remember how often Madison Avenue routinely makes us (1) *want* things we never even knew existed a minute ago, by (2) convincing us we need those things, if not in order to stay happy, alive, and healthy (hah!), than at least so we can keep up with them damn Joneses.

Third, what's his "F'n" agenda?

One thing comes out his mouth, but—just for an instant—you think you see something different twinkling in your enemy's eye. *Trust your "gut,"* it evolved a few million years before your higher rationalizing "Nah-I-only-imagined-I-saw-what-I-saw" brain. In other words, if you suspect someone has a hidden agenda, they probably do. But even without a "hidden agenda," just figuring out a person's general agenda (i.e., what motivates them, what occupies or otherwise obsesses them) can be a real challenge. In general though, "agendas" fall into six basic categories:

- *Fame Agenda*: He's got all the gossip on the latest Hollywood scandal. Knows the names of up-and-coming stars you've never heard of. Throwing their names out and seeing your lack of recognition reinforces his fantasy that he's an "insider." He drops names of people he *wishes* he knew. This is true whether he's seeking "fame" on the silver screen or just currying favor in the office. He knows the names of streets in Los Angeles although he's never been there. He uses words like "exposure," and "talent."

You'll often hear him complain about how rich and famous and powerful people don't "appreciate" what they've got. There's plenty of *Frustration agenda* here as well since he subconsciously wants to be one of those rich, famous, and powerful. This agenda type is always bitter because the world hasn't yet "discovered" them. For a man, it's that the world hasn't discovered his "genius." For women, the world refuses to acknowledge her "obvious" talent and beauty.

Offer to help him accomplish his hidden agenda to be rich, famous, and powerful (and you'll have him eating out of your hand).

- *Fortune Agenda*: It's all about the money with this person. He's a mercenary. She's a gold-digger. When they talk, it's always about money, bragging about the things they already have, lusting after what others have. Words like "capital gains," "production costs," and worries about "taxes," especially how "bad" it'll be when they're "forced" to move into a higher tax bracket flow from their lips. Likes talking about Wall Street and Tokyo.

Relationships for this type always go bankrupt since for them a spouse or companion is just one more piece of "property" to show off.

- *Faith Agenda*: He's convinced himself he's a "true believer" though this kind always have skeletons in their closet that they're deathly afraid are going to be resurrected one day. In the least, he's a hyp-ocrite and a back-stabber. Worst-case scenario: he's "born again" *Tal-iban*! Read Margaret Atwood's *The Handmaid's Tale* (1985).

He likes throwing around words like "conservative" and "family values" while he has wet-dreams of "The Judgment Day," when he'll be sitting on his much deserved ('cause he's so darn tolerant of others!) throne of gold in Glory looking down on the rest of us poor—heathen infidell!—bastards rotating on the spit. Often this agenda dovetails him into a *Frustration Agenda* the longer he has to wait for people to recognize his greatness come "The Big Payback."

- *Followers Agenda*: He's collecting a "posse," a "crew," starting his own "clique" or cult, more often than not just so he can finally get the "recognition" he thinks he deserves—*Frustration Agenda* again.

Sometimes this kind of personality also has a *Faith Agenda* and is a vig-orous recruiter for his cause—although, you can bet he's keeping a running score (notches on his Bible or Koran!) of all the souls he saved (just in case the Good Lord isn't paying close enough attention!).

He loves to organize things and loves to talk about organizing things: the office Christmas party, Little League, church events. And whatever the committee he's on, whatever the event—"Oh, don't bother!"—he's already seen to the seating arrangement. Not surprising, his infectious volunteer spirit often "guilts" others into volunteering. Oh, he's "*infectious*" all right!

At first glance you might mistake any "Father-to-Son"[7] arrangement he's involved in to cast him in the role of "obedient son." Don't be fooled. Though he may appear to be dripping with altruism, "serving others," he's only in it for himself and he's always the one running the show.

His "power" is "Expert Power"[8]—he always seems to know how to set up the microphone, where the breaker switch is when the lights suddenly go out. So when you arrive, you find he's volunteered to be "in charge" and he's already got *your* whole schedule planned out.

His kind is secretly insecure and is looking for validation outside himself.

---

7. Review "The Nine Relationships/Five Roles" above (p. 11).
8. See "The Five Types of Power," next chapter.

By assuming the badge of leadership (from scoutmaster to Master of Ceremonies) he's assured the run of things and the recognition he craves. Do I smell a little *Fame Agenda* mixed in?

In extremis, this is where our cult leaders come from.

He's always talking about past organizational successes and/or trying to involve *you* in his future plans. "Community," "brotherhood," "civil participation," "fellowship" are the kind of words he likes. If he can't put together a decent cult following outside his family, his family becomes his cult. He'll brag about how "well behaved" his kids are, how his wife is "always attentive to his every need." *Sleeping With the Enemy* (1994) anyone?

- **Future Agenda:** In his mind he has a "vision" of the future that he's trying to make happen in the present. Sometimes he's a "true believer"[9] who really expects that his version of the future will come about. (In this respect, he shares a lot in common with *Faith Agenda*.)

Other times, he's just talking "elephant shit."[10]

He always talks in future tense, staying away from present reality questions like "How much money have you actually collected so far?" and "How many people have actually signed up for this project?"

He can be political and/or religious but, unlike the *Faith Agenda*, all his aspirations are abstract. Words like "potential" and "prospective" and "possible" give him a woody.

- **Frustration Agenda:** He's mad about something and pissed at someone, maybe mad at everything and pissed at everybody. His frustration can extend as far as "God," "The Universe," and everything.

---

9. As Dr. Lung is fond of pointing out, you can't write "belief," "believe," or "believer" without sticking a "lie" smack dab in the middle.

10. Fritz Perls, mastermind behind the *Gestalt* school of psychology said that, when it comes to trying to get the truth out of people, a therapist runs into three kinds of "shit": *chicken shit* (small talk used to avoid talking about real issues), *bullshit* (lies we tell about ourselves, our abilities, and our accomplishments), and *elephant shit* (grandiose, impossible "whens" and "what ifs" we use to avoid any present and future responsibility). More on this later, in the section "Three Types of 'Shit,' Three Types of Insight" (p. 157).

This Mr. Angry freely combines elements from the first five types of agenda: he can be mad because God and The Universe don't recognize his greatness (*Fame Agenda*), because he's living in a "degenerate" world (*Faith Agenda*), because if he could only get a loan (*Financial Agenda*) or win the lottery (*Future Agenda*) he could finally accomplish his dream.

He's a complainer and a blamer. Every word that comes out his mouth is cynical. Not only is his glass half-empty . . . it's also got a crack in it!

I'm sure you've figured out by now that people often betray themselves by the topics they choose to talk about. Likewise, the very words and phrases they favor can reveal much of their hidden agenda.

Having successfully trained ourselves to recognize such word clues, part of a person's "Shadow-talk" that gives away their hidden "F'n" agenda, we can then craft our defensive/offensive strategy toward them accordingly.

Remember that it's called a "hidden agenda" because people striving after fame and fortune, faith and followers, as well as those harboring resentful frustrations, aren't always so easy to spot. People get good at hiding their secret habits, hates, and hubris. It's even possible for a person to have an agenda hidden even from themselves—*subconscious* motivations and desires that push or pull them in one direction or another without their even realizing it.

Finally, what's his "sensory mode?"

One final way in which we can use our knowledge of our five (or is that *six*?)[11] senses are to learn to discern which of the five senses others are dominated by. This is called a person's "sensory mode."

While we all use all our senses to varying degrees, each of us tends to have a preference for, i.e. "favor," one sense over the others. This unconscious preference is often reflected in our choice of entertainment—going to a movie (seeing) versus going to a music concert (hearing), versus going to a dance (touching). Our preference is also reflected in our hobbies and in our choice of careers.

A taste-oriented (dominated) person might be right at home as a chef. They could also like working with their hands (touch oriented) which is also used a lot in cooking. Though we usually associate teachers with talking (a variation of taste-oriented), hearing-oriented people actually make the best teachers since they can better determine a student's individual needs by really listening.

---

11. See "ASP" in "How to train your senses," this section.

"WHAT'S YOUR F'N AGENDA?"

What They Want	How They Talk	Key Words	The Type	Your Approach
Fame	Talk about famous people. Drop names. Complain about how famous people are always complaining.	Success. Paparazzi, Los Angeles, Hollywood, and TV.	Needs strokes and praise. Craves recognition.	Give him a way to "show 'em all." Appreciate his "genius" and talent. Compare him favorably to other famous people.
Fortune (Financial Gain)	Talk about money. Brag about things he has. Complain about taxes.	Capital gains. Production. Stocks and Bonds. Investments. New York and Tokyo.	He's in it for the money. A gun for hire. Trust him only as you're paying him better than your competition.	Hire him. Pay him well but never trust him. Others of his type: tempt with "too good to be true" offer.
Faith	Talk about the future (with veiled hints they know something you don't). Religious references.	Conservative. Family values. Judgment, law. Punishment.	Authoritarian. Born again. Taliban.	Assure him the world is going to change to fit his needs. There's a place of honor reserved for him in the kingdom to come.
Followers	Talk about organizing. How to move people and resources from place. Bringing people together. Need for strong leadership.	Community. Brotherhood. Faith. Patriotism. God-speak.	Needs validation from outside, insecure. Paranoid. Looking for love.	Give him your loyalty and love. Help him form his own cult (security blanket) or give him a trusted position in your own.
Future (Gain)	They talk about religion and/or political changes that will change everything. They are up on the latest innovations and movers & shakers.	Change. Economy. Restructuring. Rush Limbaugh. Projections. Trends.	Wallows in "elephant shit" (i.e., grandiose plans of what will happen "when/if").	Show him his place in the new world, show him how to (literally) invest in your future.
Frustration	Talk in generalities. About how people let them down. Have grandiose ideas but everyone's too stupid to see genius. Cynical.	Stupid. Short-sighted. Fair (injustice). "Old boy network"; "System's fixed"; "You gotta know someone."	Needs to get his grudge on. Lives for "the big payback." Wants revenge but he calls it "justice."	Show him how to get even and then some.

Figure 3.

We associate artists with being sight-oriented, which they are to a greater extent than most people. But what about all those sculptors and carvers dominated by the sense of touch?

Be mindful not to too quickly classify (i.e. stereotype) a person into one of these five sensory modes since people sometimes use more than one sensory mode of talking, just as they use different senses from situation to situation. However, it's true you can often discern a person's dominating sense mode simply by the words and phrases they choose to express themselves with.

For example a sight-oriented person might tell you "I *see* what you're trying to say. Could you *see* your way clear to send me a prospectus I could *look* at?" Touch-oriented people on the other hand (ahem) might phrase the same thing, "I *feel* where you're coming from! I like the way you *handle* yourself. I'd like to *touch* base with you on that again."

Other times the person's body language gives away their sensory mode. For example a *touch*-oriented person might have to *look* your proposal over but, if you study them carefully, you'll notice them literally "fondling" the folder, rubbing their hands over the cover, perhaps even bouncing it up and down in their hands, literally "weighing" your proposal.

Sometimes while they're mulling over your proposal you'll catch a *taste*-oriented person who can be caught licking or "smacking" their lips or gums, perhaps grinding their teeth (hint: look to see if the muscles in their jaw are tensing).

A *hearing*-oriented person might ask questions like, "What did so-and-so *say* about this idea?" or "What's the *word* around the office?" or "What's the *scuttlebutt* on *the grapevine*?"

Once we figure out which of the five sense modes dominates our target person, we then craft our speech and our actions to attract him to our agenda. Or, we can also use insight into his dominant sensory mode to toss a stumbling block in his path.

For example, for someone who is sight-oriented, arrange for them to have to *listen* to lengthy, boring audiotapes. Increase a touch-dominated person's anxiety by making sure he has nothing to do with his hands.[12]

Once you peg his sensory mode type, it is a simple matter to craft an effective counter strategy.

---

12. An old interrogator's trick. See *Theatre of Hell: Dr. Lung's Complete Guide to Torture* (Lumpanics Unlimited, 2003).

Know Your Environment

This means accepting, and adapting to "circumstance and flux."

Change is hard. But we have to learn to roll with the punches. "Adapt or die" is the one rule where Mother Nature refuses to compromise.

Human beings—like all survivor species—have a knack for adapting. But how well we adapt and survive is directly proportional to how well we can accurately assess where—at any given moment—we stand in the pecking order. Or, more aptly, on the food chain. By no stretch of the imagination is Mother Nature a vegetarian. She'll chew you up in a minute—the minute you fail to instantly adapt to one of her mood swings.

"Circumstance" refers to where we are. We act differently in church than we do in a tavern. What's appropriate in one venue is sacrilege—and dangerous—in another.

Martial arts adepts have a saying, "Everything works . . . but not everything works every time." In other words, in some instances a straight, solid kick to the *cojones* will end an encounter. Other times, you might have to take your opponent down with a *jiujutsu* throw. When battling back a single attacker, there are times when you might "go to the ground," wrestling him into submission. A good technique . . . unless you are fighting off more than one attacker, in which case, you cannot afford to go to the ground with one attacker as this would allow the remaining attackers to kick you while you're down. Ergo, not every technique is appropriate for every encounter. As with physical self-defense, so too with mental self-defense—and attack.

The "flux" part of "circumstance & flux" has more to do with "who" than "where," although the "where" often influences the "who."

People are a pain. But this world would be pretty lonely without them. And, as much as we might protest our independence from what others think about us and from the demands of society, we still wear a tie to that job interview. We still—reflexively—say "Bless you" when someone sneezes. Society is as much in us as we are in society. Why fight the inevitable and inexorable when you can turn them to your advantage?

You always have to take into account where you are when trying to communicate (i.e. influence) another person. Just as circumstances change, so do people depending on those circumstances. The person you have a rational one-on-one conversation with might turn into a whole 'nother person when surrounded by his "posse." And, as every guy knows, if you want to score with that fine filly at the bar, you're first gonna have to get her away from her cock-blockin' girlfriends. (That's why God created "wingmen"!)

Knowing your environment means recognizing the different demands inherent in differing times and places—whether estimating how many liters of water you'll need to make it across a desert, to whose wannabe alpha dog butt you'll have to kiss at the annual office Christmas party to make sure you still got a job going into the new year.

This is no different from two generals of old facing each other across a battlefield. The general who best knows the terrain can best take advantage of that terrain, best taking advantage of his enemy. Time and again throughout history, generals have found their knowledge of environment (or sore lack thereof) working either to their favor or their failure—from the 300 Spartans at Thermopylae, to Hannibal at Lake Trasimene and again at Cannae, Henry V at Agincourt, and Lee at Gettysburg.

THE THREE TYPES OF CONTROL

Mastering "The Three Knows" gives us the three types of control we can now exercise over ourselves, and over others if we so choose. Note how these three correspond to the three main areas where all human beings focus their attention:

Physical Control

This is first and foremost control over the body—your own, or someone else's. "Physical control" also takes into consideration how much physical influence we have over our immediate environment (thus the need to "Know your environment").

Mental Control

Metal control is not separate from physical control. In fact, one would be hard pressed to function without the other. In order to institute any serious physical training regimen one must either have a certain amount of mental will power to begin with . . . or else a really scary drill instructor! Either way, mental determination leads to physical domination.

In turn, a healthy body really is the precursor to a healthy mind. A body weak from hunger, a body racked with physical ills has little chance of engendering mental mastery. (Sure, there's Stephen Hawking—that really, really smart guy in the wheelchair, but he's the exception.) "Healthy mind, healthy body," and vice-versa.

Spiritual Control

This has two meanings: The first meaning of "spiritual control" has to do with recognizing and then influencing (i.e. controlling) the spiritual aspects of another person, either by using their beliefs to approach them, or else using their gullibility to wrangle them off into your "cult." It doesn't matter whether you believe something or not. But it's vitally important you keep track of what others around you believe—from your gullible wife who keeps sending your hard-earned wages to that smarmy televangelist, to your next door neighbor who thinks hijacking an airplane and crashing it into the building where you work is the best way to please his god.[13]

The second meaning concerns our gaining more mastery over ourselves through the full use of our five senses. This is what we call "ASP," Additional Sensory Perception, which is similar to most people's concept of "ESP" except that ASP comes not from some extra sense, operating above and beyond the five recognized senses, but instead involves the full use of those five known senses, the full employment of which often makes others believe we actually possess a "sixth sense." (More on "ASP" in the chapter on "Jing-gong: How to Develop your Senses.")

The Power to Read Minds?

This is where all the trouble you've gone to in order to increase your awareness of, and acumen with, your five senses begins to pay off. Having increased our awareness of the five senses, it will often seem to others (and sometimes even to ourselves) as if we have access to an ESP sixth sense simply because we have become more attuned to picking up on others' "shadow-talk" (Freudian slips and verbal *faux pas*) and their "shadow-walk" (body language itches and twitches).

We now perceive the *unconscious clues and cues* from their body language,

---

13. More on this in the chapter on *Junishi-do-jutsu* in Section II (p. 181).

we hear hesitations in their speech, feeling their body tremble or noting their sweaty palms when we shake their hand. Perhaps even *smelling* the lust—or fear!—exuding from their pores. Our five senses now serve us well. And often these five "sense awarenesses" are the only edge we'll need to confuse, defuse, and ultimately defeat an enemy.

Of course, wouldn't it be great if we could actually "read" an enemy's mind, knowing what he intended before he even had a chance to set his plots and plans into motion?

A July 2006 *USA TODAY* survey asked adults what "superpower" they would most like to have: one percent said they'd like to be able to walk through walls; eleven percent wanted to be able to turn invisible; another fifteen percent dreamed of having the ability to fly. But the number one "superpower" most people chose, twenty-eight percent of those surveyed, was *the power to read minds*.

We *can* read another person's mind. Again, we're not talking about pie-in-the-sky magical pixie ESP, some "psychic" extrasensory perception. We're talking about a deliberately acquired skill, accessible to every human on the planet. Thankfully, so far as survival of the fittest is concerned, most people are too busy doing really important things—like helping Howie Mandel figure out which suitcase someone else's money is in—to take the time to develop their *ASP—additional sensory perception*.

At the basic level, ASP begins with the full use of our five senses, as already mentioned, to the point where it's giving the impression that we posses extrasensory perception.

But ASP then goes on to incorporate recent discoveries about how our five senses gather information, and more importantly how we process that information to the fullest extent of our five senses—and beyond! In the following chapter on "How to train your senses" we'll teach you how to do just that.

2.

The Five Types of Power (and How to Get Some!)

HAVING THUS FAR GAINED a better knowledge—mastery!—of ourselves, as well as a better perception of our environment and better understanding of what makes our enemy tick, we are now free to learn to better recognize, protect ourselves from, and ultimately effectively wield the five types of power: Love and Respect Power, Carrot Power, Stick Power, Expert Power, and Position Power.

LOVE AND RESPECT POWER

This depends on how much you are liked by others. This is (ideally) genuine power, flowing from people who care, support, and follow you out of love and loyalty rather than those who kiss your ass for personal gain and/or from fear. This is your "support network," your "posse." Recall that, when asked whether it was better for a prince to be loved or feared, Machiavelli replied it was *safer* to be *feared* since, in the long run, it offers the prince more security. Machiavelli went on to remind us there's a big difference between being feared and being hated.[14]

---

14. More on "The Machiavelli Method" in Section III (p. 259).

"THE FIVE TYPES OF POWER"

Type of Power	Dependent Upon	Example:
Love and Respect Power	How much you are liked and respected by others.	Genuine power, flowing from people who care, support, and follow you out of love and loyalty. Your "support network," your "posse."
Carrot Power aka "Reward Power"	Your ability to manipulate others by dispensing rewards.	Exercising this kind of power, you control "the carrot" determining who gets promoted, who gets a raise, who gets sex tonight.
Stick Power aka "Coercive Power"	Your willingness to wield "the stick," to threaten and to punish others.	Pain becomes progress. Give the other guy pain and he steps out of the way of your progress! From the boss threatening to fire you, the cult leader withholds his "love" until you start goose-stepping with the rest of the "chosen" and the nagging wife who withholds sex, to the robber with the gun who threatens to blow your head off.
Expert Power	Comes from the special skills, unique abilities, or special intelligence you have access to.	You offer to share (carrot) or withhold (stick) your expertise to get your way. Often the person wielding this kind of specialized information becomes the eminence grise, "the power behind the throne."
Position Power	A person's recognized and agreed upon right to issue commands and make demands of others.	(1) *Legitimate position power* comes from your having "won" a position, either through some sort of election process, or else by universal acclamation after you "seize" power, albeit with the blessing of the masses. (2) *False position power*. On the other hand, false position power comes from simply wearing a uniform—from an actual military, police, or guard's uniform, to a cult hat, gang tattoo, to that all-powerful bureaucrat's rubber stamp.

Figure 4.

CARROT POWER (AKA "REWARD POWER")

Carrot power comes from your ability to manipulate others by dispensing rewards. Exercising this kind of power, you control "the carrot." Example: Cult offers love and "family."

STICK POWER (AKA "COERCIVE POWER")

Stick power, by contrast, comes from your willingness to wield "the stick," to threaten and to punish others, your ability to open up a can of *whup-ass*! Example: A cult leader withholds his "love" until you start goose-stepping with the rest of the "chosen."[15]

Sometimes the "stick" is only a piece of information you hold over another person. Other times you may have to resort to a more *literal* "stick."[16] Rewards should be swift, punishment swifter still. This is the secret of both Carrot and Stick power. Ancient Chinese masters knew this well:

> "Rewards encourage good. Punishment dissuades evil. Reward one to inspire a hundred. Punish one man to discourage many." —The T'ai Kung

EXPERT POWER

This comes from the special skills, unique abilities, or special intelligence you have access to. In a crisis—one naturally occurring or a crisis *you* manufacture—your expertise (special talents, skills, insight, and information) is suddenly in demand and you "humbly" accept your due. A "leader" who steps forward in times of chaos, with just the right plan (expertise and/or equipment) to "stop the madness" fits this category. From a ninja spy to a Wall Street "insider trader" when, by hook or by crook ruthless men come into possession of valuable pieces of information, information that gives them power over others, and/or influence over events (e.g., a corporate merger, the outcome of a battle), why should we be surprised that they inevitably give in to the temptation to use said information?

Often the person wielding this kind of specialized information becomes the *eminence grise*, "the power behind the throne." Ever hear of Martin Bormann? Rasputin? Karl Rove?

In medieval times, the court jester was often the most informed man in a kingdom because—thinking him the fool—everyone talked freely in front of him. The wise man can act like a fool, but the fool cannot act like a wise

---

15. See "The Cult Craft" in *Mind Manipulation* (Citadel 2002).
16. More on techniques of "Blackmail" and "Bully" in "The Killer B's," Section V.

man. Ever heard of Lenny Bruce? George Carlin ring a bell? Read Shakespeare's *King Lear* and Robert Graves's *I, Claudius*.

In Graves's novel, future Roman Emperor Claudius survives childhood only because he was afflicted from birth with a pronounced limp and noticeable stutter which causes his evil aunt to ignore him while she's busy killing off anyone who might interfere with her son Tiberius becoming Emperor. Young Claudius's infirmities cause his aunt to underestimate his potential as a threat.

We can thus use the "carrot" of feigned friendship and pretended concern to get him to open up, to lay bare his psyche, allowing us to uncover the subconscious desires, dreads, and dirty little secrets he hides even from himself.

Like a wily poker player reading the tells his opponents unwittingly bring with them to the table, so, too, we can learn to read our enemy's subconscious, allowing us to confidently double our bet (investment) . . . or fold and flee to fight another day.

We can then borrow B. F. Skinner's patented Pavlov "stick" and use it to tease the hungry hounds in our lives to not only salivate at the mere thought of playing "fetch the stick" with us, but also prod them to go around in circles chasing after their own tail! The means to accomplish this is surprisingly simple math: We either add *stress* to our enemy's life (stick approach), or we offer to take away his already existing stress (carrot approach).

POSITION POWER

Position power comes from a person's recognized and agreed upon right to issue commands and make demands of others. For example, we all agree police have the power to arrest and that the president has the power to make war. The office and rank they hold—and our consent—give them their power.

Position power is thus dependent on and derived from others who "obey" you because they believe it is their duty and/or obligation to recognize your position within the social pecking order.

There are, however, two drastically different variations of position power:

- **Legitimate position power.** This power comes from your having "won" a position, either through some sort of election process, or else by universal acclamation after you "seize" power, albeit with the blessing of the masses. Thus, historically, "legitimate" in this sense simply means the ability to get power and to hold on to it.

Julius Caesar fits this category, but so does Hitler—both "seizing" power in "troubled times" *with little resistance* because they were heralded as "deliverers" (or at least the lesser of two evils) at the time.

- *False position power.* On the other hand, false position power comes from simply wearing a uniform. This uniform can be anything from an actual military, police, or guard's uniform, to that silly hat your cult makes you wear; from your gang's tattoo, to that all-powerful bureaucrat's rubber stamp you swing around like it was the Grim Reaper's scythe!

Never mistake position for power. Mythology tells us Lucifer had power . . . but did he? He had a position in Heaven. But any "power" he exercised could be taken from him—and was!—at the whim of his schizophrenic, sexually repressed boss. Sometimes it *really is* better to rule in Hell.

Warning: Any power that depends on *externals* (e.g., the car you drive, the key you turn, the uniform you wear, or the desk *they* give you to sit behind, or the badge you hide behind) ain't worth squat since *they* can take it from you at any time. The Lord giveth, and The Lord taketh away . . .

> *Reward all those wise enough to join you, utterly crush all who oppose you and do so in so savage a manner as to completely cower any others who might dream of resisting your will.*
> —Lung and Prowant, *Mind Control*

3.

Suggestology:
The Power of Suggestion

TRUTH BE KNOWN, there's a *sixth* type of power, one that makes full—and often ruthless! use of the first five.

You see, master mind manipulators never give orders . . . they simply make "suggestions." Sometimes those suggestions are direct—even blunt. Other times, the circumstances and the sensibility of their victims require they make their suggestions less direct—but nonetheless effective.

The science of Suggestology was pioneered by Dr. Georgi Lozanov, head of the *Institute of Suggestology and Para psychology* on Budapest Street in Sofia, Bulgaria, and includes within its scope: hypnosis, propaganda, and various other means of "suggestive" manipulation.

In their landmark *Psychic Discoveries behind the Iron Curtain* (1970) Shela Ostrander and Lynn Schroeder give this definition of Lozanov's "new" science:

> Suggestology is the scientific study of suggestion. It is a method of reaching and making use of unknown reserves, powers, and abilities of the human mind. It overlaps with parapsychology.[17]

---

17. Ostrander and Schroeder, 1970, p. 292.

Dr. Lozanov himself seems to have envisioned "Suggestology" as a whole new "ology," one dealing specifically with mind *expansion*. (In the paranoia left over from the Cold War, others say mind *control*.)

Seeking any and all methods for bending (perhaps ultimately breaking and breaching!) the current boundaries of human thought and experience, Dr. Lozanov reportedly included in his research the study of Indian Yoga relaxation techniques known as Savasanna, the operating theory being "R-3" where "*R*elaxation leads to *R*elease (of doubts, fears, etc.), which in turn leads to more *R*eceptivity." In fact, some of Dr. Lozanov's subjects became so "relaxed" during his Suggestology experiments as to exhibit signs of becoming "telepathic."[18]

That some of Dr. Lozanov's subjects should respond so readily to his use of Indian Yogic Savasanna comes as no surprise since the idea of using suggestive subliminal messages was (first?) put forth by third-century Indian Yoga master Pantanjali. Pantanjali taught that our thoughts (mental constructs) were the result of our *physically* interacting and reacting to the world. For example our seeing a symbol, hearing a word, or touching an object leaves behind impressions (Skt. *samskara*) that, in turn, subtly (sometimes *subliminally*) influence our future thought and actions.

Finally! Something both science and religion can agree on: Like it or not, believe it or not, we are all susceptible to this kind of subtle/subliminal suggestion.

Thus, when a less "direct" attack is called for, master manipulators employ a variety of symbols, gestures, and innuendo word-play tactics that allow them to influence their victims on a subliminal level.

BUT WASN'T "SUBLIMINAL SUGGESTION" DISPROVEN?

Back in the 1950s there was a public panic when it was revealed that advertisers were trying to influence buyer behavior on a subconscious level by planting hidden messages in both advertisements and in movies. These messages were called "subliminal suggestions" (from the Latin *sub-limen*, meaning "below consciousness").

Subliminal suggestions works in two ways: First by creating an association

18. Ibid., p. 305

of one thing with another in a viewer's or a listener's mind. Second, the manipulator takes advantage of pre-conceived connections the person has. To accomplish this, manipulators employ a host of word-ploys, evocative symbols, and gestures already familiar to the targeted person(s).

Most people today believe that "subliminal suggestion" has been "disproven" and "discarded" by scientists back in the '50s. *Nothing could be further from the truth!*

In fact early on in the study of subliminal suggestion psychology pioneer B. F. Skinner successfully proved how his behaviorism theory of psychology could be used *subliminally* to affect noted psychoanalyst Erich Fromm, who had disputed Skinner's findings that showed just how easily human behavior could be "shaped"[19] or manipulated:

> Attending a lecture Fromm was giving, Skinner passed a note to a friend, "Watch Fromm's left hand. I'm going to shape a chopping motion."
>
> From then on, every time Fromm raised his left hand to emphasize a point, Skinner looked directly at him with a steady gaze. When Fromm lowered his hand, Skinner nodded and smiled. Within five minutes, Fromm was chopping the air so vigorously that his wristwatch kept slipping over his hand![20]

Skinner's manipulation worked because, on a subconscious level, Fromm craved Skinner's approval. Thus, Skinner's subliminal gestures were able to influence Fromm's actions.

And how about a 2007 experiment done at the University of Arizona that started out seeking to explain how President Bush's approval rating went from around fifty-one percent before 9/11 to ninety percent immediately after 9/11 and ended up giving us a vivid example of the power of suggestion:

> Participants were exposed to the letters "WTC" or the numbers "9/11" in an image flashed too quickly to register on the conscious level. Meanwhile other participants were

---

19. "Shaping" involves manipulating an animal's behavior through a serious of smaller associated tasks designed to ultimately establish a grander specific behavior in the animal. Not surprising, this same technique works on humans as well.

20. Skinner, B. F., *A Matter of Consequences* (Knopf, 1983).

exposed to familiar but random combinations of letters and numbers, such as area codes. Both groups were then shown words like **COFF_ _, SK_LL, GR_VE,** and were asked to fill in the blanks.

People who'd been shown the random combinations of letters and numbers were more likely to fill in **COFFEE, SKILL,** and **GROVE**. But people exposed to the subliminal terrorism "prompts" more often filled in **COFFIN, SKULL,** and **GRAVE**. The mere mention (i.e., suggestion, albeit subliminal) of September 11 attack or the World Trade Center is the same as reminding Americans of death.[21]

Early on, Madison Avenue realized the value of subliminal suggestion. That's why it's still alive and well and widely used today. That's why "The Pillsbury Doughboy" is modeled after a fetus (baking and giving birth being closely related in women's minds) and why the cartoon nose of popular '80s cigarette icon "Joe Camel" was modeled after male genitalia (advertiser's attempt to subconsciously associate smoking with "manly" virility).

Subliminal messages can employ any number of words, symbols, or gestures purposely designed to *subconsciously* (subliminally) penetrate into a person's mind without their normal *conscious* "gatekeeper" recognizing the messages as dangerous or superfluous, and thus turning them away.

Effectively crafting subliminal suggestions therefore requires distinguishing between *neutral* words and *emotional* words.

Neutral words, like "coffee" mentioned above, are unambiguous words carrying only one meaning. The word coffee does not evoke an emotional response in us.

Emotional words, on the other hand, have more impact because we "file" them in more than one place in our brains. For example, a word like "coffin" evokes a host of emotional reactions (unease, fear, even excitement).

Deliberately using emotional words allows the manipulator to penetrate more of our brain than using "neutral" words normally would. Thus, subliminal suggestion works best when attacking the viewer or listener on *an emotional level* versus on *a higher reasoning level*. Evoking an emotional response via subliminal suggestion is called "*subception*."

---

21. Jay Dixit, *"The Ideological Animal." Psychology Today* Jan./Feb. 2007:80–86.

Don't chide yourself. Being susceptible to subliminal suggestion has nothing to do with your being a "sucker" or being "feeble-minded" and has everything to do with how your brain naturally processes information. In other words, the reason subception works isn't about being rational or logical; it's biological.

Unlike *neutral words* which end up being tossed around and taken apart in the higher reasoning parts of the brain, *emotional words* go straight to a little place in the middle of the brain called the *amygdala,* part of the midbrain's *limbic system* where most of our emotional processing takes place. This limbic system controls "The four F's": Fighting, Feeding, Fleeing . . . and Sex.[22] This limbic system evolved earlier than the positional and philosophically "higher" areas of the brain, the cerebrum and the cerebellum and, situated as it is in our mid-brain, is literally and figuratively "closer" to the body, i.e., connected directly to the spinal cord by way of the medulla oblongata (the mass of nerve tissue at the base of the brain that controls *bodily functions* such as blood circulation and breathing).

On its way to being processed by the "higher" brain, all information first passes through this area. Any piece of information the limbic system feels is emotionally charged (e.g. something threatening, something sexually exciting) the limbic system reacts to instantly, before the information can be passed along to the higher reasoning area of the brain for in-depth analysis. This explains why we jump away from that "snake" laying in the grass (instant "flight or flight" limbic reaction) before our higher reasoning brain "realizes" it's just a harmless piece of garden hose. This also explains why when that fine young well-endowed filly struts by in painted-on jeans our limbic system reacts (crotch-wise and otherwise) before the information makes it to the higher brain who decides to "card" her.

Our limbic system instantly transforms thoughts ("feelings") into physical action and into "symptoms": making us blush when embarrassed, cry when we're sad, and makes us shake, sweat, and feel those butterflies in the stomach when we're scared. It also tells us whether to flee or stand our ground—fight or flight.

The limbic system is thus where most of our emotional processing takes place. This is where Freud's ID lives—the seat of our instinctual drives and

---

22. Vance Packard, *The People Shapers*, 1977.

desires. Truth be known, our "gut"—as in "gut feeling"—isn't in our gut, it's in our mid-brain.

Our limbic system is composed of four major structures in the brain:

> *The Thalamus* acts as "gatekeeper," sorting through and/or censoring messages going from the senses to the cerebrum (that "higher" part of the brain that controls thinking and complex tasks).
>
> *The Hypothalamus* regulates body systems, aggression, rage, pleasure and pain, and helps us learn and remember, storing sensory information.
>
> *The Basal Ganglia* control well-learned activities, like walking.
>
> *The Amygdala* (Lit. "almond," after its shape and size) regulates mood and controls emotion, and is especially adept at registering and reacting to the emotion of fear, triggering our flight-or-fight reaction.

Of course, once sensory information does—finally!—make its way to the "higher" reasoning areas of the brain you'd hope that would somehow insure we'd at least have a fighting chance of coming up with rational decisions and reasonable responses, right? But what you have to remember is that our "higher" reasoning centers make their final decisions based upon the *best available information* they have on hand (i.e. information that has already been chewed over, spit out and, in all likelihood, pissed on by that emotional "inner lizard" squatting atop our amygdala!). No big surprise then:

> The brain's wiring emphatically relies on emotion over intellect in decision making. —*USA Today*[23]

Sad to say, so far as subliminal suggestions are concerned, just because a sensation is registered in the amygdala doesn't mean that info is automatically passed along to the higher, conscious level of the brain. In fact, by examining brain scans, scientists have proven that the amygdala can be triggered by any stimulus merely *perceived* as threatening, whether a true threat actually exists or not (e.g. the image of an angry face or a loud noise). More

---

23. Dan Vergano, "*Study: Ask with Care: Emotions Rule the Brain's Decisions*," August 7, 2006:6D.

frightening still, the higher brain can often remain completely unaware of something that stimulates the more primitive mid-brain. As the article just quoted says, this is why subliminal suggestion works, because the stimulus affects us on a *subliminal* level:

> In short, the amygdala "knows" something that the organ of consciousness (whichever and whatever it is) does not.

This kind of subliminal suggestion has been further proven by experiments conducted at the University of California at San Diego in which researchers were able to increase subjects' thirst by secretly flashing *happy* faces which the subjects were consciously unaware of. Volunteers who said they were thirsty beforehand, after being exposed to the subliminal pictures, were willing to pay triple the price for the drink than another group that had secretly been shown *grimacing* faces.[24]

Thirst is controlled by the mid-brain so this is further proof that human beings can be affected by subliminal suggestion (or one might say "amygdala suggestion") provided the incoming message is (1) emotionally charged and/or (2) aimed to stimulate the person's more basic needs (e.g. thirst, hunger . . . sex?).

What about using subliminal suggestion to stimulate man's strongest emotion—fear?

During one of those notorious 1950s subliminal suggestion experiments (carried out on movie-goers without their knowledge), the word "blood" was inserted between flashing frames of a horror movie. Result? Exiting patrons—those who actually stayed through the entire movie—reported the movie to be one of the "scariest" movies they'd ever seen, even though, in actuality, the movie they saw was no more graphic and blood-splattered than other horror movies of the time.

Again we are dealing with a very basic emotion, fear. And while our higher brain knows "It's only a movie," our amygdala keeps seeing and processing the word "blood"—a danger!—over and over again.

Such experiments concluded early on that subliminal suggestions work best when they target and/or carry "emotional" messages. Therefore, rather than repeatedly flash "Drink Zap Cola"—since our amygdala can't spell "Zap

---

24. Charles Q. Choi, *"About Face." Scientific American* (August, 2006), 26.

Cola," we instead craft the simple message "thirsty" or perhaps "dry, desert," simple concepts our amygdala reacts to emotionally. (Of course, it also helps when the theater only sells Zap brand cola!)

Inserting subliminal messages into movies is touched on in the movie *Fight Club* (2001), where, at the end of the movie, if you pay close attention, you catch a glimpse of their "playful" subliminal suggestion.

Six Keys to Making Your Conscious "Suggestions" Stick

- **Simplicity:** Strip ideas to their essentials. "Uncle Sam wants you!" "We like Ike!" Obama: "Change!"
- **Unexpectedness:** First, people like novelty—things new and shiny always catch our eye. Second, if you deliberately confuse people, they'll generally hang around long enough for you to "un-confuse" them. This is part and parcel of C.H.A.O.S. Theory ("Create hassles/hardships/hazards and offer solutions"). Use "counterintuitive" examples (Read the "Friends, Romans, countrymen . . ." speech in Shakespeare's *Julius Caesar.*)
- **Concreteness:** Talk about real things people know about. Talk to farmers about crops, talk to kids about video games. It helps if you figure out the person's sensory mode (which sense dominates them) and whether they are "Watchers," "Listeners," or "Touchers," interacting with their world through what they see, what they hear, or what they touch, respectively.[25]
- **Credibility:** Ideas must be user-friendly and "testable" by the user. Having benefited someone with a small thing, they are much more likely to trust you with bigger things—more of their secrets, more of their money.
- **Emotions:** It's called "hitting their E-spot." Remember that the amygdala gets the information first. Craft your suggestions accordingly, with plenty of raw emotion. Always include one (or more) of "The Five Warning F.L.A.G.S." (i.e., Fear, Lust, Anger, Greed, Sympathy).
- **Stories:** People love a good tale. People take a good story over the truth any day.

---

25. See "Watchers, Listeners, and Touchers" in chapter 10 (p. 169).

Six Clues for Crafting Effective Subliminal Suggestions

Exactly the same as the six keys to making effective suggestions.

Six Ways to Make Your Hypnotic Suggestions More Effective

Again (big surprise), exactly the same technique used in crafting effective "suggestions." More on the power of hypnosis in chapter 9.

4.

Increasing Your Influence and Control

PEOPLE LIKE PEOPLE WHO (1) like them and (2) *are* like them. Our words draw people in. If they then find we have similar likes and dislikes, there is often ground for "bonding." If they find us immediately judgmental, they may be turned away. So the words we initially choose are the most important in any relationship—or any congame. The right words—"word play"—can be used to catch someone's attention (humorous words, provocative words, even confusing words that pique their curiosity), string them along, and then—when the hook is firmly in place—reel them in.

Having hooked our subject with our word play during "The Contact Phase" (having sized him up with the skills we've already learned in previous chapters), we can then lead him into "The Temptation Phase" where we offer him the world (or at least that little piece of it he's always had his eye on). He'll balk at first, not believing his good fortune to have found a "kindred ear" with a waterproof shoulder.

It's at this point that we move into "The Co-signing Phase," where we assure him he's justified in taking every stupid stumble, in committing every heinous act, so long as he finally gets what's coming to him. And we want to help him get what's coming to him . . .

Through "word play," temptation, and "co-signing" . . . he's putty in our hands!

WORD PLAY

Being an English major prepares you for impersonating authority.
—Garrison Keillor

We all enjoy wordplay. All our jokes are based on a slip of the tongue, misunderstood or mispronounced words, or on words with double meaning.

Likewise, a well-turned phrase can make or break a politician. (Hint: Never call New York "*Hymie-town*," at least not on the same open mike you later "whisper" about cutting off Barack Obama's balls!) By the same token, merely saying the President's full name "Barack *Hussein* Obama" means being accused of being racist or, at the very least, of trying to *subliminally* tie him to his Muslim roots.

Words are the most powerful of tools, the most dangerous of weapons.

Master manipulators use wordplay to place subliminal suggestions in their victims' minds. Such wordplay includes the manipulation of sentence structure (syntax), the "Theory of Liaison," the use of homophones.

It's also important to remember how *emotional words* can enter a subject's mind while *neutral words* are still stuck at the gate showing three forms of I.D. and giving a urine sample!

The Theory of Liaison allows that subliminal suggestions can be placed into another's mind by using words that, while by themselves are innocent, when spoken together with another innocent word create a third "subliminal" word-image.

For example, while the words "loose" and "exchange" have neutral meanings in and of themselves, when pronounced together, the phonetic ending of "loose" joins with the phonetic beginning of "exchange" to form "sex." Likewise, the *neutral* juxtaposed words "choose-examples" and "views-expected" also form the liaison "sex"—an *emotional* word if ever there was one!

In practical application, an unscrupulous seducer can liberally seed their friendly proposal with liaison words that subliminally plant the idea-image of "sex" in their listener's mind.

Likewise, using liaison, politicians and cult leaders preach to us of our "common need" (*common need* = "money").

The advent of computers allows for the creation of tens of thousands of liaison combinations. Thus during the course of a thirty-second commercial, or a thirty-minute lecture, a master manipulator using liaison can implant any number of subliminal images in their audience's collective mind.

Homophones, words that sound like other words, can also affect us on a subliminal level.

You see a beautiful woman. Do you want to *meet* her or *meat* her? Here is the basis for so much of our humor. Here is also the key to how master manipulators use word play to further confuse and control us.

Manipulating wordsmiths also use "pairing," i.e., associating one word with another, exploiting already perceived connections in people's minds. Homophones work perfectly for this.

For example, during Desert Storm, President George Bush Sr. was advised by his political strategists to deliberately pronounce Saddam Hussein's name as "Sodom," as opposed to the more proper "*Sah-damn.*" This was done in order to provoke the connection in Western minds with wicked Sodom(y) and Gomorrah. Likewise, say his name fast and Louis Farrakhan becomes "*Lucifer a con.*"

When subtlety is called for, being able to present ideas to others as suggestions, especially subliminal suggestions, is a vital skill for getting ahead in life—or, at the very least, not falling any further behind!

More important still, for self-defense, we must also learn to recognize any subliminal messages—intentional or unintentional—that could be used to overpower ourselves and our loved ones. Such messages are sure to contain thinly veiled temptations oh-so-hard to pass up.

THE NINE TEMPTATIONS OF FAUST
(AND EVERYBODY ELSE!)

I resolve to meet evil courageously, but when even a small
temptation cometh, I am in sore straits. That which seemeth trifling
sometimes giveth rise to a grievous temptation.
—**Thomas à Kempis**

Temptation is the only real Devil there is. Johann Wolfgang Von Goethe (1749–1832) knew this when he penned his masterpiece *Faust,* the story of a man (much like Goethe himself) who sells his soul to the Devil in exchange for wealth and power and pleasure and knowledge.

Accomplished poet, playwright, novelist, philosopher, student of what was then fledgling science and, most importantly, an astute student of human nature, Goethe has the Devil's pitchman[26] Mephistopheles test Faust with nine universal temptations:

- **The promise of restored youth**
- **Sensual love**
- **Rashness** (impatience)
- **Honors** (the praise of our fellow man)[27]
- **Power**[28]
- **Supernatural pleasure** ("sensual love" having failed to satisfy)
- **Regret** (the "temptation" of regret is to give in and give up)
- **Despair** (following closely on the heels of "regret")
- **Altruism** (losing oneself in service to others, too often becoming "false humility"). Since we've already established, have we not, that there's no such thing as true "altruism." Everybody gets paid, if only in "warm hugs-n-feelings."

Therefore, if you want to convince someone to do something, heed the words of Ben Franklin:

"If you want to convince, speak of interest, not of reason."

And since everyone likes a happy ending, through a final selfless act, Faust succeeds in breaking his contract with the Devil, winning his way into Heaven.

Of course, Faust's temptation is a fictional metaphor, but one all too often played out in real life, where each of us faces similar temptations. Recognizing that our enemy also faces these same temptations—especially the ones we deliberately put in his path!—gives us both insight and then inroads into his mind:

---

26. Or is that *pitchfork* man?
27. See "Hannibal's Ninety-nine Truths," Truth LVIII (p. 240).
28. See "The Five Types of Power," above (p. 28).

"THE NINE TEMPTATIONS OF FAUST"

TEMPTATION	MAJOR CONCERN	HOW TO APPLY THIS TEMPTATION
1. YOUTH	a. Staying young (when aging) b. Growing up (i.e., obtaining adult status and vices)	a. Show them the Fountain of Youth. b. Treat them like an adult.
2. SENSUAL LOVE	a. Sex (lust) b. Lasting *Eros* relationship	Become their pimp!
3. RASHNESS	Impatience, impulsive, anger-management problem	Expose his temper to the boss, public, etc.
4. HONOR(S)	Worried about "saving face," being seen as "honorable" and honest. Integrity.	Tempt him to go against his honor to save a friend and/or win the power to help others.
5. POWER	Obsessed with obtaining and maintaining "influence." Machiavelli's THE PRINCE	a. Promise him power. b. Hitch your wagon to his already rising star . . . and keep files!
6. SUPERNATURAL PLEASURE	Pleasing God and/or other unearthly powers. Sees himself as one of "The Chosen." Basks in his "righteousness."	Verify for him he's one of "The Chosen." Make him dependent on you for his supernatural "hugs."
7. REGRET	Worries about past indiscretions coming home to roost.	Give him a chance to "make amends." Help him relive his "glory days" with that barely-legal street-beagle. (Keep the videotape!)
8. DESPAIR	All is vanity. Failed life. Nothing left to live for.	If your enemy: Hand him the razor blade. If your ally: Show him his worth to you.
9. ALTRUISM	Needs to feel needed, wants to beLIEve his life has some meaning. Wants to beLIEve he's a "good person."	Help him help others. Help him spend his time and money on YOUR cause.

Figure 5.

NINE LADIES DANCING

From 1558 to 1829 England was dominated by Protestants so Roman Catholics were not permitted to practice their faith openly. According to popular lore, that's why and when ever-enterprising (some say "sinister") Jesuit priests wrote "The Twelve Days of Christmas," as a way of hiding secret instructions from the Catholic Bible inside the lyrics. This would be in keeping with the Jesuits' penchant for skullduggery and intrigue. After all, it was an eighteenth-century Jesuit stationed in China who translated the first Western version of Sun Tzu's *Ping-Fa* (Art of War) into French.

So "A partridge in a pear tree" refers to Jesus, while "twelve drummers drumming" is code for the twelve points of the Catholic "Apostle's Creed" (a forbidden teaching under Protestant rule).

Of special interest to us are those "Nine Ladies Dancing," since this phrase secretly lists "the nine ways in which one can be an accessory to another's sin." On the one hand a warning to Catholics not to be misled in one or more of these manners. On the other hand, it is a thinly-disguised training tool, instructing Catholic agents how to convert (i.e., subvert) Protestants to their cause. *Sans* any religious overtones, these nine methods can easily be adapted for our more *heathen*, modern-day use (see table on next page).

"NINE LADIES DANCING"

METHOD	MANIPULATION
By counsel:	We provide our foes with false information. We give them "The Mushroom Treatment": We keep them in the dark and feed them bullshit! No matter how hare-brained their scheme, no matter how bizarre the "conspiracy theory," we assure them they have come to a "logical" conclusion and should act on what they "know" to be the truth. He thinks us a friend when we are secretly a foe, Iago to his Othello.
By command:	Once we have won their trust and/or whenever they are otherwise under our control and we are "in authority," we send them on "suicide missions." (See "The Five Types of Power.") These are what Sun Tzu called "expendable agents."
By consent:	We give them our blessing—either overtly, or through promoting an atmosphere of "permissiveness." We bring the hookers . . . *and* the camera.
By provocation:	We "yank their chain," we stir up their emotions. We implant doubt and greed and other negative emotions to cause the person to act irrationally and/or ally themselves with our agenda.
By praise or flattery:	We inflate their ego until we can pull it along behind us like a balloon on a string.
By concealment:	We use lies of omission, we tell half-truths, and we pass gossip, rumor, innuendo, and propaganda off as fact. Like any good cult leader, we control the flow of information. We help him conceal damaging information of his indiscretions . . . but we always keep a backup disk!
By sharing:	We become his partner-in-conspiracy. We gossip with him. We keep his secrets . . . all "bloodties" for later use in extorting and blackmailing him.
By silence:	Omerta. We often do more by our *inaction* than by our actions. Our trustworthy "silence" buys us trust. He feels free to talk openly around us, free talk that, in the end, costs him dearly.
By defending a wrong that has been committed:	We co-sign for a glaring wrong/crime/sin he has committed, helping him "justify" it in his mind. He soon becomes dependent on us for his feeling of self-worth (or at least his lack of self-loathing). By co-signing for some minor wrong he has done, we can then talk him into committing a more major wrong (perhaps in an effort to rectify the first wrong).

Figure 6.

5.

Memory Manipulation

The past is truly lost if I forget today what I need to know
for tomorrow.
—**Duke Falthor Metalstorm**

REMEMBER THE LAST TIME your friend was bragging on you, entertainingly "embellishing" your heroics—lying about how big that fish was, about how good-looking that girl was you went home with last night? And, instead of correcting his exaggeration, you just "humbly" shrugged it off, since you were as caught up in hearing about *your* exploits as everyone else in the room.

Sorry, there's really no such thing as "photographic memory." Some people are just better at remembering. Others have what's called "eidetic memory" and are really good at remembering vividly. But even these "eide-tikers" don't have a photographic memory.[29] In fact, according to the most recent research, it's impossible to recall images with perfect accuracy.

We can, and should, improve our memory at every opportunity since so much of who and what we are is simply our memory. All we have is our memories. Truth be known, all we *are* is our memory. A sharp bump to the ol' brainpan and—*Voila!*—no more you, no more me. Did you forget it's called "amnesia"?

---

29. William Lee Adams, "The Truth about Photographic Memory," *Psychology Today* (March/April 2006).

What a great temptation then to realize that once you've mastered the Ultimate Control "Art of Suggestion" that you are then free not only to *alter true memories* others carry around in their heads, you're also now free to *create false memories*.

HOW TO IMPLANT FALSE MEMORIES

If we can't trust our own minds to tell us the truth, what is there left to trust?
—**Loftus and Ketcham**[30]

Our brain *is* constantly editing and re-writing our past experiences. As a general rule, we toss out the bad stuff and packrat the good—it's called "nostalgia." We especially like to get rid of any past memory about ourselves that doesn't quite fit with our present view of ourselves. This kind of "selective memory" is, at the very least, "bullshit," *in extremis*, "self-delusion." However, memories with unexpected consequence and/or strong emotions (what we call "Mama, drama, or trauma") also have a good chance of surviving the cut. This accounts for PTSD—Post Traumatic Stress Disorder.

But even after we've sifted through those memories we want to keep, when we try calling our "good" memories back up, it's still a crap-shoot. That's because:

> When we want to remember, our brains quickly reweave the tapestry by fabrication—not by retrieving—the bulk of information that we call memory. In other words, we recall the best of times and the worst of times, instead of the most likely of times. —Daniel Gilbert, Ph.D.[31]

On a grand scale, this kind of selective memory process helps explain how Hitler could so easily convince a whole nation to follow him—by "taking them back" to "the best of times" when they were a great nation, conjuring up "happy memories" which were, in fact, either reconstructions,

---

30. Elizabeth F. Loftus and Katherine Ketcham. *The Myth of Repressed Memory: False Memories and Allegations of Sexual Abuse* (St. Martin's Press, 1994).

31. *Bottom-Line Personal* (October 15, 2006), 9.

reinterpretations, or else complete fabrications of an idyllic time that never existed. *All* cult leaders (and many politicians) do this same thing: *talking* their followers back to that "perfect time" (Eden, Atlantis, the 1950s) which we can recapture if we'll just invest in the message they're selling.

Yes, this does amount to replacing real memories by implanting false memories.

Recent scientific studies have proven what police interrogators, con men and cult leaders have always known: that it's possible to implant false memories into a person's head and thereby get even the most innocent person to confess to the most heinous of crimes.

The most infamous case in modern times involving police interrogation and memory manipulation took place in Olympia, Washington, in 1988. In a scenario straight out of Salem, Massachusetts 1692, two daughters (aged 18 and 22) accused their father of having molested them.

The two daughters "remembered" this history of abuse while attending a fundamentalist Bible camp, where a charismatic cult expert lectured on how prevalent Satanic ritual abuse was, even in good Christian families.

Encouraged by the fellow camp-goers stepping forward to "confess" they had been the victims of ritual Satanic abuse and feeling peer pressure to fit in, the oldest daughter stepped forward to proclaim that she, her sister, and her brothers had been molested by her father, in her case for more than seventeen years!

Returning home to Olympia, the two girls told their stories to the local sheriff.

Their father, a church-going, upstanding member of the community, was invited down to the police station for questioning. After hours of continuous interrogation, the father confessed to being a "High Priest of Satan," to being a sodomizer of children and a willing participant in the murder, dismemberment, and cannibalization of infants. He even remembered being abused himself at age four or five. The man's stories became increasingly bizarre: incorporating infant sacrifice, Satanic ritual, and bestiality.

Before long, the accused man's wife and his two sons were also "remembering" incidents of abuse. When their memories became sketchy, their preacher and the police investigators were there to encourage them.[32] When

---

32. *Newsweek* (April 4, 1994).

questioned about his abuse, one of the sons first denied it, then "remembered" it, and then recanted. Soon the second daughter upped the ante by implicating two of her father's poker buddies.

All these "memories" later proved false!

Eventually the father would come to his senses and try to withdraw his confession, but his appeal fell on deaf judicial ears and he was sentenced to twenty years in prison.

Why would a man confess to such a heinous array of crimes he didn't commit, crimes that never happened?

False memories are more easily implanted when they are (1) traumatic and when they are (2) planted by a trusted person. Both these prerequisites came into play during the father's interrogation.

First, the father trusted his police interrogators who, ironically, were his friends and colleagues (he was a chief civil deputy for the same sheriff's department investigating the allegations against him).

Second, the father trusted his daughters who he'd described to police as "good Christian girls" incapable of lying. (Therefore, they must be telling the truth about the molestations, the police countered!)

Third, police interrogators knew the father's beliefs and were able to use what Japanese call *kyonin-no-jutsu*, turning one's superstitions and beliefs against them.

Investigating detectives (some of them trusted friends and authority figures to the man) played on the father's religious fervor, liberally loading their questions with religious references they knew the man would respond to. Simply put, the father's religious beliefs (i.e. superstitions) taught him that "demonic forces" were real and warned him that the Devil had not only the power to make people do something they wouldn't normally do, but also to make them forget they had done it. A real life version of *Faust*! These fundamentalist beliefs were reinforced by a visiting minister (a trusted authority figure) who invited the man to "get it off his chest," reassuring the confused and traumatized Christian that "confession is good for the soul."

Ironically, the prosecution's case began falling apart when their own expert on cult mind control turned against them, convinced that the father was not guilty and that he had been led to confess through a combination of leading questions and suggestive comments.

Eventually all the allegations of "Satanic abuse" remained unproven and the charges were dropped against the man's two poker buddies. By then however, it was already too late since the father had pled guilty and received his sentence.

The real injustice of the Olympia case was that no one was ever called to account for implanting the false memories of abuse into the two daughters' minds in the first place.

How police ask questions can have as much impact as the actual questions they ask. Evidence shows that even the phrasing of questions can influence answers.[33] There is a big difference in a police investigator asking an accident witness "How fast was the blue car going when it slammed into the red car?" and his asking "Did you see the cars collide?" Such leading questions are called "priming," as in priming a water pump. Thus no two interrogations are the same once you factor in (1) the personality of the person being interrogated, (2) the training and personality of the interrogator, and (3) the interaction dynamic between the two.

Tips for Implanting a False Memory

- *"Relax" your subject* by reminding them and/or getting them to talk about, some "happy time" and/or happy spot in their life. (This is an old hypnotist's trick.)
- *Don't try changing their memory all at once.* Begin by "tweaking" it a little here and there. It's called shaping.
- *Make them question their details of the actual event* first, quickly providing your own "details" of what happened—or how something "might" have happened—any time you hear them hesitate in their recollection.
- *Always show them in a good light* when challenging (and changing) their version of the event, making them "remember" what an important part *they* played in what happened, exaggerating their contribution to good things that happened.
- *Downplay anything negative or bad* they might have done or allowed to happen.
- *Inject emotion and animation* into your details, making your version

---

33 Sanford H. Kadish, editor in chief, *Encyclopedia of Crime and Justice.* (Free Press, 1983).

of the story more "exciting." FYI: This helps engage the subject's *right-side imagination-prone hemisphere* of their brain which will automatically begin creating more exciting images to replace the vague and dull—albeit real—*left-hemisphere* memories.

Could there be times when altering an existing memory and/or implanting a false memory can actually be a good thing? It *is* now an accepted fact we can alter memories, so much so that research is under way to use altered memory to help people stop overeating by implanting *false* memories in their mind of their having had a "distasteful" experience with that food in their past—in effect creating an artificial phobia.[34] The proviso is that it's likely that false memories (phobias) such as these can be implanted only when the subjects targeted are unaware of the mental manipulation taking place.

According to Elizabeth Loftus[35] of the University of California at Irvine who conducted the experiments, there's nothing to stop parents from using this technique of implanting false memories (e.g. of being averse to certain high-caloric foods) to *help* their obese children. Some worry, however, that if parents can become adept at implanting false memories about food, what else might a parent—or others?—also be able to implant in a child's mind?

Advances in technology have raised intriguing (or is that "paranoid"?) possibilities for both improving and manipulating memory. For example, at the Alpha-learning Institute in Switzerland they've developed a pair of glasses with light-emitting diodes (LEDs) that pulsate at varying speeds. Simultaneously, headphones emit a beat synchronized to the pulsing lights. This combination of light and sounds reportedly "tunes" the mind to "optimal frequencies" conducive to relaxation and concentration, thereby increasing the subject's capacity for memory, in turn making the brain more "susceptible" to learning.[36] More "susceptible" to learning . . . no comment on *what* exactly the subject might be learning and *whom* might be "teaching" it to

---

34. Rebecca Skoot, "Can Memory Manipulation Change the Way you Eat?" *Discover* (January, 2006), 30.

35. Loftus is best known for her controversial expertise at debunking "repressed memories." (See *Black Science*, 2001, *Mind Manipulation*, 2002).

36. *Learn to Remember* by Dominic O'Brien (Chronicle Books/SF 2000).

him, and for *what* reason? Recall that "relaxing" a test subject was the first step in Dr. Lozanov's science of Suggestology. The only difference being that where Lozanov used Yogic meditation to relax his test subjects, here technology is being used.

More on using the Power of Suggestion and how to create false memories in the chapter on "Secrets of Shadow-Ki Hypnosis" in Section II (p. 142).

6.

The Art of "N-timidation"

"N" IS VERY POWERFUL, perhaps the most intimidating of letters in the English language.

Add "N" to "or" and "either" (a clear choice, this or that) and you get "nor" and "neither" (a clear rejection of both options). They ask you "When? *Ever*"? You add an "N" and now they know when . . . *Never!*

Part of our gaining "Ultimate Control" requires our mastering "The Art of N-timidation."

Why "N-timidation" and not the traditional spelling "intimidation"? Because the Ultimate Control technique (art, if you will) of "N-timidation" involves our learning to wield three "N" skills: (1) Getting "N-tune," (2) Being "N-tense," and (3) Mastering the Power of "No."

GETTING "N-TUNE"

Growing out of our "Three Knows,"[37] this requires that we do six "N" things:

- **Notice:** (Another admonishment to *focus*.) Distracted by the strange, we fall to the familiar.

---

37. Review "Know Yourself," "Know Your Enemy," "Know Your Environment," in chapter 1.

- **Note:** The things I remember can only trouble my sleep. It's the things I forget that can kill me.
- **Navigate**: "Ninja 101": You don't always have to use force to go *through* a wall. Sometimes going over the wall, around the wall, even under the wall is the wiser course of action. Learn to navigate your way around obstacles, especially when those obstacles are people.
- **Nourish:** Church mouse (and Jefferson Airplane) advice: "Feed your head" and it will share its bounty with the rest of your body.
- **No prisoners.** Decide before going into any bank whether you're there to rob it or to take out a loan. If you're there to take out a loan, the way you "carry yourself" is going to be different than if you've come to rob the place. If the former, then you *need* these people, you *need* to make friends with them, which means you'll be operating on their time schedule.

If, on the other hand, you've come to get your Dillinger on, you're "on the clock" the minute you walk through the front door brandishing that Thompson. You're not there to make friends. Get in, get out, and do whatever you have to in order to accomplish your mission. They used to call this attitude "ruthlessness." No looking back. Don't let the dog outta the pen if you're scared of getting bit. In for a penny, in for a pound. Do your job and don't let your coworkers down. Or as Hannibal put it: "In for a sip, in for a sea."[38]

BEING "N-TENSE"

This means developing an intense focus. Without focus, all is lost. Being "N-tense" includes showing enough "N-thusiasm" to inspire others. Focus-plus-enthusiasm, herein lies the beginnings of true leadership.

MASTERING THE POWER OF "NO"

Ever ask yourself why others sometimes succeed while you fail? They obviously "No" something you don't:

---

38. Truth LXXXIX. See "Hannibal's Ninety-nine Truths" (p. 255).

- Perhaps they say "No" to sleeping late while you get up at half-past-ten.
- They said "No" to "Just one more round" last night.
- They "No" eating that extra donut for breakfast.

Discipline is measured by what you can do without, by what we can just say "No" to:

"Deny self for self's sake." —Benjamin Franklin

Or, as the author of *Think and Grow Rich*, put it:

"Fortunate is the person who has developed the self-control to steer a straight course toward his objective in life, without being swayed from his purpose by either commendation or condemnation." —Napoleon Hill

Author Denis Waitley in *Being the Best* (1987) says that "self-discipline does within while you do without." What's he mean by this?

Doing within while you do without means being able to focus mentally on your goal while you do without certain things to reach that goal. You may have to go without sleep, rest, that relaxing television show you want to watch, or that ice-cream sundae you're just dying to devour. . . . But in another sense, as you keep doing something mentally within, you will eventually be able to do it without—that is, on the outside. You will be able to realize your goal physically, materially and visibly.[39]

Tell yourself: No chewing your cud twice, no backing down. Tell yourself you have to master the art—it's called "discipline"—of actively, aggressively telling yourself "No!" before you can effectively influence and control others with the same "No."

This is not the same as being a "naysayer." You know who I'm talking about: that certain someone in your life (everybody's got at least one!) who's always looking over your shoulder, always ready to tell you how your latest venture is doomed to failure.

---

39. Denis Waitley, *Being the Best: A Life-changing Guide to REAL Success* (Pocket Books, 1987), 191.

In his 1998 *The Secret Power Within: Zen Solutions to Real Problems*, Chuck Norris includes these kind of negative people under what he calls "Shadow Warriors." Likewise, in their delightful and insightful 2006 *Yes Lives in the Land of No* authors B. J. Gallagher and Steve Ventura call such naysayers the "soldiers of stagnation."

These are your "Ninjas of Negativity" always waiting in the wings to undermine your N-thusiasm. Develop the discipline to just say "No" to their will-weakening whispers, their energy-draining doubts.

How to Say "No" (and Mean It!)

Nothing is more intimidating to others than our having the power to say "no." Except, perhaps, our willingness to ruthlessly wield that power!

We don't ask questions, we don't make requests, we bite our tongue all too often, all because we don't want to hear that terrible, dream-crushing, four-letter word "no".

Damn! That's cold. Indeed, a flat, icy, "No" is a sign of dominance, the ultimate sign of Ultimate Control, that one word one finger that leaves no doubt in the recipient's mind that:

- "You don't deserve an explanation."
- "You're too stupid to understand if I did lower myself to explain!"
- "I'm in charge and I don't have to explain my decisions to peons and piss ants."

Should you run into someone so stupid they don't understand why you're calling them stupid, asking you to explain to them why they're stupid, you meet them with a *silent*, condescending (and/or bored) look. Silence is *very* intimidating. (Professional interrogators call this "The Arab Method.")

Other times, when you don't want to completely burn your bridges, you may deign to explain your reason for saying "no." In which case, soften your "no" blow by giving well-prepared excuses.

Always make it abundantly clear to the person:

- How "hard" it was for you to have had "no other choice" than to say "no." (This is what's known as a "Martyr Complex" ploy, making the other person feel "guilty" for the "sacrifices" you make "just for them.")

- How your decision was made "under extreme duress" or "only after much soul-searching."
- How your "No" will somehow *benefit* them in the long run. In other words, when you say "No," you're actually doing them *a favor*. (The old "This is gonna hurt me a lot more than it hurts you" argument. A little more of that "Martyr Complex.")

For extremely bothersome—*potentially dangerous!*—people (e.g., horny NRA card-carrying, Prozac-popping postal workers from Vermont), soften them up to accept your "No" (i.e. distract them and defuse potential violence) with humor and flattery (being careful not to make *them* the butt of the joke).

Types of "No"

There are two types of "No": Your enemy's "No" and your "No."

Your "No" is carved in stone and means "Hell, no!" (or at least that's what you want him to believe in order for you to keep the upper hand in future negotiations).

His "No," on the other hand, is just a temporary inconvenience on your way to getting what you want—to getting a "Yes" out of him.

Before turning down someone's request, repeat their request back to them out loud so they'll know you understand what they're asking and won't feel obliged to keep repeating their request—and further waste your time.

After turning down their request, immediately ask them for a favor. Believe it or not, they're likely to say, "Yes."

According to David Lieberman's 2000 masterpiece *Get Anyone to Do Anything and Never Feel Powerless Again*, not only should we ask for a favor immediately after we say "No" to another person's request (since that person is then more likely to grant our request) but we should also be sure to include the word "because" in all our requests *because* it triggers unconscious acceptance. (The psychology behind this seems to be that he'll be eager to show you and himself that he's a good human being who knows how to do someone a favor, that he's the bigger man, and he's not as big a prick as you!)

Saying "No" is a reflex designed to keep us out of trouble. By the way, doing nothing is not the same as saying "No." Like acquiescing "Yes," doing nothing is passive. Firmly declaring "No," on the other hand, is active, aggressive, making us look both decisive and "N-timidating."

Sometimes, however, strategy requires we say no hesitantly and reluctantly. So it's all about how you say "No." This is where the "Martyr Complex" approach works, because we convince the person we're saying "No" to that we're actually doing them a favor.

How often have you been cautioned to sugarcoat your requests, to "let people down easy"? To be more "diplomatic"? Anytime you hear that, remind yourself that a *"diplomat"* has been defined as a man (or woman) who can tell you to "Go to Hell" in such a way that you look forward to the trip! Therefore, when it comes to telling others "No," our ideal should be to do so in such a way that they think you've done them a favor:

> "I could give you that manager's job in Hawaii, Bob. But I'm not going to. And do you know why? Because I like you too damn much! A job like that—all that sun and surf, that unlimited expense account—all that would just make a real go-getter like yourself go soft. Hell, Bob old buddy, you'd die from boredom within a week! So by saying no to Hawaii, I'm really saying yes! To Bob, the Bob we just can't do without around here!"

Or how about using his obvious "assets" as liabilities:

> "That kind of thing's not for a guy like you, not with your [high moral standards, ambition, positive attitude, patriotism]."

And that ol' tried-and-true standby, saying "No" because you don't want to obligate or burden the other person:

> "I'd feel like I was betraying your trust in me if I gave you that [loan, promotion, business contract, etc.], Bob. And do you want to know why? Because I know you trust me to do right by you. And because of what I'd have to ask for in return for it. I just wouldn't feel right asking you to make such a [sacrifice, commitment] . . . no matter how noble that [sacrifice, commitment]!"

By now, Bob—in *grateful* tears—will be begging you to let him make that noble sacrifice, take that radical pay cut, bear your love-child!

Types of "No" include:

- **The "No" Because:** Like the line you just fed Bob about doing him a favor.
- **The I'd Love to, but "No":** "I'd love to do that, but . . . ," "I'd love to just as soon as . . . ," "I'd love to if it wasn't for . . ."
- **The "No" Ignore:** You say "No" without an explanation because the person you're saying "No" to isn't worthy of an explanation. (This ploy has doubly devastating effect when used to minimize a person in front of his coworkers and friends. One, it marks him a non-entity in the eyes of onlookers. Two, it strikes terror into their hearts for fear they might be treated the same.)
- **The "No" Indictment:** Say, "No. And you *know* why." Then walk away. Of course he doesn't know why, so he's confused, worried you've discovered some heinous secret about him. And of course, anyone overhearing you tell him this won't believe him when he assures them he has no idea what you're talking about.
- **The Future "No":** Make it clear that "No" is your answer . . . for *now* . . . "But if this changes . . ."
- **The Witch's Broom "No":** Remember *The Wizard of Oz*? Nobody was getting *squat* off the man behind the curtain until they brought him the witch's broom. In other words: *Strings attached*.
- **The Big Picture "No":** He's crying for a raise until you start hinting that the company is about to go out of business. In other words: *Making mountains out of molehills?*

The Six Rules of NO-gotiation

> *Neither a fortress nor maidenhead will hold out long once they begin to parley.*
> —Benjamin Franklin

The English word "*negotiation*," originally written *negotiari*, literally means "to carry on business." From the Latin "*negotium*," ironically "negotiation" comes from the same root "*neg*" that gives us the word *negative*. "*Otium*" means "leisure," which gives us the clear warning that "negotiation" is "No fun."

Truer words have never been spoken. Negotiating is "no fun." We only negotiate when the other person has something we want. This automatically presupposes that we don't already have what we want (otherwise why would we have to negotiate?). What we "want" may be "noble" or it may simply be that we want the other person's cooperation, but the fact is we still *want* something.

Buddha taught that all suffering begins with (1) our wanting something we either don't have or (2) something we don't really need. Thus, when you *want* something, it automatically puts you in the deficit department—you no longer hold the high ground, or the upper hand.

Conversely, when you *have* something another person wants, that puts you in the catbird seat, giving you the upper hand going into any negotiation. No matter how much the other side of the negotiation table smiles in your face and offers hardy handshakes, *never forget that they're there to get all they can get and all they can get away with. So are you.* Your rationale for negotiating might be "moral" and "high-minded" but, deep down, you're still sitting there across the table from your sworn (and often sworn at!) enemy trying to play nice. You wouldn't be sitting there if there wasn't something in it for *you*. Sure, "what's in it for you" might be "world peace," but it's still something you want. And you're going to fight for "world peace" just as hard as your enemy is fighting for a *piece* of your world!

To win the "No-gotiation" game, you have to arm yourself with a lot of "*Know*-gotiation," meaning the more you (1) *know* about the person sitting across the table, and (2) *know* how the game is played, the better your chances of walking away from the negotiation table with a smile on your face.

Thus, to successfully negotiate, or *No*-gotiate, we need data. Data is both our weapon and our ammunition. Intelligence is required, both the innate kind and the gathered variety. This is nothing new, just a spin on what you've already learned about "The Three Knows"—Know yourself, Know your opponent, and Know your environment. "Environment" in this instance being your knowing what everybody at the table *wants* . . . and then figuring out what they'll *settle* for!

No-gotiation Rule One: Just say "NO!" to negotiation.

Remember: If you're willing to enter into "negotiations" it's only because the other side has something you want or need:

> We sit at the bargaining table for one reason—the other side
> has something we want.
> —*How to Negotiate,* Ronald Shapiro (2001)

That means they've already got you by the shorthairs (unless you also have something of corresponding value they want or need?). Never enter into any negotiation unless you are in a position to walk away from the table.

The difference between an amateur and a professional is that a professional knows when to walk away.

It's just like gambling. Professional gamblers know when the worm has turned: when Lady Luck just discovered that diamond engagement ring you gave her was cubic zirconium, then it's time to "cut your losses" and walk away. If you can't walk away, then you've got a gambling problem. The same with negotiating. Benjamin Franklin said it best:

> "Necessity never made a good bargain."

Some people just like to argue. They love the game more than the goal. *Don't be one of those people.* On the other hand, there's an old business adage that warns against trying to negotiate with the kind of person who, in a fifty-fifty proposition, insists on getting the *hyphen*! *Be one of those people!*

Humbly settling for second place sounds like the oh-so-politically-correct thing to do until we remind ourselves that, in a race to the finish line (or at least the tree line), the lion gets to eat lunch and the gazelle gets to be lunch!

Therefore, in order for you to master the art of "No-gotiation" there are two skills you need to devote yourself to acquiring—two goals to accomplish: (1) *Know* what you want, and (2) "*No!*" what he wants.

No-gotiation Rule Two: Whoever picks the battlefield has the power.

Gettysburg. July 1, 1863: Confederate General Robert E. Lee has boldly struck into Union territory, into Pennsylvania, where he finds himself confronting well-entrenched Union forces who've taken the high ground, placing a wide-open field between themselves and Lee's forces.

Lee's second-in-command, General James Longstreet tries to convince his commander not to attack the Union position, correctly pointing out that if Lee feigns retreat, Union forces would have no choice but to abandon their advantageous positions and give chase. Then, at any point along the way, at a battlefield of *his* choosing, Lee can engage the enemy. Longstreet's sound strategy falls on deaf ears . . .

Two days and 20,000 dead Johnny Reb's later, under cover of rain and night, what was left of Lee's forces tucks tail and retreats in earnest. It was the beginning of the end for the Stars-n-Bars, the turning point in the War Between the States, all because Lee ignored that most basic of military dictums:

> *Never let your enemy choose the battlefield.*

It would have helped if Lee had read Sun Tzu's *Ping-Fa* (Art of War) before venturing forth at Gettysburg. In fact, according to noted author and history expert Bevin Alexander:

> The answer to how Sun Tzu's Battle of Gettysburg would have differed from Lee's historical battle seems clear: Sun Tzu would not have fought the battle at all.[40]

A modern-day application of this principle? Consider the big difference between negotiating in *his* office (comfort zone/power spot) as opposed to the hallway outside his mistress' apartment; his apartment (where the least little noise bothers his neighbors) versus your *soundproofed* basement?

This is why, when fishing, police always ask, "Would you mind coming down to the station?" Home court advantage.

When you can't pick the battlefield, the next best thing is *picking apart* the battlefield. In an actual war zone, this entails seizing control of bridges and other vital avenues needed to facilitate your maneuvering and logistics, while simultaneously laying land mines and destroying lines of communication in order to deny the enemy reinforcement.

As on the battlefield, so in the ruthless boardroom, the smoke-filled backroom, and the lust-filled bedroom. Take the fish out of the water, attack his (or her) comfort zone. Confuse them until they come to you for "clarification." For example, say you peg your adversary as a *Watcher* (domi-

---

40. Bevin Alexander, "Sun Tzu's Battle of Gettysburg" *Armchair General* (July 2009).

nated by what he sees), a *Listener* (dominated by what he hears), or a *Toucher* (kinesthetically oriented); you can now manipulate rooms and rendezvous so as to keep him guessing and make him uncomfortable:

- *Touch* and otherwise crowd Listeners and Watchers, invading their space.
- Make Listeners sweat over *visual images* (e.g., a pile of dull, incomprehensible graphs, photos).
- Make a Watcher *listen* to a lecture so mind-numbing that when you finally whip out your brightly colored graphs and fast-paced videos, he'll see you as The Second Coming.

Uncomfortable chairs, poor lighting, someone continually buzzing his private pager number, as well as other distractions you can throw his way to throw him off his game. Raise the temperature of the meeting room. FYI: Research shows the human brain works best in a cool room, around sixty-five degrees.

While the No-gotiation rule is "Never give up home court advantage," there is one very notable historical exception:

In 1938, Stalin agreed to a Non-Aggression Pact with Hitler, which allowed them the following year to divide Poland between them. This was a win-win for Stalin. Unlike so many in the West, Stalin had actually taken the time to read Hitler's *Mein Kampf*, which clearly outlined what Hitler had up his sleeve. But even if Stalin hadn't read Hitler's plan beforehand, it didn't take a military mastermind to see Hitler was planning to winter in Moscow. Realizing it was only a matter of time before the Red Bear and the Black Eagle would be tearing at each other's throats, Stalin reasoned, Why fight the Hun on Russian soil, when he could just as easily fight them on Polish soil . . . with the added bonus that, once Hitler was beaten back, Poland would be given the dubious honor of becoming the newest Soviet satellite!

> What we gain in a free way is better than twice as much in a
> forced, and will be more truly ours and our posterities' . . .
> That which you have by force I look upon as nothing.
> —Lord High Protector Oliver Cromwell, 1647

No-gotiation Rule Three: The person asking the questions has the power.
The police. Your boss. Your wife. The IRS. They ask the questions while

you stutter, and sputter, and sweat trying desperately to figure out what they want you to say.

We ask questions for two reasons: *First, we need information,* and sometimes people are nice enough (or dumb enough) to just give it to us. *Second, we need to spread misinformation,* and asking questions you already know the answer to is a good way to lead the other guy around by the nose—or ears, as the case may be. In other words, we use unexpected and unusual lines of questioning to disorient and get the upper hand over our competition.

But all the questioning in the world comes to naught until we take the time to master the craft of listening to what the other guy is saying—or *isn't* saying. This is where listening to his "shadow-talk" (Freudian slips, hesitations, etc.) and noticing his "shadow-walk" (i.e. body language) begins to pay off.

Of course, should you find yourself on the receiving end of such an "interrogation," switch to stall tactics: (1) Act confused (which you probably are anyway!), (2) buy time by repeating the last thing they said, (3) exit ASAP and (4) regroup (evaluate when and why you lost control of the situation).

No-gotiation Rule Four: Control the name and you control the person.

Folks at one time superstitiously guarded their names for fear witches would use their "Christian names" to cast spells against them. Times really haven't changed all that much since, today, unscrupulous manipulators and/or identity thieves can still all too easily use our names and our coveted titles to possess us.

Conspiracy buffs worry and warn: "We're all becoming just numbers!" but when it comes to face-to-face encounters, *name games* still hold sway.

From the prettiest of pet names reserved for loved ones, to the ugliest of racial slurs reserved for those "beneath us," the names and titles *we identify with* still have power to motivate and manipulate us. Conversely, showing an interest in a person's name is one sure way of establishing early rapport with that person. Therefore, when first introduced to a person:

- Repeat their name back to them.
- Encourage them to talk about themselves.
- Start a conversation with them about their name. People love it when we talk about them. Ask about the origin of the name, where their family is from.
- Praise any famous people or notable historic sites sharing a same or similar name.

If you're in "The People Business" (and who isn't these days!), take time to study the origins of names in general and particularly the names of anyone you plan on "accidently" bumping into. People love it when you tell them something interesting and/or exciting about their name. This is made all the easier these days since you can punch it up on your iPhone. Use this information to ingratiate yourself with the person you've zeroed in on, to show you're "sincerely" interested in them.

On the flip side, you can also use such trivia against your rival, casually pointing out the fact his name means "duplicitous bastard" or "dinosaur excrement" in some obscure Klingon dialect.

Remembering a person's name is important, both as a tool and as a weapon, whether used to get closer to that person, or in order to denigrate them.

Tips to help you better remember names:

- *Take an interest* because it's in your best interest.
- *Really look at the person.* Note any unique facial characteristics, mannerisms, and traits that will help you more easily associate their face with their name.
- *Use mnemonics.* For example, let's say you want to remember the name:

    "Robert Baughman" (pronounced "boff-man"). The short version of "Robert" is "Bob" so picture in your mind a seasick BARFING (vomiting) MAN in a boat "BOBbing" up and down. Disgusting? Definitely. But guaranteed to help you remember BARF-MAN BOB . . . Bob Barf-man . . . Robert Baughman! An even better reminder would be to see this character in the cartoonish burglar's mask and striped shirt making you think "ROBBER" (i.e. "Robert"). The more colorful, "silly" (a cartoon robber) and action-filled (bobbing, vomiting!) you can make your mental picture, the easier it will be to remember the person's name.

In order to ingratiate yourself further with your new-found "friend," depending on what role you want your new friend to adopt, create a fictitious person you "once knew" who possessed not only the same (or similar) name as your new friend, but also (by implication) the same *positive attributes* (e.g., generosity, open-mindedness) you want your new friend to exhibit. This will cause your new friend to consciously (or subconsciously) want to identify with or live up to. You can also invoke the names of actual famous people sharing a same or similar name as your target, casually mentioning obscure and little known "facts" about them as suits your game plan.

What to do about a "smart-ass." Your enemy comes to the party armed with rehearsed dialogue, practiced mannerisms, a carefully crafted reputation, and enough titles, rank, and positions to choke Linda Lovelace. Worse still, he's well-studied in the "Rules of Etiquette" and feels free to insult and belittle you at every turn, secure enough to be rude since he sees himself safely insulated as he is by "decorum" and "social decency."

He "plays by the rules," so the only way to beat him is: *Know the rules* better than he does (allowing you to cash in on loopholes and trap him with "technicalities"), and don't be afraid to *break the rules!* How?

- *Deliberately mispronounce his name.* This will Make him stop his diatribe to correct you. Say, "That's a *foreign* name, isn't it?" with plenty of suspicion on "foreign." Later, should he dare challenge you on a fact or point of order, remind listeners that he's a foreigner by asking, "Is a question/tone/behavior like that considered appropriate where you come from?"
- *Ignore his ranks and titles.* Titles are a very effective form of "word slavery." We are expected to start kissin' rings and kissin' ass any time anyone puts on a uniform or flashes a commanding title—no matter how arbitrary.[41] We all do it. Who among us would dare refer to the Pope as "Mister"? Calling a nun "Miss"? Catholic priests are "Father" and you better not forget it. And what about calling the President of the United States by his first name? "Yo, Barack!" or calling a New Jersey State Highway Patrolman "Dude," or your Paris Island drill instructor "Mister"?

During the infamous Chicago Seven trial, Yippie activist and all-around trickster Abbie Hoffman insisting on disrupting the proceedings by calling the Judge (coincidentally also named Hoffman) by his first name and by "Mister," rather than "Your Honor." Order in the court!

---

41. Review "The Five Kinds of Power," e.g., Position Power (p. 31).

- *Never mistake being "famous" for having power.* In other words, don't let him intimidate you. Just because he's "famous" for putting an orange ball in a hoop or just because he's "famous" for being the third runner up on last season's *American Idol*, doesn't mean he's necessarily good for much else. He puts his pants on one leg at a time just like you.
- *Challenge his "view" of the world.* And the best way to do that is by "confusing" him and his listeners. You can do this through a combination of the "Word Play" we already talked about and "C.H.A.O.S. Theory."[42]

For example, Hindus and most other Easterners won't blink an eye if you add an "S" to the end of "God," but monotheistic Westerners will go ballistic, and be instantly distracted from their original theological argument. So to get the upper hand in any theological argument with a Christian or Muslim, simply insert "She" or "Her" when speaking about God. It doesn't matter what the subject of the initial argument was, your pious and "God-fearing" opponent will instantly forget it, in favor of smiting your "sacrilege."

Such disruptive ploys used to unbalance an enemy are known as "knocking them out of the box." "The Box" in this case is all the accepted and expected social behavior in general, as well as the specific behaviors demanded of us because of our particular place in the food chain: our socio-economic status, position, rank and uniform, or our gender. The walls of this restrictive box are constructed from names and titles, those social kowtows and taboos we are all taught to respect (i.e. *fear*) from birth. Society then uses these titles and entitlements to manipulate us beginning in childhood, putting us in the box by telling us to: "Act like a little gentleman . . ." "Behave like a proper little lady . . ." Later we're told to "Stay in your place" (the box), and "Remember your station in life. . . ."

Aren't we constantly being told how a "real man" should scratch his . . . lottery ticket, how a "proper lady" should sit. And always we're taught how to show proper respect by genuflecting to the powers-that-be. From Wall Street Ponzi schemers to politicians, would-be manipulators everywhere know they can pull our strings by using evocative challenges like: "Act like a

---

42. Create Hazards/Hardships/Hurt And Offer Solutions, e.g. start the fire and then sell fire extinguishers!

man!" and "A *true* patriot wouldn't hesitate!" to make us (and our money) follow them anywhere.

Of course we can (and already do) use these same ploys on others, freely using words, names, titles, and nicknames dreaded or coveted to control others:

- "You gonna let him get away with that? What are you, a *man* or a mouse?"
- "Do you think that's how a *true* (man/Christian/patriot) would act?"
- "What *kind* of mother are you!"
- "And you call yourself a loving son/daughter!"

Such word ploys work because, truth be known, so few of us have *cojones* big enough to challenge the status quo, to step "outside the box."

Thus anytime some rebel or malcontent does trespass social norms by challenging procedure and protocol, by questioning what it means to "be a man" or where "a woman's place" really is, those depending on such fickle social glue to hold their fragile world together are knocked out of the box, confused, and looking for someone (you?) to reinstate the reality they are so familiar (and comfortable) with.

No-gotiation Rule Five—The "4 D's": When it comes time to "get down to business" in negotiating, the key words are Defer, Demand, Delay, and Discipline.

> *Defer*: Let the other side make the initial offer in any negotiation. They just might surprise you with an offer that exceeds your wildest expectations.
>
> *Demand*: Ask for the outrageous in order to get what you really want. If you'll settle for ten, demand twenty. Give the impression your demands are not negotiable. This gives your enemy a false sense of accomplishment when they think they've convinced you to "stay and negotiate." Often they will offer concessions just to get you to stay.
>
> *Delay*: No matter how much you like their opening bid, never accept it immediately. Take time to think: Is their offer too good to be true? If I hold out, will they up their offer? Probably. Your delaying will give them time to stew—to worry. Beware, however, lest they purposely delay negotiations to their advantage, in their attempt to rattle. Turnabout being fair play and all.

Discipline is measured by what you can do without. Remember?
Never enter into any negotiation when you're desperate, scared,
or hungry. Learn to say no to your weaknesses, of which
impatience is the most deadly.

No-gotiation Rule Six: Always make mountains out of molehills.

Hindus tell this tale of a farmer who one day caught hold of a beautiful
horse wandering his property:

"Oh, what very good luck!" applauds his neighbor.

"Who can see far enough into the future to say what is
truly good luck?" the farmer shrugs.

True enough, the farmer's son no sooner climbs on the
horse than the horse bucks the young man to the ground,
breaking the young man's leg.

"Oh, what very bad luck!" laments the neighbor.

"Who can see far enough into the future to say what is
truly bad luck?" sighs the farmer, tending to his injured son.

Later that day, a warlord and his army marches through
the area, pillaging what they want from the farmers, forcing
all able-bodied young men in the area to enlist. But they leave
the farmer's son behind because of his broken leg.

The next day the tyrant and all his host are slaughtered in
a horrific battle.

"What good luck your son was spared!" declares the
neighbor.

The farmer only shrugs.

This tale tells us two things:

First, it's not what happens to you in life, it's all in how you look at
it—your *perspective*. Second, it's how you look at something compared to
something else—*context*.

Or maybe the real lesson is "Things can always get worse!" Einstein
called this the Law of Relativity. We call it ***The Law of Contrasts*** which
reminds us that we don't see things and happenings as they really are, but
rather in their relationship to other things and happenings. To a warm hand,
tepid water feels cool. To a cold hand, the same water feels warm.

Fringe political organizations often use this "Law of Contrasts" principle to their advantage. When the powers-that-be refuse to negotiate with them because of their radical views, another more-threatening "splinter, break-away faction" (that the parent organization swears they have no control over) pops up out of nowhere and begins wreaking havoc. Suddenly that radical parent organization doesn't look all that bad in comparison to the new terrorists on the block. Do *Sinn Fein*/IRA or PLO/Black September ring a bell? In other words, "Feed me or feed that bigger, uglier dog down the block!" The "lesser of two evils," one of the oldest examples of the protection racket. Yes, this *does* sound a lot like "C.H.A.O.S. Theory."

Medieval Samurai *daimyo* (warlords), finding themselves targeted for assassination by a Ninja clan would often hire bodyguards from a *rival* Ninja clan to protect them . . . only to later discover the two rival groups were actually one and the same clan—with one faction drumming up business by being threatening, until the other faction steps in, offering protection for a price. Likewise, the Middle Eastern *Hashishin* (Assassin) cult threatened and thrived for centuries, masters of just this extortion ploy.[43]

Other variations of this ploy include police using "good cop/bad cop" and opportunist politicians creating convenient enemies for us via "wag-the-dog" scenarios.

The Art of Agreeing Without Agreeing

"Agreeing without agreeing" is verbal *judo*. Your opponent jumps in the ring spoiling for a fight. He's trained long and hard, expecting you to stand toe-to-toe, meeting him blow-for-blow. How shocked and disoriented he is then when, instead of standing toe-to-toe, you duck and dodge, pivoting at just the right moment as he rushes headlong towards you—perfect timing to drop him to the floor. He pushes, you pull. He pulls, you push, and once again, he hits the canvas! As on the battlefield, so in the boardroom: Give "No" for an answer but never take "No" for an answer. Likewise, never give "Yes" for an answer. Not unless your "Yes" is just a "No" in drag!

A few "tricks"[44] for getting them to say "Yes":

---

43. See *Assassin! Secrets of the Cult of the Assassins* by Dr. Haha Lung (Paladin Press, 1997) and *Assassin!* (Citadel, 2004).

44. Tricks well-mastered are called "techniques." Techniques half-learned are merely tricks.

- **Get them to say "yes" to a little point,** and they're more likely to say "yes" to a big point. Hitler was *the* master at this.
- **Listen to them.** By listening to others—listening to their desires, their version of reality, letting them blow off steam and get it off their chests, you allow them to exhaust themselves. By listening to the other person's point of view we also see their best argument *before* they see ours.
- **Reflect the other person.** "Mirroring" tells people you're just like them. Once adept at reflecting the other person, you can take control of the communication (by adjusting the pace, tone, and direction of the conversation, gently guiding the conversation where you want it to go, leading the person into agreement with you).
- **Get in synch with the other person.** Since we tend to cooperate with people we like, those with whom we share common interests, once you determine his position and the direction his argument is taking, place yourself in synch with him by finding (1) common ground and (2) points of common interest. Pay attention not only to what others say, but to how they say it as well.
- **Watch the body language** of the person you are trying to persuade (how he sits, moves, rate of breathing, gestures) then imitate his actions and attitudes. Watch your own body language. Beginning a conversation, use wide, open and friendly arm gestures designed to grab the listener's attention. From these large gestures, gradually move inward, into smaller, more intimate hand gestures that gradually draw all the listener's focus onto you. (This is an old hypnotism technique.)
- **Don't get personal when countering a person's argument.** Attack the position not the person. Require him to defend his position, produce evidence, verify facts, and explain his reasoning.

No matter how *different* another person's argument is from yours, *agree* with them, or at least *appear to*. Use phrases like "I see your point," "I agree one hundred percent," and "It would be hard to argue with that," effectively defusing the other guy's arguments while purposely driving a wedge between the person and his argument.

To accomplish this "wedge-driving," first determine whether the person is (1) trying to *prove his point* or (2) trying to *prove himself*. In other words, does he really believe his point is worth arguing for and his position worth defending, or is he simply saying "Hey, look at me. I'm smart!"? If the latter, assure him that he is, indeed, "smart" and "valuable," it's *only* his position that's wrong.

Always leave an "honorable" way for him to downplay or otherwise distance himself from his initial argument/position should you convince him of the wisdom of doing so. Acknowledge his concerns as "valid" and, most important, *stroke his ego*. Hint: You can recognize another's need to feel important and accepted without actually agreeing with him.

Clearly show him some advantage in abandoning his position in favor of joining your team. Remember: There is no such thing as altruism. Make him choose between maintaining his position or accepting your compliments and critique of his obvious brilliance. Make him a job offer. Give him the option of promoting his argument or promoting himself. Most human beings are sell-outs, they just haven't run into a big enough bribe . . . yet.

Per Sun Tzu, always leave him an honorable—"face saving"—way out. For example, tell him, "You're obviously an intelligent person; someone must have purposely given you incorrect facts."

Likewise, to paraphrase Chinese master strategist Tu Mu, "show him a way to safely withdraw from the battle [or in this case, conversation] by creating in his mind an alternative to losing." Thus, when trying to bring a person into agreement with you, always leave him a face-saving way out of a disagreement, a way of honorably abandoning his position.

Two points of personal psychology work in your favor when attempting to do this: (1) the human need for personal consistency and (2) our desire for social acceptance.

The Need for Personal Consistency makes us all try to justify our earlier behaviors. Thus, when a manipulator points out that something we're doing or saying today contradicts yesterday's actions and opinions, we may go to great lengths to justify our actions.

Manipulators pay close attention to any inconsistencies in the other person's narrative, including contradictions between his stated goal and any effort (or lack thereof) he makes toward accomplishing his goal. Manipulators are quick to point out personal contradictions and inconsistencies in the argument of the person they are trying to persuade. They will either offer him a way to mend his inconsistencies (perhaps by showing him how your proposed course of action, your product, etc., helps him meet his goals), or else using his contradictions to further undermine his credibility.

The Need for Social Acceptance influences our decisions because, whether we admit it or not, we all care what other people think about us, especially people we look up to. The deep-seated sense of duty we feel toward authority figures (and institutions) can be invoked by manipulators in arguments with references to tribal totems, fallen heroes, and authority figures we admire, emulate, and/or seek blessings from. Thus, manipulators and naysayers never tire of reminding us of our obligations. Always remember, "duty" is a debt you owe yourself. Some call it honor. (An "obligation," on the other hand, is what other people try to tell you your duty is.)

People who are constantly snickering "I don't care what other people think of me!" already know what other people think of them.

> *There are fewer YESes than NOs to be sure,*
> *but usually all you need is one—the right one.*
> —Gallagher and Ventura, 2006

7.

Jing Gong:
How to Train Your Senses

There are even senses that are never used.
—**Voltaire**

ALL WHO HAVE EVER written on the history of Asian philosophy and martial arts always tip their hats to the pivotal part played by Chinese *Shaolin*[45] monks.

The story goes that around 520 A.D., the twenty-eighth Buddhist patriarch *Tamo*[46] traveled from his native India to what was then a Taoist monastery at *Foochow*, where he founded the Shaolin Order. After practicing meditation (Skt. *Dhyana,* Ch. *Ch'an*) for nine years by staring at a wall, Tamo had a revelation, out of which he formed *Zen* Buddhism. Tamo is also credited with teaching the monks and nuns at Shaolin a form of Indian *yogic* exercise designed to help strengthen them for staying awake during lengthy meditation sessions. He initially taught these "*kung fu*" (Ch. "hard work") exercises only for "medicinal purposes," and never intended they should ever be used, as they would be later, to kick serious ass. Or so the legend goes.

Over the course of years, several Shaolin monasteries, including the one

---

45. Often written "Shao-lin."
46. Called *Bodhidharma* in his native India, and *Daruma* in Japan.

at Foochow, fell out of imperial favor and were burned to the ground on orders of the reigning emperor. Fortunately for martial arts enthusiasts everywhere, Shaolin kung fu "boxing" (aka *wu shu quan*) survived this purge, giving birth to a thousand styles of "kung fu" worldwide.

But it was not only fighting techniques that survived from Shaolin. Techniques of mind control—both over self and others—have also been passed down to us. Called *Jing gong*, these mind control techniques are composed of two specialties: *Ying gong* and *Chi gong*.

Ying gong (lit. "body toughening") calisthenics and yoga-like exercises are used to first discipline and strengthen the body. These were those exercises originally taught by Tamo in order to help the Shaolin brothers stay awake during marathon meditation sessions. The focus here is on strengthening the body outwardly, in order that the student could withstand the rigors of monastery life and survive in a war situation when called upon to do so.

Chi gong (lit. "internal training") strengthens the internal organs and helps increase the student's overall "balance," both inside and out. These are exercises designed to purify and cleanse the internal organs and systems of the body, increasing overall health. Chi gong also helps practitioners reduce stress, relax, and cultivate "chi" energy. The practice of *Tai Chi* (aka *Dai qi quan*) fits this category.

An important component of overall Jing gong training in general, and Chi gong in particular, is the proper training of the senses. Often referred to in ancient texts as "cleansing the senses," Chi gong sense training is designed to increase a student's overall awareness through teaching them to use their five senses fully. At this level, the student's previous forging of strong body-mind awareness through initial Ying gong exercises is expanded upon.

As a result of proper Chi gong, the student's adroitness of mind not just doubles, but expands exponentially as the student first develops Ultimate Control over his own mind, before then developing the ability to exercise Ultimate Control over the minds of others.

Ultimate control over others?

Indeed, with the mastery of self, mastery of your own mind, inevitably comes the temptation to influence (i.e., master!) the minds of others. This is not necessarily a negative thing. Some scatterbrained (hence, dangerous) individuals could actually benefit from a little "mastery" from outside their own confused, even tortured, minds.

Ideally, each of us would live up to our full "Nietzschean" potential . . .

yeah, how's *that* workin' for ya?[47] In the absence of everybody on the planet suddenly growing a brain—and then, Heaven forbid, actually using that brain!—it behooves those who have been gifted (or those who have taken the time to develop the raw material each and every one of us has been born with) to help "shepherd" (i.e. guide) our less . . . *attentive* brothers.

Helping others begins with first helping yourself. Helping yourself, in turn, begins with understanding yourself and mastering those gifts you've been given. In China there is an old saying, "*Sow five, harvest six,*" meaning that mastery of our five given senses might actually grant us a "sixth" sense.

It's a simple formula: *Sensation* leads to *Recognition*, which in turn leads to *Thought* and *Action*. The trouble is, smack dab in between (1) what our senses encounter (sensation) and (2) what our brain actually "takes in" (recognition, i.e. what it recognizes and decides to think about), can be *physical defects* (e.g. hearing loss, varying degrees of blindness) and *psychological diseases* (Mama, drama, and trauma) that prevent this second stage from taking place. Then, to make us question ourselves even more, in between our perceiving and recognizing a stimulus (a sensation) and our subsequent conscious response (thoughts and actions), all kinds of *psychological detours and defects* can interfere with what messages our brain sends to the rest of our body. Our brain can even send greatly skewed information (misperceptions), either paralyzing us with fear or else kicking in our fight-or-flight reaction.

Remember the timeless, cautionary tale about "The Three Blind Men and the Elephant"? To recap: each of three blind men thought he "saw" clearly when he touched the elephant. Touching only the trunk, the first blind man declared that the elephant was like a tree. The second, running his hands along the length of the elephant's side declared the beast to be like a great wall. The third blind man, touching the animal's tail, confidently declared the elephant to be like a snake. Of course, you see clearly enough to realize how each blind man saw only part of the whole beast. Now look at the elephant in Figure 7 (next page). How many legs do you see?

If such a simple image drawn of simple black lines can confuse your eye, how much more so dynamic, constantly shifting, and interacting reality? What's that you say? "There's a big difference between some stupid drawing of an elephant and something moving around in real life!"

---

47. If you'd like to revisit Nietzsche, see the conclusion to this book (p. 355).

ELEPHANT ILLUSION

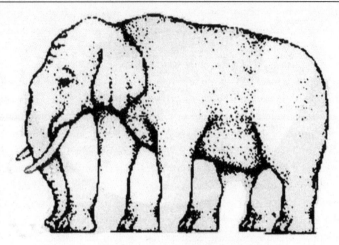

How many legs does
the elephant have?

Figure 7.

Oh really.

If you've read *Mind Manipulation* (2002) and *Mind Control* (2006), or if you've at least managed to stay awake during the first half of this book, then you know *you can't trust your senses*. For example, can you count how many black dots there are between the squares in Figure 8 (opposite)?

Now try to place your finger on one of those dots . . . Right, they don't exist. It's just your eyes playing tricks on you. Don't panic. That just means you're normal, just as screwed up as the rest of us![48] But since—win, lose, or draw—we gotta play the hand we're dealt, we have to make the best of the questionable—at best—senses Mother Nature's given us. And that means putting a little effort into fully developing those senses, before our enemy realizes it's in his best interest to do the same.

Often our senses tell us something is there when it isn't (the garden hose we mistake for a "snake") or else it tries to protect us by "ignoring" the

---

48. See the chapter on *"Yuku Mireba:* The Power of 'Seeing'" in Section II (p. 156).

SQUARE ILLUSION

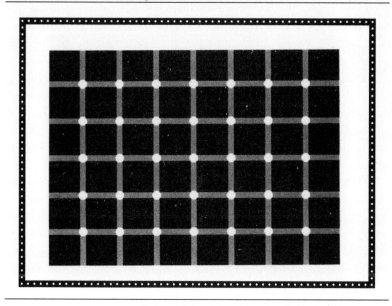

Figure 8.

obvious. But all is not lost. You can, with due diligence, gain more mastery—even complete mastery!—over your senses. At the very least, you should aim to make your senses your servants, rather than remaining a slave to them.

According to Dr. Anthony Zaffuto, author of *Alphagenics: How to Use Your Brain Waves to Improve Your Life,*[49] the key to gaining Ultimate Control (i.e., full awareness) of your senses is to (1) close off all sensory input, and then, (2) focus and concentrate all your attention on one sense at a time.

This is the same method that's been used for centuries by mind masters and mystics both East and West. It is the basis for all mind-strengthening (and mind control) disciplines, including meditation and self-hypnosis, both of which were taught to students at Shaolin as part of their overall *jing gong* sense training.

In order for us today in the West to gain better control of our senses, it is first important to understand that, despite popular belief and pop

---

49. Zaffuto (Doubleday & Co. 1974), 31.

psychology to the contrary, there's no such thing as "multi-tasking." Sorry to burst your bubble but your mind can only consciously concentrate on one thing at a time. The only reason we imagine we are thinking about and doing more than one thing at a time is because the human mind jumps from one senses-excited thought to another like a two-year-old at Toys-R-Us.

The goal is thus to train (program) our mind to switch back and forth, and to race along the myriad of connections within our brain even faster, but with more direction and purpose. In other words, we need to learn to process incoming sense information in as effortless, expedient, and efficient a manner as possible. This can be done. The mind can be trained. And it begins with training the mind by first training the five senses.

Why bother to "master" your senses? Survival. The more aware you are of your surroundings, the better your odds of outwitting and, if need be, outfighting your enemies should (when!) society and civilization go horribly wrong . . . again! And the only way to be more aware of your surroundings is to increase the attention you give to your senses since it is only through your senses—seeing, hearing, smelling, tasting, and touching—that you interact with, and receive vital information from, your environment.

Sun Tzu's "Know Yourself, Know Your Enemy, and Know Your Environment" can all be satisfied by our giving more attention to mastering our five senses:

- Mastering our senses means we've successfully set out on the road to "knowing ourselves."
- Mastering our senses, knowing how they work—or how they conspire to trick us!—means we know how our enemy's senses function as well; *information we can use against him.*
- Mastering our senses makes us more "at one" with our surroundings—upping our odds of finding shelter, weapons, and food when the time comes.
- Finally, on so many levels, a fuller and eventually full use of your senses enriches our life. Like a man born blind who has never seen a sunrise, you can't really appreciate the world around you unless you're firing on all cylinders, using the full potential of your senses. Besides, it'll improve your sex life! Hindu and Buddhist Left-Hand students of *Tantra-yoga* practice sensory awareness exercises that allow

them to develop and then direct their *prana* (vital energy) to different parts of their bodies, greatly prolonging and enhancing sexual pleasure.[50]

Focus and concentration are not synonymous. *Focus* refers to our "tightening" one of our senses (or our overall mind), sharpening it to a pinpoint directed at a singular, particular thought or object. *Concentration* means holding that captured thought or object with our mind and focused sense for some period of time.

Mastering our five senses begins and ends with focus and concentration since an increase in our overall focus and concentration is both the way in which we strengthen our senses, as well as the by-product of doing so.

HOW TO IMPROVE YOUR SENSE OF "SEEING"

Eyes given to see are not always open.
—**Voltaire**

Notice we said "improving your sense of 'seeing.'" That's because learning to "see" involves not only (1) paying closer attention to how we perceive (and misperceive) physical objects with our eyes (right, *with our brain!*), it also requires us to (2) develop our internal visualizing, what's often called "the mind's eye."

After looking at the two figures above, by now you're pretty much convinced you can't trust your eyes. But actually it's your brain you can't trust, the interpreter of what your eyes take in.

Your brain always chooses the easiest and quickest path to identifying something. Only later, when the brain has more time to closely examine the object and determine the object poses no danger, does it relax. Ah, you remember how incoming information first travels through the amygdala, before ultimately making its way to our higher reasoning frontal lobe. This explains why you jumped that time you thought you saw a snake in the grass but it turned out to be a piece of garden hose. Your brain "saw" the object,

---

50. For a complete training course in "tantric sex yoga" see *Mental Dominance* by Lung and Prowant (Citadel, 2009).

went straight to its "looks like a friggin' snake!" file, and ordered your leg muscles to jump away from the (falsely perceived) "danger." Then, once out of danger, your brain took a closer, second look, and realized it's just a piece of harmless garden hose.

So sometimes we "see" things that aren't there. Other times our *untrained* brain misses things—important, possibly dangerous things. For example your eyes pass over a seemingly peaceful park setting and fail to notice the man standing in the shadows, leaning a little too casually against the side of a tree. When's the last time you got a "gut feeling" that something just wasn't right? Often this occurs because our eyes have taken in something *novel or out of place* that our brain pushes to a back burner, in favor of something the brain is currently concentrating on. You can see how dangerous this could be if your friend leaning against the tree over there has evil intentions.

Police and professional warriors whose very lives often depend on their "seeing right" the first time are trained that the human eye first sees movement, then silhouette, and finally color.[51] We, too, can train ourselves to "see" better and, more important, actually comprehend what we are seeing—or what we have been missing!

Watch professional magicians. The hand really is quicker than the eye. Learn how magic tricks work. Go to live magic shows. Expect to be tricked because you *are* going to be tricked. Try to catch the ol' switcheroo, the misdirection. At a live magic show you expect to be fooled and you're watching intently for the "trick" . . . and you still get taken. How much more so when you're *not* watching for it, not expecting it out on the street or in your place of business?

You need to take the same attitude with you from that magic show back out into the real world: You *are* going to be tricked. So watch for it. Train your eyes (and your brain) to see trouble coming. Make paranoia your friend.

Object-Spotting Exercise: Have a friend place several small, everyday objects on the table between you. Now close your eyes while he adds or removes or otherwise rearranges these objects. Opening your eyes, try to determine what's different. This exercise will help your eyes (brain) better spot when something is "out of place" or when a novel variable has been

---

51. See *Knights of Darkness: Secrets of the World's Deadliest Night-fighters* (Paladin Press, 1998) and *Knights of Darkness* (Citadel, 2004).

added to the landscape. Cheater's hint: With your eyes closed, listen carefully and you will be able to approximate where on the table your friend changes things.

Shape-Spotting Exercise: Walk down the street, or through a park during the day, and try to spot all the objects shaped like, or composed of, circles. Now take the same walk and look for square shapes. Now try it for triangles—harder. How about diamond shapes? Harder still.

Retrace your route at different times of the day. Shadows in the morning look different at high noon, as well as in the afternoon. What about at twilight, and again at night? Notice how varying degrees of light and shadow—chiaroscuro, they call it—play tricks on your eyes. What you thought was a trash can turns out to be a squatting homeless man. Those two trees over there? One is that stranger you saw earlier in the day, but in the dark his silhouette resembles that of just another tree. In the dark, new shapes—islands of light and circles of shadow—appear where none existed during the day. Shadows can hide a person standing just inside a doorway or trick the eyes into seeing false doorways—safe havens where none truly exist.

Your eyes are dazzled and confused by the changes and, as your mind struggles to "make sense" of contradictory information, your enemies close in . . .

Mind's Eye Exercise: Study the image on page 86 for a full minute. Then close your eyes and practice keeping the fast-fading "after-image" in your mind's eye for as long as possible. Don't be discouraged when the image eventually fades. That's normal. The goal is to keep the after-image in your mind's eye for longer periods of time. As you become more accomplished at this exercise, graduate to more complex images and practice just closing your eyes and "recalling" (creating) such images out of your mind.

In India, and points East, this kind of practice image is called a "yantra." Yantra range from the simplest—a dot, or circle—to incredibly complex images known as "mandala."

In practical use this exercise will train your eye to keep more complicated images (e.g., a park scene) in your mind's eye for longer periods of time, giving your mind a chance to file away its initial impressions and (re)examine the scene more closely for potential danger and/or opportunity.

KAN-RYU "YANTRA"
MEDITATION IMAGE

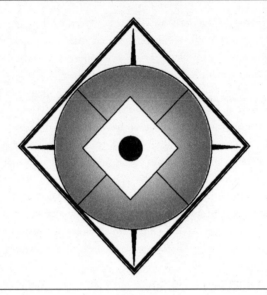

Figure 9.

HOW TO IMPROVE YOUR SENSE OF SMELL

Our sense of smell is a too-oft ignored sense. But while you might ignore what your nose is trying to tell you, others are paying close attention. Would it shock you to know that everyone, from Madison Avenue to the military use it to influence us without our ever being aware of it?

Today the U.S. military is looking for nonlethal crowd control alternatives and have developed a noxious-smelling "puke gas" that, when dispersed over an unruly crowd, makes them vomit, urinate, and defecate on themselves. In the modern war on terrorism, beyond bomb-sniffing dogs, we may now identify individuals (at airports, etc.) based on their distinctive body odor. Seems each of us exudes a combination of body chemicals as unique as a fingerprint[52] This is nothing new. Down through the years inventors have

---

52. *Business Week*, August 8, 2005:55.

designed weapons and invaders have used weapons that specifically targeted our sense of smell. For example, ancient Chinese used "stink bombs" to unnerve their enemies.[53]

Other ways in which our sense of smells leads us around by the nose:

- *Making us buy more:* Madison Avenue knows what scents first draw us into stores and then "encourage" us to buy more while we're there. For example, *Nike* recently paid for a study that concluded that most people will buy more shoes, and be willing to pay a higher price for those shoes, if the room smells like flowers. Likewise, the Las Vegas Hilton gambling casino found that its patrons spent fifty percent more time playing slot machines when the air around them was doused with a floral scent. The stronger the fragrance, the longer individuals gambled. This even works in real estate, where the smell of fresh baked bread and cookies (giving potential buyers a "homey" feeling) increased sales.

- *Manipulating our mood:* Above and beyond getting us to buy even more stuff we don't need, recent research into how we react to our sense of smell has led to several revelations, some of which might benefit us, all of which might be used against us.

- *Keeping us more alert:* The smell of peppermint or cinnamon can increase alertness, helping keep drivers awake. This according to a Wheeling Jesuit University study.[54]

- *Improving our memory:* Smells that act as memory aids include rosemary oil, basil, lemon, and sandalwood—which increase both contemplation and creative thought.

- *Making you more successful:* People whose clothes smell of pine are perceived by others as being more successful, more intelligent, sociable, sanitary, and attractive than those whose clothes smell like lemon, onion, or smoke.[55]

- *Making you more sociable and trusting:* In research done at the University of Zurich, after test subjects sniffed oxytocin (a hormone associated with lactation, social bonding, and interaction)

---

53. Seagrave (1985), 180.
54. *Men's Health* May 2006:36.
55. *Psychology Today* Sept/Oct. 2005:32.

they were twenty percent more likely to trust strangers with their money.[56]

- **_Improving your sex life:_** Research has shown that between ages eight and sixteen, girls begin to dislike the odor of male sweat. Likewise, a recent survey of adult females found that women overwhelmingly agree that a man's body odor is more important than his appearance. Men also have noses. A recent study rated unattractive women twenty percent more favorably when a room was sprayed with pleasant fragrance.[57]

FYI: Some researchers believe that an inborn olfactory sense may act as a steering mechanism guiding men and women to members of the opposite sex.[58] (Madison Avenue "dating" tip: Pairing the right packaging to the right smell, they can seduce the eye and the nose simultaneously.)

When a woman is aroused it may seem that the air between the two of you seems "thicker," as you subconsciously pick up on an increase in her sexual _pheromones_, the same way you "smell" rain coming.[59] Such human pheromones can now be bought off the shelf and are increasingly being added to perfumes and colognes. Also, many natural scents have been proven to affect us sexually. Sandalwood, for example, is considered an aphrodisiac by Hindu yogis.[60]

"Sense of Smell" dirty tricks: (1) Prior to a meeting, douse the meeting room with scents designed to relax the person(s) you will be negotiating with. If that person happens to be a woman, depending on your agenda, you might also consider sexual pheromones. (2) Prior to your rival attending an important meeting, saturate his clothing with foul-smelling odors designed to be triggered by body heat. (3) Spray liberal amounts of a woman's perfume in his car, or onto his clothing, where his wife is sure to smell them.

Sense of Smell Exercises:

Deliberately go out of your way to "practice" smelling. Fill your olfactory memory banks with different smells. Allow a friend to blindfold you

---

56. _Scientific American_, August 2005:26.

57. _Psychology Today_, ibid.

58. Bayer (1987), 34.

59. See "The Art of Seduction," in _Mind Control_ (Citadel, 2006).

60. See _Mental Domination_ (Citadel, 2009).

and then try to identify different scents they place under your nose. Hint: Aim for more natural smells, as opposed to "heavy" artificially manufactured perfumes.

The "Z-E-N Rose" Exercise is both a meditation and a way to increase your awareness of your sense of smell. When we smell something pleasant, a rose for instance, we draw our breath in to its fullest. Nostrils flared, we draw the air to the bottom of our lungs. This is how you should breathe when you're meditating. And you should learn to meditate (1) to reduce stress, (2) in order to "center" yourself for more self-control, and (3) to increase your overall sense awareness.

Most meditation techniques require you to "Sit in a comfortable, quiet place." Conversely, this Z-E-N Rose meditation you can do anywhere. A nice quiet place is great, if you have such a luxury. Filling your meditation spot with incense and other calming scents (e.g. real roses) helps in this exercise.

> *Step One: Close your eyes (if in an appropriate place to do so) and take in a full, deep breath, imagining that you are smelling a large rose, trying to draw as much of its delicious fragrance as deep as possible into your body.*

> *Step Two: As you breathe in, mentally repeat the letter "Z." In your mind, associate this "Z" with relaxing, with "getting your Z's," i.e., sleeping. Hold this "Z" breath for a few seconds before exhaling. As you exhale, think of the letter "E" for "exhale." Without giving yourself a stroke, gently force all the breath from your lungs.*

> *Now breathe in another "rose" breath as you mentally recite the letter "N" (as in "breathing IN," get it?). Think about how an "N" is just another "Z" relaxing on its side.*

> *As you breathe out this time, mentally say "ONE" . . .*

> *Continue this breathing exercise, repeating "Z-E-N" as you breathe in, out, and in again. At the completion of each cycle of three breaths count "one," then "two," "three," and finally "four."*

That's all there is to it. Probably take you three or four minutes, tops. Of course, you can do it longer if you'd like, if circumstances permit. Just start the exercise over once you complete "four."

And if you concentrate on your "rose breathing" before long, don't be surprised if you actually begin *smelling* a pleasant rose-like fragrance. This will be your proof that you have moved into a more relaxed state where the mind has created the smell from the image of the rose you have successfully held in your mind. Calmer mind, stronger senses. Stronger senses, stronger mind. How do we know this? A recent study at Massachusetts General Hospital concluded that forty minutes of meditation a day appears to thicken parts of the cerebral cortex. This is the part of the brain involved in attention and sensory processing. [61]

When possible to close your eyes doing your Z-E-N Rose meditation, augment your meditation experience (while further strengthening your senses) by *visualizing* a perfect rose in your mind's eye.

HOW TO IMPROVE YOUR SENSE OF HEARING

The smallest bones in your body, the tiny bones in your ears, do one of the biggest jobs. When you "hear," it's actually the bones in your ears vibrating in response to sound waves. It's the same thing as the Native American putting his ear to the rail, listening for the coming of "The Iron Horse"—he wasn't hearing so much as feeling vibrations. The same is true with the old woodsman's trick of sticking a knife into the ground to "hear" someone approaching.

The human capacity to hear changes over time, and not just in old age. Not surprising children and young people can usually hear better than older people (though you'd never know it when calling a teenager to do his chores!). Our hearing sensitivity begins to "dull" after age twenty-five but, until then, "kids" can hear at least one frequency we know of that older people can't. Talk about turning a negative into a positive, a British department store chain was able to isolate this frequency and used it to pipe "uncomfortable" music into the store, aimed to discourage kids from loitering. [62]

Still our ears pick up a lot more sounds than we are ever consciously aware of, a multitude of sounds, most of which we ignore, as our brain sorts through and prioritizes what it considers immediately important. This

---

61. *Psychology Today* Sept./Oct. 2006:74.
62. Reported on *Good Morning America*. ABC News June 18, 2006.

explains the "cocktail party effect": how, in a crowded, noisy room, we still immediately notice when someone casually speaks our name halfway across the room. That's because our name is important to us and our brains take immediate notice of it being spoken.

Sense of Hearing Exercises

- *Listening to some band and/or orchestra music* while you pick out one instrument and concentrate on it. Try to isolate the drum, for instance. Then do it again for the guitar, then the keyboard. It doesn't matter if you've had any formal training in music. This exercise is only about trying to discern (isolate) the various different sounds made by the instruments. This is easy to do with loud rock music, harder with more subtle arrangements. Orchestral music is excellent for this exercise.
- *Learn to lip-read.*
- *The Farthest-Away-Sound Meditation*: Begin by first using our Z-E-N Rose meditation exercise to relax yourself. Having accomplished this, now close your eyes and concentrate on the sounds immediately around you: perhaps the clock ticking on the wall, the sound of the refrigerator humming, a dripping faucet, or even the sound of an old house "settling."

After a few minutes, gently "push" your thoughts further outwards, as if "a circle of sound" is expanding out from you on all sides (like ripples in a pond). Listen for the farther away sounds—sounds outside the room you're in, perhaps outside your house. When doing this exercise outside, on your porch or in the park, listen first for birds in the area, then those farther away, and then farthest away. Perhaps you'll hear a squirrel playing in the fall leaves, or birds sitting in the trees. Extending your listening out still farther . . . now you hear that airplane high up in the sky, and a subtle sound of the wind picking up, perhaps the faintest hint of thunder rumbling in the far distance. Of course, you should also be able to *feel* this breeze on your skin, perhaps *smell* the rain coming. Having improved one sense, you will now want to use it as much as possible in concert with your other senses. As one hand washes the other, so too does one sense enhance its fellow.

HOW TO IMPROVE YOUR SENSE OF TASTE

You wouldn't expect imperial Chinese poison tasters to have had much of a retirement plan. But the truth of the matter is many of them were experts in their craft, some able to discern with just the minutest taste whether something was safe for the emperor to partake of. Likewise, an accomplished palate of a true *sommelier* can discern the subtle nuance of a hundred different wines (here again, the nose is often used to augment the sense of taste). You can, too:

Sense of Taste Exercise

- Similar to the exercise you practiced to improve your sense of smell, blindfold yourself, and have a friend give you small amounts of food—and other *nontoxic, non-caustic* materials—to taste. Note not just (1) *taste*, but also the (2) *consistency* and (3) *texture* of these foods.

HOW TO IMPROVE YOUR SENSE OF TOUCH

Your skin is your body's largest organ. Human skin is so sensitive we can sometimes feel the weather changing (air pressure, increase of moisture in the air, etc.). We can feel a potential lover's body heat increase along with their arousal.

We often show our interest through our sense of touch: lightly touching . . . and lingering along a lover's skin, slapping a pal on the back. The handshake, the hug, both "touching" signs of friendship.

We can "feel" someone walking in a nearby room by vibrations in the floor. Old-fashioned safe-crackers didn't really "listen" for the sound of tumblers falling, they instead "felt" the tumblers clicking in place through their fingertips (hence the old movie cliché of a safe-cracker "sharpening" his fingertips on sandpaper).

Ever see a Hindu snake charmer, playing his flute, making the cobra dance? Well, first of all, since that snake doesn't have ears to actually hear the sound of the flute, the music is simply for the benefit of the audience. The snake is actually "charmed" by the gentle swaying of the fakir and the tapping of his foot—which the snake "hears" vibrating through the ground.

We can spy out someone's passing or their presence by sweat left on a doorknob, by heat (and/or indentation) left on a chair, or by feeling the hood of a car to tell if the engine has recently been running.

It's not as hard as it sounds. I'll bet you can already tell when someone is worried or scared just from their sweaty palm and/or from the slight tremble you feel when shaking their hand? Some secret societies, Freemasons for example, have special handshake grasps that allow them to tell if the other person is unduly tense and/or lying (for example slipping their index finger and middle finger inside the cuff to feel that other person's pulse).

Modern-day magicians, those who specialize, in "mind reading," use a similar ploy. Rather than possessing true ESP, they are actually adept at reading the tension in a person's shoulder, arm, or hand while that person is being asked to "concentrate" about under which of several cups they've hidden an object, which the magician then finds.

Accomplished dancers—from ballet to ballroom—must use their total body-sense of touch to feel their partner's every move. Likewise, martial artists, especially those who specialize in close-in fighting (e.g., *Judo, Juijutsu,* and *Aikido*), must instantly react to an opponent's shifting position, *telling by touch*—feeling the subtle shift of balance, a settling of their opponent's weight, etc.

During the Middle Ages, Ninja, anticipating having to fight enemies in pitch dark, would strip themselves naked. That way, whenever they *touched* clothing, they instantly knew it was an enemy.

On the more benevolent side, Asian masters of traditional Chinese medicine can diagnose a person's overall health simply by feeling the patient's pulse and/or by using their hands to determine the person's *chi*-flow.[63] In much the same way, a Western doctor feels for a pulse of blood flow to an extremity (coolness and rigidity in the limb being an indication of poor circulation).

Chi masters can not only diagnose disease, they can also ferret out psychological stress by touch—recognizing tension and/or spasms, tics and twitches, in muscles.

Sense of Touch Exercises

- Learn and regularly practice *Tai Chi* and *Chi Gong*. When dancing your hands through the air during these exercises, imagine you are pushing your hands through warm water. Try to feel the still air on your skin.

---

63. Yes, this knowledge was later used to develop the grim Asian *Dim Mak* "Death Touch."

- *The* Go-Ju *Exercise*: (Japanese for "hard and soft") is simply carrying a small hard object, a rock for instance, in your right pocket and a soft object, a small piece of fur or wool, or one of those rubber-squiggly, squishy balls in your left pocket. Now when you feel stressed out, slip your hand in your left-hand pocket and squeeze the soft object several times. Conversely, when feeling like you need a short burst of energy, or when you feel the need to "center" yourself, slip your hand into your right pocket and grind the rock or other hard object into the palm of your hand.

The mind operates on very simple signals. Merely rubbing your hand across something soft (1) makes your mind identify and record the experience, and (2) in the process of identifying and categorizing the object in your hand, your brain sifts through other objects in its files labeled "hard" or "soft"; thus just one squeeze of such an object causes a dozen images of "hard" or "soft" to race across the mind, helping establish (or reestablish) a calmer or else energized and determined mind-set, respectively.

HOW TO IMPROVE YOUR "SPOOKY SENSE"

Some people who've lost their sight permanently can still "see." They seem to have an uncanny ability to correctly and consistently "guess" the movement, color, and shape of objects around them. This "spooky sense," as it's sometimes called, is more commonly known as "blindsight."

Blindsight occurs when the eye takes in images that somehow bypass the (damaged or cut-off) primary visual cortex (the part of the brain that sifts through data from our sense of sight). And even though we are not *consciously* aware we are "seeing" such images, other parts of the brain may process (respond to) this "shadow" information without waiting for it to be processed through normal channels (i.e., through the primary visual cortex).

One theory is that "blindsight" is a good thing, preventing the brain from going into "sensory overload" by "filtering" the vast amounts of information coming into the brain via the eyes at any given moment. Thus, at any given moment, our brains are receiving—and responding to—not only a flow of conscious "sensory" information, but an "extrasensory" flow of data as well that we are not aware of. As a result this unconscious flow of information allows us to change our behavior and make decisions without our ever knowing why we did.[64]

Thus it's possible for us to find ourselves unconsciously making decisions, adjusting our behavior to fit information that we are *not consciously aware* we are receiving. Furthermore, we often think we "predicted" something was going to happen—perhaps avoiding disaster—even to the point of congratulating ourselves for being "psychic" when, in reality, it wasn't ESP, it was ASP: the additional uses of our already existing senses' ability. Seeing us act or react to "unseen data" (perceptions that have thus far eluded their notice), others might also be in awe, also believing us to have "ESP."

Coincidentally, a recent discovery sheds light on how a naturally-occurring process might give others the impression we possess ESP. It involves what are known as "mirror neurons," special brain cells buried deep inside our skulls that seem to read the minds of others and know their intentions.[65] These mirror neurons are brain cells that fire in response to the "reflection" of another person. For example, when you watch someone lift a cup to take a drink, the mirror neurons in your brain activate just like they would if it were *you* lifting your cup to take a drink.

Neuroscientists believe these mirror neurons are what make us feel empathy and compassion for other human beings, and cite research showing that autistic boys' mirror neurons fail to fire in this way, and may account for an autistic child's lack of social interaction and communication skills.[66]

Perhaps there's something to the fact ancient Hindus equated the "sixth sense" with the use of the heart *chakra* (i.e. center of feeling and compassion), which we might also think of as our simply being "empathetic" to the suffering of others . . . which brings us right back around to those recently discovered "mirror neurons."

As science continues to uncover such new information, or at the very least continues to find credence in wisdom intuited by mind-masters of long ago, we may one day find that all of us do indeed possess some sort of ESP—"extra SENSES potential," or, in other words, using the senses we were born

---

64. Susan Kruglinski. "What You See Is What You Don't Get" *Discover*, February, 2006:13.

65. See: "Step by Step, Your Brain Mimics His Moves" by Ker Than. *Psychology Today* July/August 2005.

66. Ibid., 29.

with to their fullest potential. So, until then, we need to put effort into developing the first five, if only to show we deserve a sixth.

Six Sense Exercise:

Repeat the exercises for the eyes, the ears, the nose, your sense of touch and taste. And then repeat them again!

> *Restless man's mind is, strongly shaken*
> *In the grip of the senses. . . . Truly I think*
> *The wind is no wilder.*
> *—Bhagavad-Gita*

A final thought on the subject of mastering your senses: So if you weren't born with ESP, or haven't yet mastered those cool Jedi mind tricks . . . fake it till you can make it! Use every trick in the book (especially in *this* book!) to convince your enemy you possess abilities to crush him, up to and including supernatural ESP powers.

But in the end, nothing is better than actually devoting the time and attention it takes to develop your own mind. Begin by making your initial goal the full mastering of your five senses.

And if along the way you inexplicably discover yourself with the ability to "hear" other peoples' thoughts, to bend them to your bidding through your mesmerizing gaze alone, and if objects suddenly start levitating around the room . . . well, I'm sure you'd never give in to the temptation to use such special mind powers for selfish, evil, twisted gain? Then again, what was it that Oscar Wilde said?

"I can resist anything but temptation."

II.
Maintaining
Ultimate Control

Conquest is easy. Control is not.
—Khan Noonian Singh

IN THE FOURTH CENTURY B.C., roughly around the same time Sun Tzu was penning "All warfare is based on deception" in his *Ping Fa* (*Art of War*), over in India a man named Kautilya, a high-ranking prime minister to the Nanda kings of India's Magadha region, was feeling a little "under-appreciated" by his employers. Increasingly frustrated by their shortsightedness, one day Kautilya packed his bags and defected to their kingly rival, Candragupta Maurya.

Candragupta was a lot smarter than the Nanda. Recognizing Kautilya's genius insights, heeding his new counselor's advice, Candragupta quickly swallowed up the lands of the Nanda and became Emperor.

During his life Kautilya wrote his thoughts down into the *Arthasastra* (*Principles of Politics*), a treatise on the art of governing that is often compared with Plato's *Republic* and Machiavelli's *The Prince*. In fact, Kautilya is often referred to as "The Eastern Machiavelli."[67]

---

67. Though, since he lived a couple thousand years before Machiavelli, perhaps Machiavelli should be called "the Western Kautilya"?

The *Arthasastra* expounds on politics and economics and how to stay ahead of the game in both. Kautilya saw clearly: A king has only two goals, (1) to keep himself in power, and (2) ensure the prosperity of the people (thereby keeping himself in power!).

Thus, for Kautilya, ruthlessness is the order of the day and moral considerations have no place in politics. He thus championed the use of spies, psychological warfare, and propaganda. According to Kautilya, intelligence was paramount and propaganda, both overt and covert, should be used to disrupt an enemy's army and capture his capital:

> He advised the king to follow only that policy calculated to increase his power and material resources, and he felt no scruple in recommending dubious and sometimes highly unjust and immoral means to achieve that end. For this purpose he sketched an elaborate system for recruiting spies and training them.[68]

All propaganda is therefore intended to teach a simple lesson: All who support the king's goals will reap great benefit. All who oppose the king will reap the whirlwind!

Covertly, propaganda agents should be sent to infiltrate the kingdoms of both present *and potential* enemies, spreading defeatist gloom and doom among enemy troops; planting rumor and misleading news (a.k.a. "disinformation") among enemy civilians:

> Like modern propagandists, Kautilya was much preoccupied with techniques for sowing fear, dissension, and confusion in the opponent's ranks (psychological warfare) and for showering blandishments on allies without becoming excessively dependent upon them.[69]

Overtly, propagandists raise the standard of the king as high as possible with their praise, proclaiming the king to be the embodiment of all that is good, convincing the people that the king can literally do magic, announcing that God and the Prophets are all on the king's side! Within the king's own

---

68. David L. Sills, Editor. *International Encyclopedia of Social Sciences.* (Doubleday, 1970).
69. Ibid.

kingdom, internal propaganda is used to manipulate a king's subjects in order to stimulate their support for state policies.

Masters like Sun Tzu and Kautilya knew the importance of a good turn of phrase, knowing that the right word whispered in the right ear (or shouted from a balcony) at just the right time could prevent a war. Of course, the opposite effect is also possible, with a single golden-tongued rabble-rouser . . . well, rousing the rabble. "Friends, romans, countrymen! I come not to praise Caesar but to bury him . . ."

Whether performed as "propaganda" and "disinformation" on a global stage, or playing out every morning around the water cooler as back-biting gossip, rumor, and innuendo, words have the power to wound, even to kill, should the wrong ear overhear the wrong word at the wrong time.

"An eye to every keyhole, an ear to every crack" is the rule of thumb for any conqueror wishing to remain unconquered himself for long. Information is power. Intelligence, both the innate kind you're born with, and the gathered variety you take deliberate steps to obtain in a timely fashion, are the bread and butter of power. It's how you gain Ultimate Control; it's how you maintain Ultimate Control. Now that you've exerted your control, first over self, then over others, you must now consolidate that control. In other words, having gained their "attention," you now have to *keep it*!

Through the power of your voice—whether whispered in another's ear, shouted from the rooftops, or words simply texted across town, to gain power, to maintain Ultimate Control . . . you have to *reach out and touch someone*.

> **Many have fallen by the sword, but not as many as by the tongue.**
> **—Jesus, Son of Sirach**

8.

Zetsu-Jutsu: Mastering Others with the Power of Your Voice

Good words are better than bad strokes.
—**Shakespeare,** *Julius Caesar*

POETRY OF THE EIGHTEENTH-CENTURY Romantic Movement was specifically arranged to create a trance-like state in listeners (as well as in those reciting it). Many religious chants and hymns are also designed to draw listeners into a hypnosis-like state, placing practitioners into a tranquil state where they can more easily commune with the gods . . . or else simply making them more susceptible to the cult's underlying message.

It's no secret that our voices alone have the power to put another person (or ourselves) into a hypnotic trance. Ancient peoples respected and feared the power of words. Thus we have tales of heroes going in search of magic words that would grant them great power: "Voilà", "Abracadabra," "Open Sesame," or "Aum."

Some of these mysterious sounds and words were believed to accomplish magic, others, to freeze an enemy in his tracks—or even drop them dead. The Indian *Kama Sutra* for example speaks of magical verses that have the power of "fascination" and makes reference to them appearing in an even more ancient Indian text, the *Anunga Runga* (*Kamaledhiplava*).

Down through the ages, many "words to conjure by" were sacred or forbidden. In India, these sacred sounds are known as *mantra*. Yogi practitioners maintain that reciting mantra can grant chanters all kinds of magical abilities (called "*siddhas*"). As a result, mantra formulas, from single syllables to lengthy scrolls are found throughout the Far East, in the religions of Hinduism, Tibetan *Lamanism*, and Buddhism.

One theory claims that mantra are the original sounds first made by primitive man to express basic emotions (fear, surprise, love, etc.) and that this accounts for why mantra are recognized subliminally by the more primitive parts of our brains. In other words, mantra vibrations act as codes that stimulate the brain on a subconscious level—in effect, acting like a TV remote control, changing our moods and our energy levels.

Any accomplished mind manipulator knows the potential of the spoken word and so uses specially chosen words and phrases that put us under their spell before we know it.

Worldwide, down through history, the power of words wielded by masterful (and often menacing!) wordsmiths are well documented: Rasputin, Charles Manson, Rush Limbaugh. From words that incite riots ("Burn, Baby Burn!") to words designed to quell riots ("Can't we all just get along?"), words have the power not just to raise people up off the couch but to *raze* cities!

Out the mouth of an accomplished politician, the right words all too often lead us into the wrong war. In a minute we'll examine how words can even incite others to commit crimes. And, despite what they tell you, a masterful—and unscrupulous—hypnotist *can* convince a person to do acts you wouldn't normally think of doing, up to and *including murder*. (More on this in the next chapter: "Secrets of 'Shadow *Ki*' Hypnosis.")

In Japan such masters are called *Sennin*, their art is *Jumon-no-jutsu*, the "Way of the Word Wizards," sometimes referred to as *Zetsu-jutsu*.

Zetsu-jutsu is the art of thrusting manipulative images, thoughts, and emotions into the mind of another person. To develop the ability to craft such "mind-daggers," sennin must first master a variety of lesser arts and skills that give them insight into the manner, means, and motivations of the human animal.

Not surprising, in the hands (or rather "mouths") of such masters, words literally became dangerous tools. Sennin themselves keep such word tools in two separate boxes: Tatari and Imi-kotoba.

- *Tatari* are curses, powerful spells that spell certain doom. Demons known as *Dons* were thought to possess this power to curse—or bless—with a single word, with a single whisper to literally hold a person "spellbound," making them perform tasks without their knowledge and/or against their will.[70] As we'll discuss in a minute, the use of "cursing" words, even when stripped of their "supernatural" component, still have the power to enrage, wound, and, in some instances, even kill! Western science calls the use of such words *Dyshemism*.

- *Imi-kotoba*, on the other hand, are "taboo words" and, in Japan, include words that must never be spoken during sacred ritual, nor in the vicinity of shrines, negative words such as "*blood*," "*sweat*," "*meat*," "*grave*," and "*cry*." Due to the rivalry between religions, words specific to Buddhist practice are also forbidden to be spoken at Shinto shrines. Should this occur, an often elaborate ritual is required to "cleanse" the site.

Down through Japanese history certain other words, outside the sacred, were also forbidden. For example, during what amounted to Japan's middle ages the word *ninja*—meaning simply "to enter by stealth"—merited the death penalty (since it was considered an insult to the Japanese people in general and to the Samurai's chivalric code of *Bushido* in particular to even suggest any respectable Japanese would ever think of engaging in such underhanded acts (sneaking into another's home, theft, spying, back-stabbing murder) as Ninja were often (rightly) accused of doing.

But even without the threat of immediate decapitation, as was the case in medieval Japan, "forbidden" words can be used to influence and gain Ultimate Control over others.

> "If you have no honey in your pot, have some in your mouth." —Benjamin Franklin

Our words are simply vibrations. Every time we speak we literally reach out and touch someone. The vibrations of our voice travel through

---

70. Ancient "nonsense"? For modern proof see "The Control of Candy Jones" in *Mind Manipulation* by Lung and Prowant (Citadel, 2002).

the air and enter the ear of the other person where these air vibrations then literally touch the eardrum, causing it to vibrate in synch. This vibration in turn travels along electrical signals to the brain where they are then interpreted as either "noise" or "music" or else words—words that can instantly challenge us, confuse us, make us hesitate and obey, or else invoke any of a dozen variations of helpful, harmful, or distracting emotions. Thus, before you can be "touched" emotionally by soothing words or sentimental music, you must first literally be "touched" physically by those vibrations.

This is why we say that a piece of music or the words of a speech—"I have a dream!"—*touched* us. Other times we might tell someone that their words of concern "touched" us. In fact, the words we speak do in fact literally touch other people, just as their words "touch" us. Fingernails on a blackboard, a scream of terror, a racial curse, all these can lead to a *physical* reaction. Why do you think they call it a "blood-curdling" scream?

Consider: I have a thought in my mind. I voice it. The sound of my voice (vibrations) travel from my mouth to your ear and you are affected. From mental thought to physical action. With just my words alone, depending on the words I choose, I can affect you.

Just as different individual words can affect different people in different ways, so too can such evocative words be classed into two categories, the same or at least similar to those wielded by Japanese sennin:

- *Dyshemism,* words used to wound, disable, and sometimes kill others, and
- "Word slavery," words used to cower and control others.

DYSHEMISM: WORD WEAPONS

Our enemies stab at us—and all too often successfully wound us!—with words. The technical term for this is *Dyshemism*, words used as weapons.

These "word weapons" fall into two basic types: "purr," words designed to attract, pacify, and placate us, and "slur," words that stab into us, hurtful and confusing words designed to repel and wound us. Also known as "stroke or choke" words, "pushers and pullers," "attractors and detractors," these two types of word weapons can further be broken down into three distinct categories of "White Talk," "Black Talk," and "Gray Talk."

White Talk ("Purr Words" and Positive Strokes)

Yet words do well/when he that speaks them pleases those that hear.
—Shakespeare, *As You Like It*

White talk is "positive" talk, words and phrases designed to draw another person to us, either because such talk makes us look *so good* or because we've used such talk to purposely make any alternative look *so bad*.

White talk allows us to *associate* ourselves and/or our cause with something or someone our targeted subject already has good feelings about. Thus, in order to get close to the targeted person, we adopt his hobbies, his persona, his professional and political likes and dislikes, all in order to *associate ourselves in his mind with something he already likes and somebody he already likes*.

Recent studies have proven what professional con men have always known: that people are more easily and more often persuaded by the opinions and behavior of those who are like them. Across all communication modes, people are usually more successful at winning over members of their own sex. Men overall are slightly more swaying than women because we tend to perceive men as having higher credibility and expertise. The exception to this would be when the subject under discussion is "stereotypically feminine," for example, child care.[71]

One way to make someone "like" you is to learn what "trigger words" they unthinkingly (unconsciously) respond to. These are social, cultural, and religious words and catch-phrases, or else words with more personal—perhaps even subconscious—meaning to the person:

- **Words that make him feel safe on the one hand**
- **Words that galvanize him to action on the other hand**

As soon as we find his particular positive trigger words, we can use these proverbial short hairs like marionette strings, making him dance where we choose. This is where the time we've previously invested in gathering intelligence on your enemy pays dividends.

We talk to him on his level, *crafting mental images that make him relive past pleasure or else imagine pleasures to come*—pleasurable images that have already

---

71. *Scientific American Mind*, July/August 2009.

triggered an emotional (amygdala) reaction from him long before his more suspicious analytical mind ever gets a chance to take a more critical look at them.

With our words and actions we make him associate us with everything good in his world:

- We *unconditionally* approve of him.
- We encourage his plans—the more unrealistic the better!
- We believe what he believes.
- We like what he likes. When he sees us coming, he drops his guard and holsters his suspicions because he "associates" us with pleasure.

"Association" is one of the most powerful tools in the manipulator's arsenal. Whether or not others "like" us is directly connected with whom and what they *instantly* "associate" us with. When you walk in the door, does the other person immediately "associate" you with something pleasant or something painful? Like it or not (admit it or not), we all "pre-judge" others by their appearance and by their actions.

Say for example you dress like a cowboy. Every time I see you, every image of every cowboy (or wannabe cowboy) I've ever seen (or heard of) flashes across my mind. If my past experiences (or perhaps only what I've *heard* about cowboys) is negative, your looking like a cowboy will cause me to associate you with negativity. Of course, the opposite could be true. Depending on my past experiences (or, again, only on what I've *heard*) seeing you dressed up like a cowboy could unleash all kinds of *positive* images in my head.

Yeah, it's called "*prejudice*" and every single human being on this planet does it (*mostly* subconsciously) every friggin' day of their friggin' lives. And the time you're going to spend denying you do this would be better spent understanding this *natural reaction* before your enemy uses this *natural reaction* to manipulate you!

Mind-control experts, for example professional hypnotists, put this "association response" into practice using a technique known as "the anchor" to gain their subjects' undivided attention. It works like this:

- *Ask your subject a question that makes them remember something pleasant* ("What's your favorite flavor of ice cream?").
- When the person responds "strawberry," *immediately repeat their*

response: "You like strawberry," while simultaneously making a gesture toward them with your hand, either with fingers splayed and dancing, or while holding a small (preferably shining) object in your hand. This causes your subject to subconsciously associate (and replace) your voice for their own inner voice, the one that brings them pleasure by reminding them how much they love strawberry ice cream. Pairing your words with a specific gesture/object also associates that gesture with your command voice, a pleasurable (confident and comforting) voice the subject will be all too willing to follow into deeper levels of relaxation and cooperation (i.e., hypnosis).

- Use this same "agreed upon" gesture every time your subject says something you approve of, further associating it in their mind with pleasure (i.e., being approved of).

Once you've linked (associated) both your voice and gesture with pleasure in the subject's mind, simply saying "strawberry" along with the specific gesture will be enough to place your subject into a light "hypnotic trance." (Perhaps you recall our mention of the dirty "shaping" trick Skinner played on Fromm, in our discussion on subliminal suggestion?)

Black Talk (Slur Words, Cuss Words, Bully Words, and Stereotypes)

Whereas White Talk uses positive words designed to attract others to us, Black Talk is more negative and designed to repel, wound, and literally strike down our enemies. Shakespeare called this kind of talk "*Ethiop words*," words intended to do harm, to make an enemy stumble back, stunned, perhaps even making him a sitting duck for your follow-up verbal (and physical?) *coup de grace*.

Black Talk are all the words that should make you want to wash your mouth out with soap: bullying words, slanders, slurs, cuss words, and having no hesitation in "playing the race card" when prudent and profitable.

We use Black Talk in a direct attack against our enemy: either when engaged in direct conflict, or else when attacking his character and undermining him from afar. In this way, Black Talk corresponds to Sun Tzu's *cheng*, a direct, conventional attack (as opposed to employing indirect means, *chi*, which better fits the *modus operandi* of "Gray Talk").

TYPE OF WORDS	PHYSICAL REACTION
"Blood-curdling" scream	Signs of fear, "Flight or Fight" (paleness, dry mouth, sweating), flinching, cringing, paralysis, death.
Racial/ethnic slur	Signs of anger (and/or fear), face contorted in rage (or fear), fighting stance (e.g. muscles tensed, fists "balled up," etc).
Soft, "cooing"	Smiling. Sexual arousal (wide eyes, licking lips, Increased nervousness).
Authoritative, firm	Positive: Increased focus of attention. Negative: Increased anxiety.
Authoritative, soft	Relaxation (introduction to hypnosis).*
Authoritative, loud & pointed (e.g., "patriotic speech")	Increased heartbeat, muscle tension.
Nostalgic (e.g., "the good ol' days," also music)	Melancholy, listlessness. Sadness.

* See *Secrets of "Shadow-Ki" Hypnosis*, next chapter.

Figure 10.

"Slur words" are the most used form of Black Talk. These include everything from common "Fuck you!"s to tried-and-true social ("Jerry Springer trailer trash!"); religious ("Devil-worshipping pagan!"); political ("pinko commie bastard!"); sexual ("flamer!"); racial ("honky mo fo!"); and ethnic ("chink!") insults.

Ironically, many common English slur words used today, even some of our most vile racial and ethnic slurs, had benign origins:

> *Nigger* comes from the Latin niger, meaning simply "black." In fact, two nations in modern-day Africa, Niger and Nigeria, have the same origin.
>
> *Dago* is a corruption of the common Spanish family name "Diego" and was originally applied as a slur against Hispanic peoples before becoming associated with Italians.

Wop was a generic U.S. Immigration Department acronym
meaning "With-Out Papers" before becoming specifically
associated with Italians.

Gook is a proper Korean noun meaning "person."

Other slur words came about as the result of powers-that-be promoting
the propaganda that city dwellers are somehow superior to people who live
in the countryside:

- *Civilized*, for "civitas," meaning "city." Thus the beginning of the myth
  that city dwellers are better than "un-civilized" country folk.
- *Savages*, simply "forest dwellers," another synonym for the uncivilized.
- *Heathen*: Back when feudal lords kept all the good land to themselves,
  many landless folk fled into "the heaths"—bogs, swamps, and other
  worthless land.
- *Villains*: From the root "villa." *Villains* at first simply referred to poor
  serfs living in the "village" surrounding and servicing feudal estates
  and castles (*villas*). *Villain* became synonymous with *criminal* because,
  to make ends meet, the serfs—virtual slaves under the feudal system—
  had to resort to stealing and poaching just so their families would
  have enough to eat. Apropos, *danger* comes from a word meaning
  "dominated and ruled by a master."

Many present-day slur words developed their current meanings in
medieval times and were used as weapons to reinforce the dominance of the
feudal system in general and the Catholic Church in particular. How'd these
words end up "slurs"? Simple: Church clergy and feudal royalty were the only
ones who could (and in many instances *were allowed to*) read and write. Thus:

- *Profanity* means "outside the temple," that is, anything not approved
  by the Church. *Occult* means pretty much the same thing: "O" =
  "without," "cult" = "church."
- *Pagan*, from a root meaning "trees." This slur was applied to warrior
  tribesmen in Northern Europe who worshipped "the old gods" outside in groves of trees, who refused to come inside a (Catholic)
  church to worship this strange new god who carried no sword and
  couldn't even outrun his enemies!

- *Heretic* comes from a root meaning "choice." Ironic, considering the only "choice" the Church gave "heretics" when burning them at the stake was *"regular* or *extra crispy?"*
- *Vandals* were bold Teutonic warriors, admired even by the Romans. Rhineland Vandals conquered Gaul (France), Spain, and then conquered Rome's old foe Carthage in North Africa. Their name didn't become synonymous with wanton destruction (and graffiti) until they sacked the "Holy City" of Rome in 455 A.D.

Finally, here's a couple ironic ones:

- *Cretin*, originally meant "Christian."
- *Idiot* originally meant "those who *don't* hold public office." (Heh-heh-heh.) Use *that* piece of information the next time someone tries to tell you "Times haven't changed!"
- And . . . next time someone tells you to "Go to Hell!" thank them. Our word *Hell* comes from the Scandinavian goddess Hel, ruler of the Viking underworld which was not nearly as bad as the later, less imaginative, less hospitable Christian version that stole her name.

Whether for defensive or offensive purposes, it is worth taking the time and effort to familiarize ourselves with the origins of as many of these slur words as possible. *One*, so we can more effectively use them to discomfort and distract our enemy and, *two*, to turn the tide and gain advantage in a conversation/confrontation where one of these words rears its ugly head.

For example, you're at a party and somebody throws a slur in your direction. Instead of giving them the satisfaction of seeing you lose your cool, you smile it off by informing them (and the gathering crowd) of the proper meaning and use of the word—stifling Mr. Pottiemouth's arrogance and showing your brilliance, both in a single stroke!

"Cuss words" inserted into a "polite" conversation are always a shocker . . . and a good way to gain control of a situation. For best effect, don't scream the cuss word at the other person, instead, softly "mutter" the cuss word, making the other person pause in the midst of their diatribe to ask, "What did you say?" Seize on his hesitation to *repeat your initial argument*.

Cussing is also a good way to jump-start a stalled negotiation, "taking it up a notch," since most people will take your sudden use of "profanity" as a sign of *frustration* (i.e., you are at the end of your rope and about to "walk"), or they will see it as *potential physical violence*, since cussing is a form of verbal "violence." (Review "The 6 Rules of "NO-gotiation" in Section I.)

"Bully words" are used by some people to muscle and manipulate their way through life.

It's not beneath these bullies to use stereotypes, play the race card, and use other "control freak" tactics designed to get them the upper hand: Playing the "race card" is becoming more and more popular—and potentially more profitable.

The race card trumps every other card on the table because, even if the other players in the game suspect you're "full of it," they won't call your bluff for fear of being labeled "racist," "chauvinist," "sexist," "insensitive," or "politically incorrect."

Generically, "playing the race card" means cashing in on anything you can make the other guy feel confused and uncomfortable about, and hopefully guilty enough to shell out some greenbacks. This includes:

- Getting paid for real, imagined, or manufactured ethnic and racial slights and slurs someone uses against you
- Collecting on your particular "disability" (*everybody's* got at least one these days!)
- Making the boss scared of firing you for fear of discriminating against any of the above, or against your "sexual orientation" (whether the one God gave you or the one that friendly priest pointed out to you that summer you volunteered as an altar boy)

According to one former Heisman Trophy winner NFL Hall-of-Famer, you can practically get away with murder (make that *two* murders!) if you hire a smart lawyer who knows when to play the race card.

But most important, you can still play the race card to get better service at Denny's restaurant!

"Stereotypes" are easy to use, since they feed into expectations and images people already possess—about others and about themselves. Not only can we "plant" a stereotype into one person's mind in order to poison them against another, but recent research shows that stereotypes can also be used directly against the targeted person themselves.

Recent research has shown that people who are the object of stereotyping can adopt the negative traits attributed to them. In other words, "planting" (or triggering already existing) *images* of a stereotype in a person's mind reinforces that image, especially if they already hold the stereotype about themselves—whether consciously or subconsciously. In one study, subjects' performance scores on a test of general knowledge decreased when the stereotype of "supermodel" (associated with "airhead" and "dumb blonde," etc.) was activated. Conversely, subjects' performance scores rose when the stereotype "professor" (educated) was associated with them. In the same vein, when a stereotype of "elderly" was activated, subjects actually walked more slowly.[72]

Simply put, when you "subtly remind" people of their shortcomings by making them "associate" (there's that word again!) themselves with stereotypes, they tend to take on the characteristics of that stereotype.

Gray Talk (Gestalt, Gossip, and Side-talkin')

> *There are three great things in the world: There is religion, there is science, and there is gossip.*
> —Robert Frost

Where White Talk is designed to attract us, and Black Talk repels us, Gray Talk's purpose is to confuse. Often the best defense is a *confusing* offense! Gray Talk includes gossip, rumor, and innuendo. People love jumping to conclusions and gray talk helps them set the bar as low as possible.

Rooted in the *Gestalt* school of psychology is the observation that people have a natural urge—perhaps need—to complete things. Crossword puzzles for example, trying to remember who wrote that song you woke up humming. Completing things makes us feel less useless. Even a small win is still a win. Gestalt tells us that if you show a person this:

●

● ●

---

72. *Psychology Today*, October, 2001:28.

They'll form a "triangle" in their mind every time.

We plant confusion in enemy ranks by sowing "disinformation," revelations that (1) *appear authentic,* (2) *are exactly what our enemy wants to hear,* and (3) *is preferably information the enemy "discovers" through efforts of their own.*

We also encourage the spread of false information about our enemy via gossip, innuendo, and rumor designed to sway public opinion to our cause while effectively slandering our foe's agenda.

When our government does this it's called "Public Service Announcements." When an enemy government does it, it's "propaganda." When the media does it, it's called "the nightly news."

But when you don't own your own television network, or own a piece of the government, it's simply "gossip" and "rumor."

Don't despair; both gossip and rumor are respected (or at least *feared!*) tools in our mind-control black bag of tricks.

Consider: A masterful Merlin casually passes his hand through the air, scooping up unseen essence, which soon becomes visible to the eye as a pulsing ball of blue light. Under his attentive, unwavering eye, animated solely by his mental command, this orb of energy gradually coalesces into a tangible physical form befitting the will and whimsy of the magician.

In the same way, "word wizards," using mental manipulation, give birth to their unseen thoughts—first as simple words and phrases that stir others to wonder, to speculate, to doubt, and to *gossip*—giving *voice* to what was merely thought. Ultimately, stirring others to take action.

Thus, through hints and innuendo, subtle suggestion, subliminal sway, and a myriad of mental maneuverings, these word wizards alchemize once intangible thought and ephemeral dream into physical effect. Having mastered the power of the word, they now wield the power to create—and destroy!—with but a whisper.

History is full of examples of how fear, fueled by uncontrollable coincidence and happenstance, becomes superstition, becomes ritual, becomes cult—which, if surviving long enough, grows into a religion wielding the power of life and death. So, too, history is replete with examples of how the intangible dreams and desires of singular-minded men—tempered by trials, sharpened by a constant whetting of will—grow into the towering spires of empire.

What begins as thought, when fueled by emotion—positive or negative—expressed through voice, inspires action, can all too soon become reality.

As natural a process as steam becoming water becoming ice, so, too, is gossip—with just a little help—become rumor, become "truth," manifesting to measurable physical effect.

To get people talking and keep them talking—talking about what and who *we* want them to talk about—that is the goal of gossip. People are perpetually "hungry" for juicy gossip. Once the table is set, you can then freely offer up selected entrées designed to further excite their appetite for "news." Inquiring minds want to know. Having gotten them talking, now drop hints about where they can uncover more information ("information" that you plant, of course).

People appreciate things more when you make them work for it. Likewise, information (i.e., gossip and rumor) is somehow more real when you make them search and "discover" it themselves. It makes them feel smart. And their desire to tell everybody how smart they are for "tracking down" and "discovering" the information will make sure that information—*your* information—will be spread far and wide! The term "eating out of the palm of your hand" comes to mind.

In other words, the best way to get someone to use your idea is to make them think it's their idea.

The secret to spreading good gossip is *never* let it be discovered that you're the source for the gossip. Always maintain (1) distance and (2) "plausible deniability." In others words, don't tell someone directly the "information" you want them to spread. Instead, point them in the right direction—to the person, file, or Web site—for "the real story" where they'll "discover" the info you planted. (Just tell yourself you're doing them a favor since, as previously mentioned, it makes the "discoverer" feel smart.)

You can do this by "casually" asking a coworker if they know anything about a disturbing piece of information you overheard while sitting in a toilet stall:

> "No, I didn't see the two men doing the talking—somebody from accounting, I think. Anyway, they were saying someone who works *here* is listed on a Web site for sexual predators! No, I didn't catch who they were talking about, but the Web site address was scumballs.com. I'm gonna have to look that up as soon as I get a chance . . ."

What's the odds the first chance your coworker gets he/she is making a beeline to that Web site . . . a Web site *you* set up (or an already established sleaze site you anonymously contributed your enemy's name, address, and uh . . . *shoe size* to), where they'll find the name of your enemy target prominently displayed.

These kinds of ploys are variations of "side-talking": not talking directly to a person, but rather allowing a person to "accidently overhear" a snippet of conversation, or "find" a scandalous piece of information sure to spur them to go on a hunting expedition to discover more facts—gossip they will be sure to pass along to others in the course of bragging about how good a "detective" they are.

Shakespeare highlights side-talking ploys in *Much Ado about Nothing* (1598–99), where a group of friends scheme to finally get constantly bickering-but-meant-to-be lovebirds Benedick and Beatrice together by allowing both to "accidently overhear" how the one secretly loves the other.

The "hypocrite's gambit" is another variation of side-talking. Here you talk to the targeted person about someone else who just happens to have the same type of attitude or behavior you're really trying to get the person you're talking to directly to change. Merely getting the person you're talking to, to agree that the "other" somebody's attitude or actions need changing, puts your listener on the road to change. This roundabout method often works because no one wants to be thought a hypocrite, especially to themselves. Psychologists call this *cognitive dissonance*[73] and it spurs him toward change in order to bring his words in sync with his thoughts and actions.

Side-talking employs all the despicable tactics we've studied so far—slurs, stereotypes, cuss words—all of which we want others to "associate" (there's that word again) with our enemy. Side-talking also uses innuendo, implication, influence, and the power of suggestion.

The "power of suggestion" is defined as "The process of including uncritical acceptance of an idea or course of action"[74] and it has been theorized that certain parts in the hypothalamus, at the very core of our brain, are activated by suggestion. Could this be the key to hypnosis?

---

73. When two competing, contradictory ideas won't fit in the limited space inside your head.

74. Goldenson, 1970:1274.

"Lyin' by Implyin'," also sometimes referred to as "dropping lugs," relies heavily on suggestion.

When an adroit manipulator is weaving a story together, "facts" just slow down progress.

Say for example that your goal is to undermine an office coworker. First, make friends with the biggest office gossip you can find. Now, shaking your head sadly, "absentmindedly" comment:

- "Too bad about Bob. Guess God's got a longer memory than the rest of us . . ."
- "Just because Bob's made *some* mistakes in the past . . ."
- "Darn! I was hoping Bob had put all *that* behind him . . ."
- "I really thought Bob had it *under control* this time . . ."

You'll know this ploy has taken root when the other person replies, "What do you mean?" Catching yourself, quickly shrug, "Oh, nothing. Forget I mentioned it. Nobody wants to reopen *that* can of worms again!" Exit immediately.

Trust the office gossip to "investigate" and—as people are prone to do—"fill in the blanks" where necessary to make the story more "juicy."

Don't forget *Gestalt* says we all love to fill in the blanks, *and* we tend to fill in the blanks in *predictable* ways. Complete the following sentence:

"Charlie's parents had three children: April, May, and_____."

Did you answer "June"? The answer is "Charlie," but most people will answer "June" because, in the same way our brain makes those three dots into a triangle, so too, our thinking, and thus our speech, follows *predictable* patterns.

Our brain is lazy. When our brain hears several statements it accepts as true, chances are it will accept—unquestionably—the next statement as true, too. Example: "Bob's such a good worker. He's always on time, always will-ing to help others. . . ." That's *three* true statements in a row. Now without missing a beat add, "Too bad about *that incident with the kid*."

Some people hide a big lie behind the heap of a lot of little lies. Others hide a lot of little lies in the shadow of a great big hulking lie. Either way, most people hearing the lie(s) are too busy, telling themselves "I'll check into it later"—but they never do.

Often "Lyin' by Implyin'" leans on the fact that a single word can imply so much. For example, saying the word "really" in different ways:

- "Really!" (with eyebrows raised, implies *surprise and interest)*
- "Really." (said in a flat tone with flat facial expression, implies *disbelief)*
- "Really?" (with sly smile and narrowed eyes, implies *suspicion* and perhaps a willingness to *conspire*)

Another way of casting aspersions and suspicions your enemy's way is by using "The White Elephant Ploy." The argument goes that if you *want* someone to think about a white elephant tell them "Don't think about a white elephant!" The old argument is that as soon as someone tells you "Don't think about a white elephant!" your mind latches onto this image and, try as you might, you can't get the image of the white elephant out of your mind. "Reverse psychology" if ever there was such a thing!

Likewise, once we hear a slur or slander *associated* with a person—especially a sensational or emotional slander—it is almost impossible to get that image out of our mind. Tell the truth, what's the *first* thing that comes to mind when you hear the name "Michael Jackson" or "O.J. Simpson"? "The King of Pop," "NFL Hall of Fame Running Back-slash-movie star"? Or did something else come to mind first? Tell the truth.

Lyin' by Implyin' also allows you to twist words until your aunt cries "Uncle."

Got a ruthless plan you fear a needed confederate might object to because it will bother their conscience? Scoff at their concern and remind them that "conscience" is spelled "*con*-science."

Got a religious fanatic in your face, high on telling you what he believes? Point out to him that "You can't spell 'believe' without a *lie* in the middle."

While such ploys might seem simplistic, perhaps even childish at first glance, it is directly to the still "childish" part of our many-layered mind that such ploys speak; that part of our mind least able to discern fact from fancy and defend itself.

WORD SLAVERY

The proper words can make people take actions. "Sticks and stones can break my bones, but words . . . ?" Words can do all sorts of things. For instance, words of praise can make you work harder, run faster, or behave in a jollier way. A word of criticism can do the opposite. Whether or not we believe the words, they do their work. "Something always sticks" is the way the Romans put it. The word, being an exteriorization of a thought, is the key to our behavior.
—Hans Holzer[75]

Words can be used not only to wound and render others ineffective, they can also be used to literally enslave another person—this is aptly called "Word Slavery" and happens every time you can control what words are allowed to come out of another person's mouth.

In October 1972, New York radio station WBAI aired the late comedian George Carlin's amusing and *enlightening* routine in which he mouthed those infamous "Seven words you're not allowed to say on the air": shit, piss, fuck, cunt, cock-sucker, motherfucker, and tits.

The all-powerful Federal Communications Commission (FCC) was not amused. Nor were they the least bit enlightened. Created in 1934, the FCC is composed of five members appointed by the president (yeah, guys like George W. Bush!) to regulate all interstate communications, including the licensing of radio and television stations. Piss off the FCC and they'll jerk your license. No FCC license means kiss your radio or television station good-bye.

It's the FCC's job to censor words that are "too obscene" to say over the airwaves. In other words: "Five people determine what you cannot hear and see."[76] For example, in 2004, the FCC decided not to fine rock star Bono for declaring "This is *fucking* great!" at the January Golden Globe Awards, determining that the lead singer of the rock group U2 had used the offensive word as an *adjective* not as a *verb*.

The original "censors" were Roman "census" takers, magistrates in charge of taking a census of the empire every five years. These censors doubled as spies for the government, taking the pulse of the empire, taking note

---

75. *ESP and You* (Hawthorn Books, 1996).

76. "How the FCC Saves You from Indecency" by Nat Hentoff, Village Voice, May 25,1993.

of both morale and morals (e.g., celibacy, inhumane acts of cruelty against children, animals, and even slaves). Fifteen hundred years after the collapse of the Roman Empire, the only thing that's changed is that today most "censors" are *self-appointed*.

Any time you can make a person think twice before they speak, write, or publish certain words, opinions, or knowledge—in effect controlling their actions—you're half way to controlling their thinking.

Brainwashing 101: What a person does is what they are. Controlling a person's *actions* is the first step to controlling their *thinking*. Or as another controversial comedian Lenny Bruce once put it: "If you can't say 'Fuck,' you can't say 'Fuck the government!'"

Control what comes out of a person's mouth and you control that person. A person afraid to speak is a person afraid to protest. A people prevented from speaking will never find a common voice.

That's why so many of us are defined and confined by "Word Slavery," and so easily manipulated by the words we hear:

- Words that move us to tears
- Words that shock and anger us
- Words that lull a baby to sleep
- Words that lull adults into a false sense of security
- Words that convince us to buy things we don't need, and to buy into ideas we'd be better off without
- Words that can heighten our awareness
- Words that can hypnotize us.

Wily word wizards use a variety of Word Slavery ploys to manipulate us: from confusing our brain with "abstracts" and playing on the vanity we attach to our names, to their attempts to constrict and censor what words and ideas freely flow from our lips and pen.

Concrete versus Abstract Words

One way to spot wily word wizards is that they avoid "concrete" words, words with agreed upon, unambiguous meanings: "Five hundred dollars, Friday morning at nine," preferring instead to use more vague, less restricting, more abstract words and phrases, words with different meanings for different people in different times and places: "Oh, three or four miles as the crow flies," "Sometime next week . . ."

For example, ask two people the meaning of "love," "patriotism," "family values," and you'll get *three* different answers. Manipulative word wizards wallow and thrive in wavering vagaries, half-truths, and innuendo. Their non-stop barrage of vague and abstract images goes directly to the right intuitive side of the brain, avoiding the more analytical, reasoning left side of the brain that's more adept at dealing with more concrete images.

Facing down such a "slick" talker, counter-attack by placing concrete hurdles in his path. Make him cough up a specific plan of action, make him commit to specific dates, times, and amounts.

When a politician or some other slickster tries to "pull your chain" with purposely evocative phrases like "morals" and "family values," make sure his idea of "morals" and "family values" is the same as yours.

The Name of the Game Is the Game in the Name

A landmark study done at State University of New York at Buffalo concluded that we are attracted to anything that reminds us of us. In other words when people feel good about themselves they also feel good about anything (associated) with themselves: a word that sounds like their name, numbers significant only to them (e.g. their birthday).[77]

This (often subconscious) attraction/association affects many of the choices we make. For example, a man named George or Geoffrey is forty percent more likely to become a *geo*logist than someone not named *George*. Likewise, a person named *Dennis* is more likely to become a *den*tist. This extends to numbers. Those born on March 3rd (3 + 3) are more likely to live in a town with a name like Six Forks.

Knowing this secret allows us to "seed" an enemy's environment with subliminal "word friendly" suggestions and reminders, words that mean something only to him, getting closer to our mark (target) by seeding offers with words and phrases they know their mark will respond to—if not consciously, then subliminally. For example, a man will be more susceptible to a woman named Jill if he'd once been dumped by another woman named Jill he never quite got over. Likewise, he will be more inclined to buy a policy

---

77. *Popular Science,* July 2002.

from Puma Life Insurance simply because, "Hey! 'The Pumas' was the name of my old high school football team!"

This tendency of attraction/association may explain the phenomenon of *synchronicity*, where events are connected by *meaning* rather than by any other discernible (physical) cause and effect.

A Pair of Dirty Birds

What comes to mind when you hear the phrase "a pair of tits"? Sure, but "a pair of tits" is also the proper term for two small plump long-tailed *titmouse* birds.

So how do words like "tits" become taboo?

Language taboos, like all other taboos, arise from our natural aversion to something (e.g. excrement), our superstitious attitudes towards objects and ideas (e.g. "Never speak the Devil's name lest he appear!"), and sometimes simply because the words become associated with a defeated people. For example, most of our "vulgar" English words today are dirty because 1,000 years ago a bunch of Vikings-turned-Frenchmen known as the Normans beat the hell out of the two German tribes Angles and Saxons (hence *Anglo-Saxons*) running England (back then known as *Angleland*) at that time. As a result, the French language of the conquerors was elevated in both court and in commerce, while the German-based language of the conquered was identified with the vulgar lower classes. Ironically, the word *vulgar* itself originally meant "common people."

The best example of an innocuous word fallen into disrepute is the word *fuck*, originally from the innocuous German/Dutch *fokken* (lit. "to breed cattle"). Before the Norman Conquest of 1066, *fuck* was considered proper "English" (i.e., Anglo-ish).

To proper English-speaking people today, *fuck* is the bugaboo "F-word," though if you ask the average person "Why the fuck is *fuck* such a dirty word?" most would be hard-pressed to give you anything close to an adult answer.

Today, if you stand face-to-face with a non-English-speaking Chinese and—with a big, friendly smile on your face—say, "Fuck you!", *so long as you smile*, that Chinese man will smile back at you because the word *fuck*—like all vulgar words—has only the meaning *we* give it. That's right, any social rules governing "vulgar" and "obscene" words are largely a matter of geography and of time. For all you know, that smiling Asian gentleman might just have told you to go fuck your mother in Chinese but, so long as he's smiling and you don't speak a word of Chinese, you'll never know it. You could be listening to that Chinese cussing up a storm, and/or you could be looking at the raunchiest of Chinese pornographic writings . . . and it would all just be Greek—or rather Chinese—to you: the words meaningless, the writing obscure hieroglyphics.

Bertrand Russell once observed "Sin is geographical." The same holds true for "cuss words" (but, of course, you'll never convince the FCC of that!). In other words . . . the meanings of words are in your mind—and in your enemy's mind.

In the same way the things we think we "see" are actually *reconstructions inside our heads*, so too everything we ultimately "hear" inside our head is "filtered" through any number of personal and social "filters"—"Mama" (nurture), "drama" (personal problems), and "trauma" (Your Uncle Michael inviting you down into his basement to play with his pet dik-dik).[78]

For example, you wouldn't blink or think twice if someone read you a list off of "A cat; a donkey; a female dog; sporting equipment; a blessed saint; a big red rooster; a hairy dam builder; a noisy bird; fruit chock fulla protein; Richard Nixon; and a couple little, albeit obese, birds."

But if, on the other "vulgar" hand, someone rattled off: "Pussy; ass; bitch; balls; Peter; a big red cock; unshaved beaver; pecker; nuts; Dick; and a big fat pair of tits!" you'd be shocked—but perhaps only because "fat" is no longer "politically correct"!

Obviously, whether or not a word is obscene or even politically incorrect depends on *context*, where the word in question appears in connection with other words, and most importantly, how *we* interpret it or—wait for it!— how *others* interpret those words for us.

Thus we become slaves to words, victims of "Word Slavery," without realizing it. Word Slavery can be both active and passive. *Active Word Slavery* has us parroting popular words and slogans because they are socially or politically expedient, and even necessary for survival—"*Sieg Heil!*", "Yes we can!"

Conversely, *Passive Word Slavery* is us being equally fearful of using words deemed insensitive, politically incorrect, and "vulgar" and "obscene" by the reigning powers-that-be. Since politics change (around here, every four years), sensibilities and sensitivities to what is and what isn't "vulgar" and

---

78. Dik-dik: A small African antelope. Admit it, you *thought that* was a dirty word, didn't you!

"obscene," or at the very least "politically prudent," also tends to change. Within our lifetimes we've seen this happen. Before the 1980s' AIDS crisis, you never heard the word "condom" spoken on television; now it has become commonplace on TV shows, as have the words "fart" and "poop." If Oprah can say it on television, it must be okay.

The Bible tells us that "it's not what goes *into* a man's mouth that profanes him, it's what comes *out* of his mouth".[79] Control what comes *out* of a man's mouth and you control the man. Make a man fearful of speaking certain words, and you cause that man to hesitate, whether on a grand political scale, or when in a one-on-one debate with your rival. Where good men hesitate, bad men seize an opportunity to rush in.

USING RUMOR AND PROPAGANDA

How to influence people was an old quest long before Dale Carnegie wrote about it.
—Hans Holzer[80]

Yeah, I know. "Propaganda" is a new, big, scary word and you hate learning new, big, scary words. Don't panic. "Propaganda" is just a "rumor" on steroids. And I'm sure you know all about "rumors"? *The Encyclopedia of Human Behavior*[81] defines a rumor thus:

> An unverified report or account that circulates primarily by word of mouth. Rumors may be wholly false or may contain an element of truth that is usually distorted or exaggerated. Though they often circulate in the form of gossip and may be deliberately "planted" at any time, they tend to occur in greatest profusion during periods of public crisis when reliable information is hard to obtain.[82]

Rumors are what fully blossom when you plant innuendo and gossip deep enough. It has been calculated that if, at midnight, everyone who was

---

79. Matthew 15, see also Mark 7.
80. Hans Holzer, *ESP and You* (Hawthorn Books, 1966).
81. Robert M. Goldenson, Ph.D. *The Encyclopedia of Human Behavior* (Doubleday, 1970).
82. Ibid.

told about a murder told two other people within 2 minutes, that by dawn, everybody on Earth would know about it.

Why do rumors spread?

> The predilection for accepting opinion or even rumor as fact is a familiar and widespread human failing. —J. Paul Getty

The reason for this is most people are too busy (lazy) to check, let alone double-check, the facts of a rumor. Besides, most of us will choose an *interesting*, even if slightly implausible, rumor over the cold hard (boring) truth every time!

Three things help us start and spread effective rumors:

> First, *disguising the source of the rumor*. In other words, take pains now (to avoid more pain later if caught!) to insure any rumor you start cannot be traced back to you. The ideal, of course, is to allow a despicable rumor you start about one foe to be traced back to yet another of your foes! It's always a joy when you can maneuver your enemies into doing your dirty work for you!
>
> Second, "3-D" your target. Make sure the "information" contained in your rumor *Demeans*, *Dehumanizes*, and ultimately *Demonizes* your target—making him appear dangerous, perverted, a religious, social, and moral outcast. Just making him look "foolish" won't cut it, since sympathy all too often transforms fools into "tragic figures" that people at first pity . . . and then help.
>
> Third, always include an emotional element in your rumor to make your rumor stick in the listener's mind. Always construct your rumor around facts that evoke an emotional reaction from listeners, preferably one of the easily manipulated emotional "Warning F.L.A.G.S."[83]

Like urban legends, rumors survive best when you include this emotional element.

Studies on the phenomenon of urban legends show that these bizarre tales survive because they tap into basic emotions, fear and disgust.[84] Urban

---

83. Fear, Lust, Anger, Greed, and Sympathy.

84. *Psychology Today,* March/April 2002:21.

legends are like campfire ghost stories, strange anecdotes, and cautionary tales passed from one person to another that people swear on a stack of Bibles are true, although no one can point to any specific place or time the actual event occurred.

Example: Live on stage, rocker Ozzy Osbourne once bit the head off a chicken . . . or was it a bat? . . . and drank its blood . . . or was that Alice Cooper . . . no, wait, it was the band KISS! Everyone "knows" this really happened—especially that guy you know who once dated this chick that was actually there, and saw the whole thing, Dude! (Must be the same girl who accidently ate some watermelon seeds and nine months later gave birth to a watermelon . . . or was it an alien? Or was it an alien watermelon?)

Rumors not only help us undermine foes, but can also be profitable. Prior to talking a potential community of suckers . . . uh, "investors," out of their hard-earned dollars, wily confidence men "pre-plant" rumors slandering any competition while opposite rumors praising their get-rich-quick investment plan are likewise circulated throughout the targeted community.

Controversy swirled around the 2002 Academy Award's top contender *A Beautiful Mind*. Producers of the movie charged that rival producers were behind rumors that the Nobel Prize–winning physicist on whom the movie was based was both a bisexual and an anti-Semite.

The accused producers vehemently denied allegations they'd started such rumors and counterattacked, accusing the producers of the movie themselves of having initiated the rumors in order to garner the sympathy vote from Academy members. Recall that Sympathy is one of the emotional "Warning F.L.A.G.S." Also keep in mind that winning an Academy Award adds *millions* to your movie's box-office and subsequent video sales. (How many rumors—okay, bald-faced lies—would *you* tell for a million dollars?)

Success! You can tell you've given birth to a good rumor when the little bastard shows up one day on your front porch full grown; when people start telling *you* the rumor *you* started!

All concerted efforts at propaganda begin as rumors, some deliberately planted in preparation for more advanced future propaganda, others occurring spontaneously (in lieu of real information being available), but both kinds helped along by propagandists with agenda.

The classic office rumor goes something like this: You casually mention to the office gossip that "Bob certainly seems to be doing better since he finished *the program* . . ." Then you quickly change the subject when quizzed "What program?"

Drug problems? Emotional problems? Marital problems? No one seems to be sure, and you can bet they aren't going to ask "Poor Bob." Just to be on the safe side, not wanting to upset Bob, they start avoiding the "troubled" man.

Eventually this rumor makes its way around to Bob's boss who may then decide to "take it easy" on Bob, just until Bob works out his problems. The boss then assigns Bob's pet project to the next man in line . . . *you!*

Never become the source for gossip or rumor (or, rather, never get *caught* being the source of gossip or rumor). Always maintain plausible deniability. In other words, do not tell someone directly the "information" you want them to spread. Instead, point them in the right direction—to the person, file, or Web site—for "the real story" (i.e., where they'll "discover" the info *you planted!*).

This kind of "Suggestion" is at the heart of a ploy known as "Lyin' by Implyin'," or, as it is called in today's jargon "dropping lugs."

For example, say your goal is to undermine an office coworker. First, make friends with the biggest office gossip you can find. Shaking your head sadly, absentmindedly comment or your co-worker's incompetence.

The more sketchy a rumor the better. Rumors work best when you allow others to fill in the blanks. The same with propaganda:

> The function of propaganda does not lie in the scientific training of the individual, but in the calling of the masses' attention to certain facts, processes, necessities, etc., whose significance is thus for the first time placed in their field of vision. —Adolf Hitler, *Mein Kampf*

Master spy chief William J. "Wild Bill" Donovan, head of America's WWII counter-spy force the Office of Strategic Services (OSS) which after the war became the CIA, knew the value of propaganda, making it a vital weapon in his overall war arsenal:

> To break the enemy's will the OSS pioneered psychological operations, targeting German soldiers and civilians with cunning propaganda and disinformation. To penetrate Axis-occupied countries [Donovan] led a coordinated effort that

was in his view a modern version of medieval siege tactics: Propaganda was the opening wedge, followed by espionage, sabotage, and guerrilla warfare, all paving the way for invasion by conventional forces.[85]

Since World War II, propaganda has been a dirty word. Yet the concept of propaganda is hardly a twentieth-century invention. Propaganda as a tool and weapon of both religious and government policy has been known and used since ancient times:

> No doubt propaganda has existed ever since primates have been sufficiently articulate to use it. Artifacts from prehistory and from early civilizations give evidence that dazzling raiment, mystic insignia, and movements were used to advertise the purported majesty and supernatural powers of early rulers and priests.—David Sills[86]

Persian dictator Cyrus the Great used propaganda against the Greeks. Turnabout being fair play, Alexander the Great used propaganda as he swept across the Persian Empire, just as his father Philip II of Macedon also used it to "soften up" Athens to his rule. Likewise Genghis Khan's conquests were to a great extent aided by propaganda (i.e. fear!). "Heralds" rode ahead of his horde, warning of the futility and fatality of any daring to stand in the way and oppose the coming of the Khan.

Ancient propaganda ploys concentrated on spreading myths and legends of a king's invincibility and infallibility. Little has changed. The most successful political and religious leaders either had/have a natural talent for propaganda or were/are smart enough to employ wily advisors adept at crafting and spreading easily memorized political slogans, or religious parables, proverbs, and commandments from their particular gods—all meant to excite and/or cower the people.

Our modern word "propaganda" comes from the Latin *Congregatio de Propaganda Fide* (Congregation for the Propagation of the Faith), "*La Propa-*

---

85. Barnet Schecter, *"The OSS in Greece,"* Armchair General, September 2009: 26–27.

86. David L. Sills, Editor. *International Encyclopedia of the Social Sciences* (Macmillan, 1968), Vol. 12.

ganda" for short, a powerful group of Cardinals in charge of promoting the Roman Catholic Church since 1622.

But why should the Church have all the fun? As the "art" of war became more sophisticated, systematic approaches to *secular* propaganda began appearing. As already alluded to, systematic approaches to propaganda had appeared in Athens as early as 500 B.C. But not until that (in)famous Florentine Niccolo Machiavelli (1469–1527) penned his *The Prince* (1513), following it up with his *Art of War* (1520), outlining how to ruthlessly gain and then maintain power, was propaganda accepted in the West as a vital and indispensable part of both military and political conflict.

Considered by many to be "the father of modern political science," Machiavelli wrote that a ruler was justified in using any means necessary to maintain the stability of his lands, including cruelty, force, and all forms of deception such as propaganda. According to Machiavelli, a virtuous prince maintains power not by crushing his subjects when they rise against him, but by preventing his subjects from becoming rebellious. To accomplish this, the prince utilizes propaganda and the institutions of religion to keep the people satisfied. (More on "*The Machiavelli Method*" in Section III.)

Even before the ink was dry, Machiavelli had become required reading, his writings influencing not only ambitious political and religious leaders, but social philosophers and even playwrights.

While works of fiction, many of the plays of William Shakespeare (1564–1616) were inspired by real events and reveal both his skills of observation as well as an astute familiarity with the use of psychological warfare and propaganda.

In *King Richard III* (1591), Buckingham plants rabble-rousers in town to stir up popular support for Richard's coup. In another propaganda ploy, Richard leaves a note designed to undermine Norfolk's morale prior to battle pinned to the man's tent. And just prior to the Battle of Bosworth Field, Richard gives a propaganda-laden speech, inciting his men, assuaging their consciences and destroying their doubts.

Still, Richard's self-serving propaganda pales in comparison to the awe-inspiring (and all-inspiring) rally given by Good King Harry to his men prior to the 1415 Battle of Agincourt as recounted by Shakespeare in *Henry V* (1600).

Over in *Hamlet* (1603), the vengeance-driven Prince of Denmark has a troupe of actors perform a play (written by his hand) designed to unnerve his traitorous uncle. And what are Iago's whispered rumors and the suggestions of infidelity he successfully plants in the mind of the Moor in *Othello* (1622) if not pure propaganda?

Mark Antony's rabble-rousing, sarcastic speech in *Julius Caesar* (1623) gradually turns the crowd of listeners into a mob ready to burn and kill in order to avenge Caesar's assassination. *Macbeth* (1623) sees a man led astray by the prophecy (propaganda) of three witches—augmented by the wily whispers of his ambitious wife.

Today, propaganda is an intrinsic factor in any military campaign. Yet you need not be attached to the military to be affected by it. Each of us are also affected on a daily basis by propaganda beamed at us by a variety of groups, some political, some religious, many with questionable, shadowy agendas.

Whatever their goals—obvious or hidden, global or just down the street, politician or professional con man[87]—the same tried-and-true tactics and techniques of propaganda are used by anyone and everyone with the knowledge and knack.

Tools and Techniques of Propaganda

Well put-together propaganda is specifically designed to attack all three of Sigmund Freud's levels of the mind: rational and logical arguments engage the *Ego*; pleasurable promises appeal to our child-like *Id*; and moral arguments target the higher reasoning *Super-Ego*.

Propaganda arguments fall into two categories, depending on their intended target audience:

- *Strategic propaganda* is aimed at a mass audience, and carries a more generalized message (e.g., "The enemy is bad!"). This category of propaganda uses commonly shared symbols and universal archetypes that affect everyone (e.g., all Americans).
- *Tactical propaganda*, on the other hand, is more specific, more finely tuned and aims to get us to do specific things (e.g., "Buy this car!" "Buy this war!"). Tactical propaganda uses the same images in addition to images and symbols that have special meaning within a specifically targeted group (e.g., a minority or a specific religious group).

---

87. I know, probably redundant!

Whether strategic or tactical, all propaganda must be adjusted to the particular level of understanding of those being targeted:

> All propaganda must be popular and its intellectual level must be adjusted to the most limited intelligence among those it is addressed to. —Adolf Hitler, *Mein Kampf*

Thus, depending on its intent and intended audience, a typical propaganda ploy can include the use of suggestion (overt and subliminal), innuendo, and rumor on both a personal and/or mass scale.

Propaganda aims to accomplish one of two goals:

- *Integration propaganda* helps form people into more easily manageable units, causing them to hold the same opinion about a specific thing. This makes it easier to control them and, when need be, to focus their collective energies against the enemy.
- *Agitation propaganda* incites us to do a specific action.

Both integration propaganda and agitation propaganda use one or more of the following arguments:

- **"Us versus Them":** You're either with us or against us. There's only two kinds of people in the world: Brothers . . . and others! There is no middle ground. "They" are different from us. "They" don't think like us, ergo "They" are less deserving of life and land than us.
- **Taboo and terror:** They have committed atrocities—crimes against humanity. They trample our traditions and commit taboo acts that are an affront to both man and God.
- **Exaggeration:** We purposely inflate the number of the dead killed and oppressed by our enemy to make matters sound worse than they really are. We skew statistics. Remember: If you torture numbers long enough, they'll confess to anything!
- **Inflated stakes:** Our children are at risk! Our way of life is being threatened! We are shown how we will be directly affected by any failure on our part to act.
- **Demonization:** The enemy isn't human. He is a Godless beast! He's subhuman. His barbaric acts have cost him his humanity and his right to live (thus he can be slain and his lands seized without any guilt attaching itself to us).

- **"God is on our side":** We are good, "they" are evil. God loves us more than he loves them.
- **Turnabout's fair play:** Payback's a bitch! They did it to us, we are justified in doing it to them twofold. This is also where you turn an enemy's propaganda against him, using his own words to indict him—since he's probably saying pretty much the same thing about us!

What makes these propaganda arguments so effective is that they all contain a *portion* of the truth. Humans have a lazy habit of thinking that if A, B, C are true, D must also be true. Con men count on this.

Hide little lies inside a big truth. Wrap big lies in a lot of little truths.

> To influence the masses rather than one single subject is of course more difficult, but certain key words, slogans, tones of voice, and emotional circumstances are all part of the hypnotist's "one-step . . . two step . . . three step" formula; it is just applied to a broader audience. —Hans Holzer

For propaganda to be successful, the propagandist must determine their audience's mind-set: their susceptibility to physical and psychological inducements (i.e. threats and bribery).

First, what is likely to be your audience's initial attitude to your strategic, overall message? Does the targeted audience have a predisposition to the message you're offering? Is it something they (secretly) want to hear? Your message is designed to replace (or at least modify) the person's present belief. Does it strike a chord with him? Have you been sure to wrap any bitter message pills in sweet propaganda—easy-to-swallow symbols and phrases the audience recognizes, identifies with, and has been known to respond favorably to in the past? For example, you don't want to use any pie-in-the-sky "New Age" terminology when trying to get your message across to traditional Christians. A practical application of this principle comes from when usually black-robed Jesuits first began their missionary work in Asia they opted to wear saffon-orange colored robes so Asians, unfamiliar and suspicious of this new faith "Christianity," would initially think the Jesuits were familiar Buddhist priests. Foot in the door . . . money in the collection plate.

Second, what inducements (bribes or threats) does your offer carry? In other words, what does the audience have to gain or lose psychologically and/or physically by accepting your message? This includes economic induce-ments, bribes of money, and lucrative job opportunities on the one hand, threats of losing the same on the other hand. Physical inducements can also include promises of security, sex, and material wealth.

Psychological inducements people are most likely to respond to include offers for fulfillment of personal (perhaps secret) desires, promises of recog-nition, promises of increased social acceptance, prestige, and power. At the opposite extreme, your propaganda can threaten to take all these things away if your agenda is not embraced.

Propaganda: Coming Soon to a Brain Near You!

An agitator who demonstrates the ability to transmit an idea to the broad masses must always be a psychologist, even if he is only a demagogue.
—Adolf Hitler, *Mein Kampf*

What is the future of propaganda?

According to some experts, tomorrow's mind-slayer media manipulators will move away from propaganda aimed at mass audiences and more toward crafting different versions of a message for each audience segment (race, demographic). This is known as the "Dear Mary" approach and is already used by direct-marketing copywriters. As technology increases and privacy decreases, mind-slayers armed with data from credit card and tax records, medical databases, and other sources will be able to target individuals with propaganda personalized to suit that particular person.

Wherever the person turns, he will be confronted in print (such as newspapers or magazines he subscribes to), via television shows he watches regularly, through the video games he plays, and at the Web sites he most fre-quents.

For example: You set your clock-radio to awaken you at 7:30 A.M. and the moment it comes on you hear a message targeting you specifically with a subtle—perhaps subliminal—message in the form of an ad or a piece of news. At the newsstand, your favorite newspaper and/or magazines carry a cover story of the same news or a blatant ad for the same product. The plac-ard on the side of the bus you take every day to work or on that billboard alongside the same road you drive to work holds the same message.

PROPAGANDA PLOYS AND PLAYS

Identification ploy	Go out of your way to identify yourself and your cause with the common man, be "just plain folks"—anything to win the hearts and minds of your target audience. Use "Mirroring."
Argumentum *ad populum* ("argument to the people")	Frame your appeals in everyday language meant to appeal to the common folk and to common sense (i.e. "sensibilities held in common" with whatever group you happen to be talking to).
Bandwagon ploy	Assure him/her/them that "Everyone's doing it" and *you* don't want/can't afford to be left out, do you This appeals to our need to be accepted, to be "one of the boys," to be "normal" and to be part of the crowd.
Testimonial ploy	You associate yourself in people's minds with the rich and the famous (movie stars, sports figures, war heroes) who entice your listener to buy whatever the "rich and famous" are endorsing—in this case, *you*.
Transfer ploy (aka "guilt by association")	A "Cutting-at-the-edges"[1] ploy in which a person is held in suspicion by their associations, and attacked simply for the company they keep, or the company you can make others think they've been keeping.
Name-calling ploy	These label others as "bleeding hearts," "communists," "Godless pagans," and/or other societal taboo slur words.
Stroking ploy	The opposite of the former name-calling ploy, here we use acceptable societal "prestige" and "purr" words, terms such as "patriot," "true American," and "an example to us all" to attract and flatter members of the target audience.
"Purr" generality ploy	Rather than stick to the facts and address specific solutions to specific problems, generality ploys use emotional pleas and always speak in vague terms. They use *evocative but unclear* terms like "justice," "family values," and other societal "virtue words" to jerk our chains.
"Slur" generality ploy	Slur generalities include defaming another with loaded (often vague) terms: "New-Ager," "un-patriotic," "pagan," "Godless," "occult-oriented," and with phrases like "waffling," "wishy-washy," and "soft on crime."
Faulty reasoning ploy	Includes pointing out the other guy's bad statistics (or what we can make to look like bad statistics), his use of faulty cause and effect, false analogy, and defective comparison. The statement "Crime has risen 90 percent since he took office" may be true, but no causal connection—no cause and effect—has actually been established
Assumption ploy (aka "begging the question")	You emphasize (accuse) that "No one in his right mind would support such an unfeasible plan!" But has it been *shown* to be "unfeasible" or are we being asked to *assume* it is unfeasible?
Selective memory (aka "lying by omission")	We're all pretty good at remembering what bolsters our own agendas and all too quick to forget to mention pertinent facts that reveal the downsides of our agendas. Predictably, we play down any successes of our opponent while harping on his every falter and faux pas.
Pressure ploy (aka "Limited Time Offer")	These force listeners to choose between two "clear" extremes (e.g. between good and evil) although the issue may actually be blanketed by gray. No compromise can be allowed to be considered. Religious cults' "limited time offer" falls into this category.
Semantics	Use word play (homonyms, vague definitions, etc.) to confuse and wear down your audience.
Argumentation ad hominem ("argument to the man")	When all else fails, propaganda attacks are made against the person himself, whether he's a candidate running for office or the salesman endorsing a rival product. The current term for this is "swift-boating."

[1] See *The Musashi Method*, Section III.

Figure 11.

These media masters are already "laying in wait" to ambush you at work, having already used a "Cutting-at-the-Edges"[88] approach to make sure all your coworkers are standing around the water cooler talking about the same news or product.[89]

Even today, think how easy it is for a propaganda message to be infiltrated into entertainment. For example, how many times a day do you hear repeated the joke Jay Leno told last night?

If this is indeed the future of propaganda, then what does the future hold for individuals in regard to propaganda? Scant, unless we learn to master propaganda before it masters us!

We start by reminding ourselves that our reputations precede us. How many times have we been warned to watch out for a particular salesman, an opposing attorney, or even a rival ball team, simply because they are known to be tough customers? *That* is propaganda!

Remember, ancient Celtic shaman cultivated a power called "glamour," an overpowering personal presence that, coupled with specially chosen words, could accomplish dazzling effects, from disrobing a lover to disarming an enemy. Our "personal propaganda" works in this same way. At the most basic level, our personal propaganda is how we carry ourselves: our walk of alertness that turns aside muggers, our aim of confidence that makes the salesman lower his price.

How we carry ourselves tells the world we are tough customers—that we won't put up with their bullshit. Word gets around and the wolves no longer come sniffing at our door. For the most part, criminal mind-slayers are a mangy lot, culling the human herd by targeting the weak and the unwary. By studying the tactics of these human hyenas, we make ourselves less of a target for their mind-manipulation ploys. (See "Looking Out For Number One: Bring in the Ringer!" in Section III)[90]

---

88. Coined by master Japanese strategist Miyamoto Musashi (1594–1645), "cutting-at-the-edges" involves attacking the peripheral of an enemy's world (family, friends, etc.) when you cannot attack him directly. See the "Mastering the Musashi Method" section (p. 177).

89. For more on these kinds of media "backdoor" propaganda techniques, read *War and Anti-War: Survival at the Dawn of the Twenty-first Century* by Alvin and Heidi Toffler. Little, Brown & Company, 1993. (Hint: They're called "backdoor techniques" for a reason!)

90. Recommended reading: *Winning through Intimidation* by Robert J. Ringer. Crest/Fawcett edition, 1993.

The V.A.L.U.E. of "Personal Propaganda"

A rose by any other name . . . "Personal Propaganda" is just another name for "flattery"—something *you* use every day, something used on *you* every day. And just like other forms of propaganda, "flattery" used between individuals follows all the rules—or lack of!—used when propaganda is played out on a grand scale between nations.

There's an old adage: "All talk between men and women is foreplay." If you think "flattery won't get you anywhere," (1) you obviously need to get out more often and, (2) you've obviously never heard of Casanova, Don Juan, or read the *Kama Sutra*, all of which praise the power of flattery.

When we're talking about flattery, we're talking about *talking*—inserting just the right compliment, morale booster, and motivator at just the right juncture in our boardroom, barroom, and bedroom negotiations.[91]

Have you ever noticed that (1) men and women talk differently and (2) they talk differently to one another than they do to members of the same sex. Initially, up to a certain point, men and women talk about the same things. The top five things both men and women like talking about—in order of importance—being:

> *Home life*, especially their kids. (Always ask to see the pictures and "flatter" them by way of their fine-looking family.)
> *Health* (*Theirs*, not yours. Be sure to *empathize*, flattering them on how well they look or, if you can't do that with a straight face, flatter them on their resolution to eventually start to begin to consider the possibility of maybe someday working out!)
> *Job* (Usually about how much their job sucks. Again, try to *empathize*. Don't get in a pissing contest just because you know your job sucks even more than theirs!) If nothing else, flatter them on being able to put up with all the B.S. at work.
> *Career* hopes and plans. Flatter them on their "focus" and "foresight" to be able to so clearly see the future. Flatter their "determination" and "ability to set goals" (they haven't got a prayer of ever starting, let alone coming close to finishing!).

---

91. And what's the first of "The Six Rules of 'No-gotiation'"?

Personal growth. (*No, this doesn't mean how much their ass has grown since the last time you saw them!*) Flatter them for what they plan to get around to doing just as soon as the world stops plotting against them!

Beyond these initial five, talk priorities begin to diverge for men and women. They still talk about some of the same things, for example, "recreation and travel," "the opposite sex," though the sexes vary in the order of importance for these, eventually diverging altogether as women add "clothing" and "shopping" on the women's list, and men add "sports" and "politics."

We deliberately flatter someone by talking to them about things you know they're interested in, whether male or female. We flatter others with our attention, especially when we compliment them on their insight, eloquence, and expertise.

When you flatter, be specific. Don't compliment her (or him) with generics like "pretty" and "smart," instead pick specific parts of her (or his) physique (eyes, laugh, etc.) and personality (attitude, sense of humor, etc.). When trying to flatter, "VALUE" when talking to women (and some men!):

Vulnerability: Showing someone is always more effective than just telling them. Show her you're emotionally approachable, you have feelings and you're secure enough in your manhood to show those emotions. Tell her how you cried like a baby when . . . you saw the injured puppy, or the ending of *Sleepless in Seattle* (1993), *The Piano* (1993), and *The Notebook* (2005). (Go easy on the blubbering. There's a thin line between being "sensitive" and being a "wimp"!)

Altruism: I know, we told you, "There's no such thing as altruism." Which still holds true. That means you gotta practice sincerely faking it, showing her how you go out of your way to help everything from kids and charities to stranded motorists.

Loving: Whip out those feelings again. Show her how you care for Grammie, and kids, and lost puppies.

Uniqueness: She's one of a kind. You've never met another woman like her. She has a unique way of looking at that boring subject. Yada-yada-yada. You got the idea.

Empathy: You feel her pain. You value her incredible insight and you'll defend her right to bitch-bitch-bitch about her ex-boyfriend. Gigolo Rule Number One: You have to hit her "E-spot" before you can hit her "G-spot". "E" = "emotion," "E" = "empathy."

Charisma: The Art of Selling Yourself

For I must tell you friendly in your ear, Sell when you can,
you are not for all markets.
—**Shakespeare,** *As You Like It*

The "Art" of charisma has gone by many names down through the ages. Ancient Celts called it *glamour*, a presence so overpowering, so magical, as to dazzle the mind, hence our modern usage of "glamour" as a synonym for beauty and style. The French, on the other hand, call it *je ne sais quoi* (lit. "I know not what"), that air of confidence and aura of caring that makes those around you *feel* important and blessed just for being in your presence mixed in with just a dash of *panache*, a flamboyance in both style and action. In Yiddish it's called *chutzpah*, bold self-confidence and daring.

Think of life as a commercial for yourself. Most people have no idea what they're really selling. Accomplished salesmen wink, "People pay more for the sizzle than for the steak." "Charisma" *is* that sizzle. Before you can sell a product, you have to sell yourself. This takes us back to "The Three Knows," slightly modified to "Know Yourself," "Know Your Customer," and "Know Your Market" (Who's buying what today?).

When we make people like us *and* like themselves for liking us . . . *that's charisma!*

"Political correctness" be damned! Let's review the cold, hard, occasionally prejudiced and self-serving facts of life:

We like people to like us.
We like people who like us.
We like people who are like us.

Conversely, people *dislike* us because:

They think *we* dislike *them*.
They are intimidated by us.

We're their rivals for the same lover or for the same parking space.

They *think* we're their rival for the same lover or for the same parking space.

We've given them a real reason to hate us. (We've beaten them out or beaten them up sometime in the past.)

They *think* we've given them a reason to hate us. (Cue theme from "Twilight Zone"!)

They hate *everybody* and we're stuck being part of "everybody."

So what can we do to *make* people like us more?

- *Project strength and confidence* without being overpowering. "Strength" + "confidence" = "Charisma." Confidence and power are both attractive and intoxicating. Offer to let them "share" your strength and confidence. Convince them "We're stronger together."
- *Be "vulnerable"* without being weak. Nobody likes a wimp. (We equate weakness with *need*, and "need" means you want something from *me!*)
- *Be approachable.* Sure, then people come to you with all *their* time-wasting problems . . . but sometimes they also come to you with timely *warnings*.
- *Make eye contact*, without being rude. Eye contact links us with others. Remember to smile with your eyes when faking sincerity.
- *Ask others for help.* Asking others to help, and for their opinion, shows you respect and value them. Making people *feel* useful encourages them to *be* useful.
- *Make them feel good about themselves* (which in turn makes them feel good about *you* making them feel good about themselves).[92]
- *Speak positively,* about yourself (it pays to "advertise" . . . without bragging, of course), and about your plans (that they can be a part of—*if* they're smart enough). Most important, speak positively about *them*, without sounding condescending.
- *Keep the emphasis on them*, even when shamelessly promoting yourself and your agenda. At least make them *think* you are still talking about them.
- *Use "matching" and "mirroring,"* i.e., imitating and mirroring their

---

92. Uh-oh! I smell a "cult" brewing! Or at least a fan club stewing.

actions and speech patterns (without mocking), in order to further establish rapport with them.

Information vs. Dis-information

All human conflict—be it bloody war or equally merciless boardroom "No-gotiation"—comes down to information versus dis-information. In the propaganda game it's not "either/or" when it comes to putting our "positive" propaganda (designed to make you and your cause look good) versus "negative" propaganda (designed to make your enemy look like the piece of $%I + he is!).

In propaganda, as in all human conflict it all comes down to information versus dis-information: the facts of the matter versus the facts we want others to *think* matter.

Dis-information is as simple as distorting facts and figures and then force-feeding them to your foes. Any time you can further distend and distort your enemy's perception of reality, the further you hinder and incapacitate him, preventing him from getting the upper hand in life in general and "No-gotiations" in particular.

To create dis-information we freely use all the "good information" we've learned to manufacture so far, from hints, innuendo, rumor, and bald-faced lies, to planting doubt in his mind to increase his anxiety, exaggerating and amplifying his problem(s), in effect, turning his molehills into mountains.

Flipping the script, we turn his mountains of concern and suspicion into molehills, down-playing any doubts he might have about us or about our offer. This approach can also be used to make him drop his guard, leaving him vulnerable to our real attack.

Sometimes all it takes is choosing the right words, the right "turn" of phrase to turn mountains into molehills, molehills into mountains. Notice that "molehills" are always followed by *periods* (or, at worst, a *question mark*). "Mountains" are always chased by *exclamation points!*

MOUNTAINS	MOLEHILLS
Permanent!	Temporary.
Significant!	Insignificant.
Critical!	Marginal.
All-consuming!	Isolated incident.

MOUNTAINS	MOLEHILLS
Disaster!	Challenge.
Complete collapse!	Glitch.
Impossible!	Doable.
Never!	Soon.
Mandatory!	Optional.
"It's now or never!"	"*Chill-lax*, dude. It can wait."

Think of this as emotional *ju-jitsu*: When he pushes, you pull. When he pulls, you push, turning his own force and momentum against him.

When he starts complaining about how bad and unfair life is—agree! And then convince him things are even *worse* than he suspects.

Or, he's optimistic. "Things are definitely looking up!" Again, agree with him. Point out all the good things in his life (just be sure to take your humble portion of credit for things getting better!).[93]

When agreeing (or at least appearing to agree) with someone:

- Make eye contact.
- Raise your eyebrows to show interest.
- Smile. (Remember to smile with the eyes as well.)
- Keep nodding in agreement. Augment your nodding with an "Ah!" each time you want to appear to agree with a specific point they are making.
- Point your finger at them each time you want to appear to agree with a specific point they are making.

The more you agree with *them*, the more they will begin agreeing with *you*. (It's called give and take . . . *they* give, *you* take!)

Keep agreeing with them, gradually leading them to their conclusion (which just happens to be your agenda). Just make sure they think it's their own idea and never let them realize you've been herding them in one direction by slowly but surely limiting their options.

"Fewer and faster" is the key. Limit his choices and give him only "limited time offers."

---

93. Yes, this *should* remind you of the section on "The Art of Agreeing Without Agreeing" (p. 73).

Continuously thank them for "clarifying the issue for you" and for "setting you straight." Sincerely fake this.

Make them think they've already done/are doing you a favor. Studies have shown that people are less quick to object and more likely to agree and to do other things for you, if they think they've already done you a first favor. This approach is called "The Law of Inertia" i.e. "Objects in motion tend to stay in motion."

No matter how different your opinion is from his, no matter how adamant he is in his disagreement with you, keep smiling, nodding, pointing your finger while repeating, "So you agree with me. So you see my point. That's great, that's great."

First, this will stifle the flow of his diatribe when he has to stop in mid-rant to clarify/protest that he *doesn't* agree with you. Second, the more you force him to openly disagree with you, the more you make him look like the bad guy.

9.

Secrets of "Shadow *Ki*" Hypnosis

*Hypnotism, and the act of depriving another person of
choice or use of will, does constitute one of the most
loathsome forms of black magic.*
—Israel Regardie[94]

IN JAPAN THE WORD *kuro* implies the dark and the mysterious, something hidden in the shadows and not (fit?) for common viewing. For example *kuro-kakure* means "skullduggery" in general, harkening to a dark and hidden agenda.

Likewise, *kuro-ki* ("shadow-*ki*") *also* refers to things mysterious and hidden (perhaps for good reason!). "*Ki*" is the Japanese rendering of the Chinese "*Chi*," the mysterious life-force that both surrounds us and fills us, animating us. This *ki* is impersonal. Thus the same ki that might be used by a practitioner to heal another (by strengthening the weaker's life force) could be used by someone with evil intent to unduly influence or else completely overpower the weaker (i.e. less perceptive, less alert) mind of another. The ability to wield ki-force to influence and overpower another (e.g. through hypnosis) is called *ki-dol.*

---

94. Israel Regardie, *The Tree of Life: A Study in Magic* (Samuel Weiser Co., 1994).

Ninja in medieval Japan practiced an art known as *yugen-shin*, "the mysterious mind," which embraced any and all techniques for "overshadowing" the mind of an enemy, up to and including hypnosis and self-hypnosis, the latter practice helping Ninja improve their control over self, while the former allowed then to mentally influence—and dominate—their foes.

Despite their bloodthirsty reputation, Ninja preferred non-violent means to accomplish their ends. Hypnotism helped them accomplish this ideal. When violence was unavoidable, however, Ninja could use hypnosis and self-hypnosis to strengthen their own resolve—as well as their swordhand!—while undermining the resolve of foes by not only hypnotizing actual enemies, but also by compromising those close to a reclusive enemy.

As a side benefit, Ninja mastery of yugen-shin helped foster the belief—and fear!—in others that all Ninja possessed the power to control others with just a thought. Post-hypnotic suggestions to "forget" may be the truth behind tall tales of a Ninjas' possessing "magical powers," for example, their ability to "appear" and "vanish" at will.[95]

Likewise, the use of self-hypnosis allowed these knights of darkness to relax themselves physically and calm themselves mentally in preparation for dangerous missions. Ninja trainees were each given a post-hypnotic mantra-like trigger word that when spoken aloud (or even thought of) in times of stress, fear, or pain triggered their fight-or-flight adrenaline response. Self-hypnosis was also used to enhance an agent's mental concentration, for example, enhancing the memory of a Ninja entrusted with a special message. Often such carriers—whether Ninja operatives or unwitting draftees—would be given messages they were not consciously aware they were carrying until another agent at a prearranged rendezvous spoke a code word triggering a post-hypnotic suggestion to remember the information.[96] On the flip-side, agents could be given a hypnotic trigger-word to make them forget information they carried if captured.

Is *yugen-shin* still being practiced today in Japan?

Consider that, while stationed in Japan, Lee Harvey Oswald participated

---

95. The Ninja strategy of making others believe you possess magical powers is known as "The One-Eyed Snake," based on the adage that "a one-eyed snake still bites" (i.e. an enemy superstitiously believing you possess magical powers is the next best thing to actually possessing such power). See *Nine Halls of Death* by Lung and Tucker (Citadel 2007).

96. See *The Control of Candy Jones* by Donald Bain (Playboy Press, 1977).

in a study group (some call it a cult) dubbed "The Sleeping Tigers" lorded over by a mysterious Dr. Fujisawa, reportedly a master of ancient Asian techniques of mind control—including hypnosis—busy adapting such techniques to his mysterious "New Age" agenda.[97]

During a trip to Japan by then-President George Bush Sr., it was alleged that Japanese intelligence used a "psychic assassin" of *ki-dol* to make Bush sick enough to vomit during an important state dinner, causing the American President to "lose face" (i.e., honor and respect) in the eyes of Asian people, ensuring he would then feel obligated to give economic and political concessions to Japan in order to regain his lost face.[98]

A "psychic" attack? Sound too far-fetched that a government-backed intelligence agency would spend time and money on such projects? Well in 1995 the U.S. government finally acknowledged the existence of a series of top secret "Mind-X" ("X" for "experiment") programs going under several names down through the years but finally settling on "Stargate."[99] This CIA-sponsored program, designed to collect and, if possible, *create* "psychic spies," operated from the mid-'60s up through 1988. One such "Mind-X" program consisted of a secret unit of eight or more men, each recruited because he had scored high on ESP tests. Taught to control their ESP ability through meditation, biofeedback, and a cocktail of specialized drugs, these psychics were initially employed for "remote viewing" (e.g., pinpointing the location of enemy bases and hostages and/or reading the minds of enemy leaders and scientists) but were later "upgraded" to include attempting to use their psychic abilities to kill enemies from afar. Don't laugh. *Your* tax-dollars went to pay for this.

Stargate was eventually discontinued after it kept coming up short in attempts to turn "psychic *spies*" into "psychic *assassins*." Keep in mind this was considered legitimate research after Western intelligence discovered Soviet intelligence was already pouring millions into training "psychic agents."

---

97. Get the whole "Oswald and the Sleeping Tigers" story in *Mind Penetration* (Citadel 2007).

98. *Strange Universe*. Syndicated TV, November 12, 1997.

99. No relation to the 1994 Kurt Russell movie *Stargate* and its subsequent spin-off TV-series' *Stargate* and *Stargate Atlantis*. Although, in conspiracy circles, the argument has been made that, by surreptitiously promoting the movie and TV series of the same name, government propagandists help stifle any meaningful discussion of real project Stargate experimentation. Likewise the NSA's "*Echelon*" satellite array, a disinformation variation of which was figured prominently in Steven Segal's 1995 movie *Under Siege 2: Dark Territory*.

One of the methods for training these agents to "release" their innate psychic abilities was hypnosis and self-hypnosis. Thus, while a useful tool in the hands of ethical therapists, in the hands of unethical con men, cult leaders, and rogue government agencies with hidden agendas, hypnotism can be a frightening weapon.

HYPNOTISM: TOOL OR WEAPON?

The possibility that hypnosis has been used and even now is being
used by oppositional forces is quite real.
—**1966 confidential CIA report**[100]

On March 29, 1951, a thirty-three-year-old man named Hardrupp shot and killed two people in Copenhagen during a botched robbery. When arrested his defense was he had been repeatedly hypnotized into committing the robbery by a man named Nielsen. After a sensational trial, Hardrupp was found guilty but was only sentenced to a mental asylum with possible release in two years. Nielsen the hypnotist, on the other hand, was tried and convicted and received a life sentence for committing murder by hypnotism!

Predictably, prosecutors had argued the commonly held belief that it's impossible to make someone do something while under hypnosis they wouldn't normally do. However, the defense's expert witnesses, including Paul Reiter, former governor of the Denmark insane asylum and later head of the psychiatric department at the Copenhagen City Hospital, testified that when Hardrupp had committed the crime he was clinically insane since he was in "a semi-conscious state while deprived of his free will by repeated hypnotic suggestion."

According to Dr. Reiter, any person is capable of committing any act while under hypnosis so long as the hypnotist presents the crime as being for a worthy purpose. In this instance Nielsen had convinced Hardrupp that the money from the robbery would be used to combat communism!

Speaking of communism, it's not surprising that during the Cold War, intelligence forces on both sides of the Iron Curtain took an avid (rabid?)

---

100. From *Mind Controllers* by Dr. Armen Victorian. Vision Books/Satin Pub. Ltd. Great Britain, 1999. 2000 Lewis International USA edition.

interest in the "dark side" of hypnosis, both as a tool/weapon unto itself and as an augment to "brainwashing."

In his highly informative *Mind Controllers* (1999) Dr. Armen Victorian documents how, beginning in the 1950s up through the 1970s,[101] the U.S. intelligence community, primarily CIA and Department of Defense (DOD) collaborations, had successfully accomplished the following using hypnosis:

> Test subjects were convinced to steal and then make false confessions.
>
> A soldier was successfully hypnotized to abandon his post.
>
> Another soldier was hypnotized into revealing secret information.
>
> Under hypnosis still another soldier was convinced to strike his superior officer.
>
> Under hypnosis one test subject fearlessly picked up a dangerous snake.
>
> Another test subject obeyed when ordered to throw acid in someone's face. (FYI: the test subject did not have knowledge the acid was fake.)
>
> Test subjects were made to shoot themselves. (Subjects did not have knowledge the gun was empty or else loaded with blank cartridges.)

Victorian takes especial interest in two types of CIA/DOD hypnotism experiments:

> The first, *"pseudo-hypnosis"* (hypnosis administered to test subjects without their knowledge). The second, "RHIC" (*"Radio Hypnotic Intercerebral Control"*), experiments designed to remotely control individuals using hypnotic suggestions broadcast through a tiny radio-like receiver implanted in the test-subject's head.

Admittedly, it's often hard for the average person to even wrap their minds around the idea of "hypnotism," let alone hypnotism used (or abused) to make someone do some offensive, dangerous, or else heinous act either without their knowledge or totally against their will. Truly frightening!

---

101. That we *know* of!

No wonder all the "experts" keep telling us: "It's not possible to make someone do something against their will while hypnotized. It's impossible to make someone commit a crime—let alone murder!—while under hypnosis."

These "experts" keep telling us this (1) in the face of a mountain of evidence to the contrary and, (2) because if the average person knew what hypnotism was capable of they'd be screaming for it to be outlawed!

WHAT IS HYPNOTISM?

Whether you know it or not, you yourself have been in a hypnotic state literally thousands of times. Anytime you've caught yourself daydreaming or being absent-minded, you've been under a form of hypnosis.

Don't chide yourself for being "scatter-brained" or "weak-minded." This just means you're normal. Ninety percent of people can be deliberately hypnotized to some degree and of that number, fully ten percent are highly suggestible and thus susceptible to being placed in deep levels of trance.

How does hypnotism work? The truth is *no one knows*. There are several competing theories for *how* hypnosis works. What we do know, however, is that hypnosis does work, and has been and continues to be used to hamper and even heal a number of human ills.

Not everyone knows how to fix their auto, that's why we have a mechanic. Still most of us can change a tire in an emergency, right? In the same way, just because we don't know exactly how hypnotism works, doesn't mean we can't take advantage of its benefits by learning how to put someone under.

First off, always remember that *effective hypnotism begins and ends with the power of suggestion.* And haven't you already familiarized yourself with—if not mastered?—"Suggestology: The Power of Suggestion" from Section I? If not, this might be a good time to review.

The comparison between hypnotism and your finding yourself "absent-minded" is appropriate since, during hypnosis, our usual controlling *conscious* "higher" mind is temporarily asleep or otherwise "absent," while our "lower" *subconscious* "shadow mind" (responsible for emotion and motor control) is still awake. Under hypnosis, our higher brain goes to sleep while our lower brain, accustomed to being given commands by our higher brain, begins taking orders from the hypnotist. In other words, our lower brain simply substitutes the outside commands of the hypnotist for the commands of its (now) sleeping higher brain. Three things are necessary to make hypnotism possible:

> **The subject's focus is narrowed** to the point where only a single precise source of information is coming into the subject's brain—information controlled by the hypnotist who now literally defines reality for the victim's subconscious mind.
>
> **The subject believes in the process** of hypnosis and in the hypnotist. Thus the hypnotist establishes rapport with the subject *before* commencing the session.
>
> **The subject must be willing to suspend critical thought,** accepting loss of logic and accepting temporary distortions in normal (waking) cause and effect, and in their perception of time and space. For example, a hypnotized subject can be given a post-hypnotic suggestion to forget the number seven. When awakened from the trance and asked "What is three plus four?" the subject readily answers either "six" or "eight." Asked how many fingers he has, the subject correctly responds "10" and often seems unbothered by the fact he has an "extra" digit when asked to count his fingers.

Any time such discrepancies in logic appear, truly hypnotized subjects either attempt to rationalize them away or else simply ignore them. This is known as "trance logic" and is often seen in cults where members go to great extremes to rationalize the bizarre and often contradictory actions of their leaders.

HOW TO HYPNOTIZE OTHERS

Let's assume you're not interested in a long-winded seminar on the history and ethics of hypnotism. We'll just assume since you obviously like reading Dr. Lung books[102] that you're already basically familiar with the history of

---

102. Relax. Having good taste is not a prerequisite for learning hypnotism.

the use (and misuse) of hypnotism but are more interested in actually acquiring hypnotism skills that you can use (or, Heaven forbid, abuse) today.

Admit it. You've always wanted to learn how to hypnotize someone ever since you were a little kid and you saw one of those ads in the back of your favorite comic book. "Amaze your friends! You too can become a master of Hypnosis!" Heck, they even sent you one of those cool "Patented Hypno-coins" "master of hypnosis" and, yeah, your friends really will be "amazed." Like that "force" that both Luke Skywalker and Darth Vader used—albeit toward drastically different goals—so too anyone can be guaranteed to put anyone under just by twirling it in front of their face. Well, you can still, however, learn "the power" to hypnotize others . . . what you do with that "power" once you acquire it . . .

How to Spot a Good Hypnotism Subject

Professional hypnotherapists don't pick their hypnotism patients, the patients pick them. The mere fact that a person would seek out a hypnotherapist in the first place points to (1) their believing in the power of hypnosis and/or (2) their being "desperate" for help.

Stage hypnotists on the other hand use their knowledge of body language and personality typing to help them spot the most susceptible subjects. The stage hypnotist's greatest skill is the ability to spot those people most likely to obey his commands without question. Stage hypnotists therefore select only the best subjects from a group of volunteers, those with a predisposition to obey. People don't volunteer unless they want to take part in the show. Stage hypnotists are careful to avoid those people "volunteered" by their friends. The best subjects for hypnosis appear enthusiastic, cooperative, outgoing, and funny. They are natural hams.

"Listeners" (as opposed to "Watchers" or "Touchers") make excellent hypnosis subjects since they pay special attention to words.

A quick test of a subjects' ability to take commands:

Have the group hold their arms straight out. Note those who respond immediately, without questioning looks on their faces. Eliminate those whose arms begin wavering after thirty seconds.

Having spotted a promising subject(s), the stage hypnotist then uses a combination of psychological and physical ploys to "put them under."

Choosing Your Hypnotism Approach Strategy

There are three main approaches used to induce a hypnotic state:

The Single-Point Focus captures and holds the subject's attention on a single object (e.g., a light, a swinging pendulum, a metronome, or a hypnotic coin)

The Command Approach gives the subject direct instructions and works especially well where the hypnotist is seen as an authority figure

The Imagery Approach (aka "The Subliminal Approach") uses analogies, symbols, and metaphors to separate the subject from his external environment. This approach is effective for use with those patients who resist the command approach. Imagery approach induction allows the mind-slayer to craft commands designed especially to capture and hold the attention of the subject through use of his favored speech style:

Tell Watchers: *"Picture* in your mind . . ."

Tell Listeners: *"Listen* to the sound of my words . . ."

Tell Touchers: *"Feel* the *soft* breeze on your face, *smell* the flowers . . ."

The Imagery Approach is effective because it is difficult for a person to resist suggestions he does not *consciously* know he is receiving. That's because the suggestions you use are disguised in symbolism that only the *subconscious* mind registers. This subliminal approach is favored by the unscrupulous—con men, cult leaders, and Madison Avenue.

How a subject views the hypnotist determines which of these hypnosis strategies will work best. Once you establish yourself in your subject's mind as an authority figure, the Command Approach—direct repetitious orders used in connection with Single-point Focus—often works best.

If the subject is on an informal or personal basis with you, the hypnotist (where subject and hypnotist are seen as equals), the Imagery Approach, augmented with Single-Point Focus, works best.

Speech-Induced Trances: More "Power of the Voice"

The most important aspect of any hypnotic induction is the voice of the hypnotist. This would probably be a good time to review the chapter on "*Zetsu-Jutsu*: Mastering Others with the Power of Your Voice" (p. 101).

All hypnosis techniques first relax the body and then narrow the mind's focus, making the hypnotic subject oblivious to external stimulation, except for the voice of the hypnotist.

The human voice alone can produce a hypnotic state because the preverbal "lower" brain remains in awe of the "higher" brain's verbal ability. That's why, before beginning, you should first determine your subject's "type"—Watcher, Listener, or Toucher—and mirror it when giving suggestions. (More on this in the chapter "Watchers, Listeners, and Touchers", later in this section.)

When inducing a hypnotic state by speaking:

> Avoid interruption in the flow of your words.
> Speak in short separate sentences tied together with "and".
> Speak in a rhythmic monotone "singsong" as pleasantly as
>   possible, stretching out any soothing and relaxing words:
>   "looossse . . . sleeepy . . . deeeply."

When giving hypnosis commands, follow these guidelines:

- Break complex goals into simple, more manageable ones. Use small steps to accomplish one goal at a time.
- Keep suggestions simple and concise, believable and desirable.
- Use positive words wrapped in clear and appropriate imagery.
- Repeat suggestions in order to reinforce them.
- Use synonyms as much as possible (the same words repeated over and over lose meaning).
- Avoid vague time periods such as "soon" or "in the future." Instead, give definite time suggestions: "When I snap my fingers" or "Upon awakening."
  And, most importantly,
- Always include a post-hypnotic suggestion, for example a "trigger-word" that produces instant re-hypnosis any time the subject hears it.

Putting Them Under: Basic Hypnosis Method

To place another person in a light hypnotic trance:

Begin by having him sit back or lay down in a quiet, comfortable place.

Now spend a few minutes guiding the subject in a slow, deep breathing exercise. You can use your "Z-E-N Rose" meditation for this, instructing your subject to breath in while visualizing "Z," exhale on "E," etc. This not only helps calm the subject, but encouraging them to concentrate on the "Z-E-N Rose" *mantra* forces their mind to focus on a single point. Also, verbally guiding them through this "meditation" gets them used to obeying your instructions.

Once you see the subject visibly relax, say to them:

"Thank you for helping. Now when you're ready, take another deep breath and remember the feeling you feel right before waking up after a really good night's sleep, when you feel yourself half-awake, half-asleep, oh, so comfortable and warm that you just want to lay there, all warm and relaxed, barely touching the bed, floating on a warm cushion of air, one part of you wanting to move, the other savoring the warm, relaxing, comfortable sensation of floating on a warm bed of clouds . . . so you reward yourself, resting relaxed, warm and comfortable, allowing your body to float, allowing your mind to drift comfortably from thought to thought . . ."

Do not rush your relaxation of the subject. The more relaxed your subject becomes, the deeper their hypnotic trance. Having relaxed your subject into a light hypnotic trance, gently draw his focus to the specific subject and/or suggestions you want to work on.

A light hypnotic trance state is actually better for learning suggestions than a deep trance.

Types of Hypnotic Suggestions

Having successfully induced a trance, the hypnotist is now free to choose what sorts of suggestions will be given to the subject. The kinds of hypnotic suggestions given vary with their intended goals:

Relaxation suggestions are designed to place the subject into a state more receptive to additional, more complex, suggestion.

Trance-deepening suggestions take the subject to deeper levels of trance, opening him to deeper conditioning.

Imagery-building suggestions reinforce the trance state with pictures of reality drawn by the hypnotist.

Direct Command suggestions order the subject to do specific things, such as change his behavior.

Post-hypnotic suggestions are orders given to the subject that he carries out after being awakened from the actual trance. Mind-slayers often refer to post-hypnotic suggestions as "time bombs," and with good reason!

HYPNOSIS DIRTY TRICKS

About a Svengali taking advantage of an unwilling Trilby:
it can happen that an emotional, gullible person in
need of masterminding may fall under the spell of a stronger,
positive personality.
—Hans Holzer[103]

In the hands of the unscrupulous, hypnotism was and is a formidable weapon. Down through history sinister groups such as Islamic *Hashishins* (Assassins) of the medieval Middle East reportedly used hypnosis to "inspire" their followers to homicidal and suicidal acts. There are even reports of them hypnotizing (i.e. effectively "brainwashing") captured Crusaders who were then released after being "programmed" with post-hypnotic suggestions designed to be triggered when the repatriated Crusader heard a specific code word whispered, or was confronted by a specific sign or symbol, or even when he smelled a special blend of perfume.[104]

---

103. Hans Holzer, *ESP and You* (Hawthorn Books, 1966). Svengali and Trilby are characters from George du Maurier's 1894 novel *Trilby*.

104. See *Assassin!* by Dr. Haha Lung (Citadel 2004) and *Knights of Light, Sons of Darkness: The History & Heresy of the Order of the Knights Templar* by Robert Baughman (Promar Productions 2009).

Likewise Chinese *Moshuh Nanren*, Vietnamese "Black Crows," Indonesian "Nightsiders," and Japanese Ninja have all been accused of using similar ploys involving hypnotism.

When true hypnotism couldn't be mastered, Ninja are said to have resorted to "One-Eyed Snake" strategies that mimicked real hypnotism. Many of these fake hypnosis techniques are still used by unscrupulous mind manipulators and, to a lesser extent, by ambitious stage hypnotists.

While clinical hypnosis is now a respected tool used by both the medical and psychiatric communities, the type of hypnotism the average person is familiar with is audience-participation stage hypnosis. When it comes to using hypnosis, mind manipulators hedge their bets by not only studying the legitimate techniques of hypnosis used by doctors and psychologists, but also by studying the tricks of the trade of these stage hypnotists.

While most stage hypnotists are simply honest showmen capable of inducing true hypnosis, there are some who resort to chicanery rather than taking the time to master true hypnosis to accomplish their effects. These stage "tricks" fall into two categories: Psychological tricks and physical tricks, with much overlap.

Psychological hypnosis tricks

With rare exceptions, the process of hypnosis requires at least a minimum of cooperation from the subject. In a clinical setting, it is important the patient agrees to be hypnotized.

On stage, not only do most[105] volunteers want to be hypnotized, but they are willing—to some extent—to play along with the hypnotist. Often, even if an individual is not truly hypnotized, if he sees others appearing to be hypnotized, he will play along with the crowd, even to the point of sometimes convincing himself he *is* truly hypnotized. For this reason, when a stage hypnotist chooses a group from the audience, you can bet at least one of them is a "shill," a confederate whose job it is to convince the other members of the group that the hypnotist actually has the power to hypnotize them.

The old saying among stage hypnotists is: "If you can hypnotize one, you can hypnotize one hundred." In other words, people tend to go along if they see someone else doing it.

---

105. Occasionally the stage hypnotist will encounter a wisenheimer whose sole reason for volunteering is to muck up the act.

Hypnotists also play on subjects' egos by assuring them that "the more intelligent you are, the better you respond to hypnosis." Since no one wants to look stupid—especially in front of a crowd of people—they "go along to get along."

Physical hypnosis tricks

Initially the hypnotist must get his foot in the door. If the hypnotist can convince the subject that he truly possesses the power of hypnosis, the subject's skepticism will disappear and he will truly be drawn into a trance.

Unscrupulous hypnotists have a variety of physical tricks they use to accomplish this.

> One hypnotist rigged his subject's chair to emit a slight electrical current, making anyone sitting in it "tingle" as soon as the hypnotist started to "put them under." This tingling sensation convinced the subject the hypnotist had "the gift."
>
> Other hypnotists give suggestions to their subjects that they will smell a certain odor (secretly sprayed in the air by the hypnotist).
>
> Others will be made to touch items coated with sugar and then touch their fingers to their mouth right before the hypnotist suggests they remember the taste of a birthday cake.
>
> Itching powder has been used to induce the suggestion of itching.
>
> Hypnotists often keep a mint in their mouth, breathing this soothing vapor into the subject's face in order to relax them. Others spray a light vapor of ether, chloroform, or other calmative agent onto the victim in order to make the victim light-headed. To accomplish this the hypnotist hides a small squeeze-ball up his sleeve.
>
> Modern, more technologically savvy hypnotists can flood the room with relaxing positive ions or with very low-frequency (VLF) sound waves specially tuned to make a victim more susceptible to the hypnotist's commands.
>
> When all else fails, the hypnotist can bulldog a subject by pinching the back of the subject's head and/or squeezing the side of his neck to constrict the victim's brain. Even slight pressure can cause dizziness and loss of consciousness as the victim passes out into a "trance." This is a very dangerous practice, used only by the most unscrupulous of manipulators.

10.

Yuku Mireba:
The Power of "Seeing"

To "LOOK" IS NOT necessarily to "see." Optical illusions are proof of this. As we've already discussed, we all believe our senses are bringing us accurate information. But our senses lie. We misperceive. And misperception is a real bitch, sometimes convincing us to lay our hard-earned money down because we're so God-awful-certain we know which nutshell the pea is under, oftentimes placing us in real danger because we never see that figurative or all-too-often literal sucker punch coming.

Ultimately, to gain Ultimate Control—first over self then over the minds of lesser men—we must learn to "see" with our entire being, not just with our eyes, but with our other senses as well,[106] and, ultimately, to learn to process incoming information correctly to finally "see" clearly with our mind. Japanese sennin mind-masters call this *yuku mireba*, the power of "seeing" and it requires we master the skill of "seeing" beneath the surface of things, to what others are trying to hide from our sight—both our outer eyes, as well as our "inner eye."

---

106. This would be a good time to review the chapter on "*Jing-gong: How to Train Your Senses*" (p. 77).

THREE TYPES OF "SHIT,"
THREE TYPES OF INSIGHT

According to Fritz Perls (1893–1970), founder of the Gestalt school of psychology, there are three kinds of shit you are likely to run into while talking with people: chicken shit, bullshit, and elephant shit.

Master mind manipulators become adept at first spotting (before you step in it!) all three of these types of "verbal shit," and then using these types of crap to woo their target audience.

Learning to spot what kind of verbal shit a person favors tells you a lot about that person's overall personality:

- Chicken-shitters are fearful of human contact, and often harbor secrets by which they can be extorted.
- Bull-shitters are opportunists. They will lie to promote themselves and their agenda.
- Elephant-shitters are full of plans that have no hope of ever coming true. These types can be approached with the promise to help make those dreams come true. Other elephant-shitters are approached by reinforcing their victim identity, telling them something like, "You could have done better if so many people hadn't been against you."

THE THREE TYPES OF SHIT

	Type of Shit	How to Smell It	What It Hides
	Chicken Shit	Clichéd small talk, devoid of actual information	They're trying to avoid emotional contact, fearful of revealing too much about themselves.
	Bull Shit	Out-and-out lies	Told for one of three reasons: (1) To conceal the truth and cover wrongdoing, (2) to protect someone, or (3) in order to gain something (e.g., money, prestige, sex, etc.)
	Elephant Shit	"Big talk," grandiose plans	Avoids confronting reality and responsibility (e.g., what you'll do when you win the lottery).

Figure 12.

157

SHINIGAMI: "YOU'RE ONLY AS SICK AS THE SECRETS YOU KEEP"

Secrets bleed like blood.
—Hannibal the Conqueror[107]

In Japanese folk religion a *shinigami* is a death spirit that rises from the underworld to collect souls—literally, something that comes back to haunt us. Metaphorically, shinigami refers to those "dark secrets" we all keep that, left untended, never quite buried deep enough, eventually rise and return—always at the worst of times—to haunt us.

We all harbor such secrets. If not secrets about ourselves, then secrets we vouchsafe for loved ones.

Merciless manipulators are relentless in digging up such secrets—the darker those secrets, the better—from the stuff of tabloids, to the stuff of terror.

Part of our *yuku mireba* training involves learning to "see" the shadows that would elude the light, learning to "see" what secrets others are trying to keep hidden from us. Once having shined light to these shadows, perhaps we will use this new-found knowledge like a friend (or at least a trusted psychiatrist) to help those harboring such secrets. Or perhaps we will use these newly-discovered secrets to harm them—like the *dependable* enemy we are! Better a faithful foe than a false friend.

By "shadow" we mean those stumbles and stutters in our lives we prefer to keep hidden away from polite, prudish society, our "nightsider" face, full of desire and possibly spite that we keep hidden, the shadow self we're afraid will somehow, someday, inadvertently show its teeth to the world.

This is our "I know what you did last summer" stumble, our "What happens in Vegas . . . just followed your drunk ass home!" secret. Can you say "blackmail" waiting to happen? Fear is our most useful tool for fouling our foes:

> Intimidation—motivation through fear—is an ever-present head game played in a myriad of ways. If you give it some thought, you might be shocked to find that a large percentage

---

107. Truth XIV (p. 224). See Section III for all 99 of Hannibal's "Truths."

of your actions are motivated by fear. You may be motivated by the fear of physical harm, the fear of losing someone's love, or the fear of being embarrassed, to name a few. Some of these fears are valid, but most are not. It's the preponderance of unfounded fears which unnecessarily disrupts your life. —Robert Ringer[108]

In their informative study of the Japanese mafia, *Yakuza* authors David E. Kaplan and Alec Dubro relate how one enterprising gangster sent out thousands of letters to prominent Japanese reading simply: "I know what you did and I will reveal your secret to the world unless you send me money!" Despite the fact no specific wrongdoing or actual secret was mentioned in the letters, despite the fact that no specific extortion amount was mentioned, the money was soon rolling in from those fearing someone had discovered their dark secret . . . whatever it was!

While there seems no limit to the number of silliness, sadness, and sodomies human beings try to sweep under their rug, or skeletons they try to cram up in their closet, in general we can distinguish seven categories of "dark secrets" humans try so desperately to keep hidden, some just as ephemeral, yet just as frighteningly haunting as a true *Shinigami:*

Birth Secrets

At one time being born a "bastard" all but assured that your life was pretty much over before it began. While we no longer blame the children for being conceived outside marriage, an unwed mother is still today often looked down upon with disdain, and some individuals and families—especially those from more traditional cultures—still go to great lengths to keep such things secret. Sometimes this requires sending the girl away to "visit relatives" in another state, then quietly putting the baby up for adoption. This leads to another birth-related shock, finding out (or being made to think) you are adopted.

Unwanted pregnancy can also end in an abortion, which, while legal, isn't something the young woman (or her family) wants broadcast.

---

108. Robert J. Ringer, *Looking Out for #1* (Fawcett/Crest 1977), 73. See also "Looking Out for Number One: Bring in the Ringer!" in Section III (p. 320).

Lately we've seen an increase in the West of incidents of the Middle Eastern tradition of "honor killings," where it falls to the brother or father of a young girl to murder her in order to erase the "dishonor" she's brought on the family name by something as simple as marrying outside her religion—let alone, getting pregnant.

Body Secrets

We all have an image in our minds of "the perfect body." Unfortunately, none of us seem to have this body. For teenagers, zits and freckles can undermine self-confidence. For the middle-aged, it's hair-loss or being fat—the latter often judged by others to be the result of lack of control or laziness.

Manipulators learn to "see" and then exaggerate and exploit the smallest of body defects and deformities—real or imagined—both in the minds of the insecure individuals and/or in the minds of insensitive people around them. "Body Secrets" often segue into "Health Secrets."

Health Secrets

Despite all our outward show of concern, illness is still seen by many as "weakness" on the part of the sick person. Other times illness is seen as something the person brought on himself (for example through drug abuse or lifestyle). When illness is combined with a sexual element, it is doubly useful to your enemy. For example, AIDS is (still) seen by some as "God's punishment" for a "wicked and immoral" lifestyle. Likewise contracting any STD is your "punishment" for committing adultery.

The first step in crooked cult "faith-healing" is convincing the person they actually have an illness. The only thing better than dealing in physical faith healing is tampering with mental illness, since the manipulator doesn't even have to produce any physical evidence. (Unlike those "psychic surgeons" who have to at least palm some bloody chicken organs in order to remain convincing!)

The next best thing to making a foe doubt his own sanity, is making those around him doubt it for him. A classic "cutting-at-the-edges" ploy using this strategy was played out during the 1972 presidential campaign when presidential hopeful George McGovern's running mate, Senator Thomas Eagleton, resigned from the ticket after someone leaked to the media the fact that Eagleton had been hospitalized three times for treatment of emotional exhaustion and depression.

Whatever Eagleton's actual qualifications, the assumptions about his mental dependability made him a political liability, and effectively sank McGovern's campaign.

Failure Secrets

Failure to achieve a dream of success makes many people frustrated and then bitter before their time.

Internally-motivated people often torture themselves when they fail to meet their goals. This can then lead to a vicious cycle of self-doubt, hesitation, and further failure.

Externally-motivated people often feel they have failed to live up to others' expectations (e.g. parents, spouse, etc.). Mind-slayers get close to such people by promising to show them how to satisfy others.

Recently, with the meltdown on Wall Street, we've seen brokers and others willing to do anything (up to and including suicide) just to hide the shame of their financial failures. Of course, uncovering such a failure before it's made public puts a ruthless manipulator in the catbird seat so far as either extorting those involved and/or convincing those in dire straits to take chances and make deals they wouldn't normally think of taking and making, all in order to regain their flagging wealth (and prestige).

Sex Secrets

From Hawthorne's *The Scarlet Letter* to the Clinton-Lewinsky scandal, sex has always been a hot potato—or in Clinton's case, an even hotter cigar!

Politicians in the public eye always seem to have secrets they'd rather not have seen by the public eye. Take for example the recent case of Nevada senator John Ensign who went public that he'd had an extramarital affair . . . but only after the husband of the woman with whom he was having the affair demanded hush money. A possible contender for the 2012 Republican Presidential nomination, ironically (or predictably?) Ensign was a member of the evangelical Christian *Promise Keepers,* a group that promotes strong "family values."[109]

In addition to the "sin" of adultery (seen, at the very least, as a weakness in character), there are a host of other sex-related wounds in which a wily manipulator can twist the knife:

---

109. Reported in *The Week*, June 26, 2009.

- **_Unexpressed sexual fantasies_** can lead to secret guilt, humiliation (if revealed) and, when unearthed, can open a person to blackmail.
- **_Feelings of importance and inadequacy_** can lead people to go to extremes, from hiring a prostitute to jumping out of a plane to prove they're macho.

Since sex is often seen as the . . . measure of a man's worth, feeling that we just don't . . . measure up can undermine a man's self-confidence and lead to feelings of frustration, anger, even violence.

Woman can likewise feel inadequate, imagining (or being made to imagine) that her actions or inactions have driven her lover into the arms of another. Feelings of inadequacy often feed the fear of losing a lover, this in turn fuels suspicion and jealousy. Sex and jealousy go hand in hand. Making a person doubt his/her loved one's devotion drives a wedge between the two. The bigger the wedge, the more easily a manipulator can slip in.

- **_Homophobia_**, fear of homosexuals and/or the fear of being (thought) gay can be a powerful slander against a person, either (1) because others believe it, or (2) because the person being targeted _fears_ others will believe it.

Another consideration in the same vein is the effect of a loved one being (or, again, even being thought) gay has on family and close friends. Mothers and fathers wonder "Where did _we_ go wrong in raising him?"; siblings fret it might be "genetic" and "run in the family"; while spouses think, "I drove them to this! If only I'd done more in the bedroom!" and begin to doubt their self-worth as wife or husband.

Even longtime friends have been known to abandon one another if one is thought to be gay, fearing people will think, "If your buddy is gay, you must be gay too!"

Manipulators with this kind of "insider" information are not above using such rumors to drive a wedge between friends and family, further undermining their intended victim's support network.

- **_Molestation_**, actual or alleged, can also be used to both discredit a victim's credibility with others and even make the targeted people doubt themselves.

Even false allegations of child molestation can devastate a family and ruin a person's reputation and career. The media are quick to plaster a person's name on the screen when he's *accused* of a heinous act (e.g. rape, child molestation), yet when's the last time you saw a news agency run a follow-up story when the charges were dropped?

A second way molestation can be used is to convince your victim that he himself has been the victim of molestation as a child. For example, a ruthless manipulator targets a rival businessman by convincing the businessman's teenage daughter to go to the authorities with "repressed memories" she has suddenly "recalled" of being molested as a child by her father. Too far-fetched? Have you so soon forgotten the example of the 1988 Washington state case where, after attending a fundamentalist Bible camp which featured a "cult expert" lecturing on how prevalent "Satanic ritual abuse" was "even in good Christian families," two young daughters became convinced they'd been the victims of child abuse years before by their father, leading to the breakup of their family and the subsequent imprisonment of their father.[110]

Crime Secrets

From those paper clips we stick in our pockets as we're leaving work, to our son's shoplifting problem, there's always somebody watching, a "friendly" face willing to look the other way and/or help us sweep it under the rug with a conspiratorial wink. What they never tell you is that (1) trying to cover such things up usually turns out to be twice as much trouble as the actual crime itself and, more importantly (2) you've just put your career, your family's future, perhaps your life itself, into the hands of someone who, at their merest whim, can sink you.

Death Secrets

Death always leaves unresolved feelings. Psychologists call this "lack of closure." These unresolved feelings leave us vulnerable and invite every ill-intentioned ilk of con man, psychic, and cult leader to get their foot in the funeral-home door. Feeling "responsible" and "guilty" (justified or not) over the death of another often leaves an opening large enough for an opportunistic manipulator to drive a truck (or at least a hearse) through.

Often those walking away from a deadly accident experience "survivor's guilt" ("Why did they have to die when I didn't?"). The suicide of a loved

---

110. See the "Memory Manipulation" chapter in Section I (p. 49).

one likewise always leaves behind guilt in the survivors (i.e., "I should have seen the signs . . ."). Where guilt doesn't occur naturally, manipulators are quick to create it.

When their intended victim is too squeaky clean and doesn't have any true *Shinigami* dark secrets his enemy can use against him, it's necessary for the manipulator to create dark secrets or, when all else fails, resort to "cutting-at-the-edges" by unearthing the dark secrets (actual or manufactured) on the targeted victim's friends and relatives.

PUTTING SOME LIGHT ON "SHADOW LANGUAGE"

It has been estimated that as much as seventy percent of all communication between people is non-verbal, carried on without the use of words, through our body language (e.g. facial expression, posture, gestures, movement, etc.). Even when we do use words to communicate, a large percentage of our communication is not through the actual words spoken, but rather our tone, patterns of speech, and the types of words we favor to convey our meaning.

All this adds up to our "Shadow Language." Thus Black Science is as much "muscle-reading" as it is "mind-reading."

Medieval Ninja relied on being able to read the body language of others in order to spot approaching danger. In addition, as part of their sixth training "Hall"—the Art of Disguise—Ninja mastered nuances of posture, walk, and gesture in order to disguise their own body language. This physical skill was further augmented by skills taught in the Ninja's ninth training Hall dedicated to the Art of Mysticism.[111] Here a Ninja learned how to disguise his *wa* (lit. spirit, presence, intention) when approaching a foe. Sword Adept and master strategist Miyamoto Musashi also lectured at length on the importance of studying "attitude," i.e. the body language that can betray one's intent. (More on "The Musashi Method" in the next chapter.)

Modern self-defense experts also know the importance of both reading the body language of others as well as learning to project their own body language into an "attitude" of confidence intended to dissuade attack.[112]

---

111. For a complete course in all aspects of Ninja training see *Nine Halls of Death* by Lung and Tucker (Citadel, 2007).

112. Dirk Skinner, *Street Ninja: Ancient Secrets for Surviving Today's Mean Streets* (Barricade Books, 1995).

Yet even without any formal training in martial arts or psychology,[113] it's simple for most folks to determine when another person is happy or depressed, excited or bored, simply by looking at that person's body language. This is hardly new—500 years ago Shakespeare spoke of it in *Macbeth*:

> There's no art to find the mind's construction in the face . . .
> Your face, my thane, is as a book where men may read strange matters.

The "Body-type-determines-behavior" theory was first formally put forth (in the West at least) by the Greek Hippocrates (460–370 B.C.). Since then the practice (art?) of determining personality and intent through observing physical appearance and actions (what we today just call "body language") has gone through numerous incarnations down through the centuries, with various physiognomy-based insights, prejudices, and stereotypes passing into and out of vogue. For example, it was once believed criminals could be identified by their "beady little eyes," "sloping" foreheads, and their lack of earlobes.

In the 1940s and '50s, psychologists maintained they could determine a person's overall personality by classifying them according to body shape into one of three "somatotypes": ectomorphic, endomorphic, or mesomorphic.

> **Ectomorphs** are tall, thin, and poorly muscled. They tend to be brainy—your basic nerd stereotype. We always suspect them as being up to something. Think Basil Rathbone as *Sherlock Holmes*.
> **Mesomorphs** are short and stocky and have a lot of muscle. They tend to be more physical-minded. We worry they may get angry (physical!) at any time. Think Robert Blake[114] as *Beretta*.
> **Endomorphs** are round-faced and overweight. Big surprise, these people are thought to be more sedentary, lazy. Think John Belushi, who, ironically, was quite active as SNL's *Samurai*-everything (but, unfortunately, quite active in drugs as well . . .).

Quiet as it's kept, we still maintain many of these stereotypes and prejudices: "Fat people are jolly" (which John Belushi obviously was); "People

---

113. And any good martial arts school is going to teach students that psychology ("The Three Knows") is their first line of defense . . . and offense.

114. Acquitted of killing his wife by the way . . .

with high foreheads are deep thinkers" (which Basil Rathbone actually had and the fictional Sherlock was described as having); "Blondes are dumb" (or, on the other hand, perhaps Anna Nicole Smith really was a *great* enough actress to have fooled us all?); and "Redheads have wicked tempers"; and the size of a man's nose—or is it his foot?—reflects the size of his . . . well, you get the idea.

Beyond these generalities (a much nicer term than "stereotypes and prejudices") are actual subconscious signals ("tells") the body gives off that are often at odds with what the conscious mind is doing and saying.

Physical "tells" include such easy-to-spot clues as changes in breathing, direct eye contact (or lack thereof), and physical tension (muscle tics, fingering objects, etc.). Verbal "tells" include stuttering, hesitations, and Freudian slips of the tongue. All of these non-verbal indicators are "tells," or unconscious body language signals we all give off.

Some off-the-cuff "tells" you can instantly use to "read" other people:

- **The Face:** *The Kama Sutra* advises that among the arts to be studied if you really want to be good at manipulating others is "the art of knowing the character of a man from his features." Today science recognizes "micro-expressions" all of us subconsciously give off when we're trying to hide the truth.[115]

Even without special training, we can learn so much just by taking the time not only to "look" at the other person's face, but also to "see" what it is "TELLing" us. For example, is he pale from fear, or blushing from embarrassment or guilt? Which of the easily read "10 Basic Emotions" can we see on his face: Joy, Anger, Interest (aka Excitement), Disgust, Surprise, Contempt, Sadness, Fear, Shame, and Guilt?

- **The Eyes Have It:** Totally beyond our control, our eyes widen in surprise, narrow in suspicion. That's why Arab businessmen often wear dark sunglasses when "NO-gotiating," so as to not tip their hands by displaying not-so secret interest when their pupils dilate.

---

115. See *The Truth About Lying* by Dr. Haha Lung. Publication pending.

Is he afraid to make eye contact? Many believe that blinking is a sign of guilt and lying; actually, it's often the opposite—liars often try to "stare you down," blinking less than normal.

Here's your guideline:

- **We look upwards** when we're trying to remember or imagine seeing something. Ninety percent of people look *up and to the left* when remembering, *up and to the right* when creating images in their minds. In simplest terms: Left = memory, Right = imagining and creating.

    Thus, when it comes to figuring out whether someone is lying or not, the rule of thumb is: If they're looking to the left it means they're actually remembering something that happened. Looking to the right usually means they're lying their ass off!

    By watching where a person's eyes go when asked a question, we can often figure out whether he is being truthful or lying. Review and reinforcement: We look up and to the left when we're *remembering* something we saw (e.g. a picture). We look up and to the right when *creating* a picture—or creating a lie. (More on "How to Spot a Liar" in a minute.)

- **We look to the side** (towards our ears) for sounds. Again, to the left to *recall* a tune and to the right when trying to *imagine* what something or someone might sound like.

- **We look down** (towards our nose, hands, and body) when recalling things we touched, tasted, or smelled, and sometimes when recalling *emotional* hurt. Thus we look down and left to recall the *smell* or *feel* of leather, down and right to imagine what something might feel, smell, or taste like.

- **Head angle:** Is his chin up (determined, defiant) or downcast (passive, possibly guilty)?

- **The Hands:** Are his knuckles clenched white in stress or anger? Are his fingers drumming in nervousness or impatience? Is he wringing his hands in anxiety? Are his hands trembling with fear? Are his palms sweaty? Does he keep brushing off imaginary pieces of lint from his clothes (trying to brush away guilt and responsibility)?

- **Gestures:** Gesture "tells" include:

    The unconscious tapping together of a person's thumb and
        index finger (making the "OK" sign) can be a tell that

person secretly wants to agree with you, if only to avoid an argument.

Rubbing the body and smoothing out wrinkles in clothing means he's trying to do the same to the lies he's telling you.

Palms unconsciously flapping out from the body can indicate "I don't know."

That almost imperceptible shrug the person is unaware he is doing may be an indication he is unsure about what he is talking about and/or has subconscious doubts. FYI: Some people have a "micro-expression" where they "shrug" with the corners of their mouths instead of with their shoulders—means the same.

If you doubt the power of simple *deliberate* gestures, watch how "flipping the bird" can change the mood of a whole room full of people! Yet even deliberate gestures can have hidden (even subconscious) meaning to different people. That's because the meaning of gestures varies in meaning from place to place. The American two-finger "V for victory" means "screw you!" in England and Australia. (You may recall the uproar a visiting President George Bush Sr. caused when he flashed a cheering Aussie crowd what he thought was the "V for victory" sign—palm inward!)

- **Posture:** Is his spine straight (confident, alert, determined). Of course too-rigid a back can be a sign of discomfort and/or that he's hiding something from you. Slouching can mean he's either tired or else feeling defeated—a sign you've won the NO-gotiation.
- **Personal distance:** "Casual" conversation takes place with individuals standing three to five feet from one another. Closer than this is known as "intimate distance" and indicates either friends confiding or else conspirators in cahoots.

The distance between people can even help you pinpoint a person's culture of origin. Anglo-Americans are generally more space-and distance-defensive and less touch-oriented than many cultures. Middle Easterners, for example, stand closer than Americans when talking—close enough to (1) feel one another's breath (and to note any change in normal *breathing patterns* as a possible indication of deception) and (2) read one another's eyes. Men in other cultures embrace and kiss upon meeting, something pretty much taboo in North America.

- **Walking**: Is their step brisk and light ("carefree") or slow and shuffling (weary, concerned)?

Yuku mireba "Seeing" (not just "looking" at) another's body language can also give us clues to their overall "sensory mode," i.e., their primary approach to taking in information.

Watchers, Listeners, and Touchers

People can be classified into three "sensory" types, depending on their primary mode of gathering information:

1. **"Watchers"** take in information primarily through their eyes and are thus dominated by what they see;
2. **"Listeners"** are ruled by what they hear; and
3. **"Touchers"** process information primarily through their senses of touch and taste.

We all use all three of these sensory modes at various times, yet each of us tends to favor one style of information-gathering more. This becomes a vital component to our personality. Consequently, becoming adept at recognizing which sensory mode a person favors takes us a long way towards our goal of fashioning an "approach" to that person. On a more immediately practical, mundane level, being able to recognize sensory mode in others can help us with our day-to-day relationships.

Don't worry, you won't have to guess whether people are Watchers, Listeners, or Touchers. They'll be glad to tell you in several ways.

First, watch what they do. Watcher's minds tend to wander when forced to *listen* to others talk. They like to read (because it involves using their eyes). They tend to have good handwriting, to doodle while thinking, and are good spellers (although they often need to actually write the word out or close their eyes to recall what words look like).

Watchers are good at remembering faces (but not names). They notice details (like your lodge pin, college ring. That fine-looking "Watcher" at the bar already noticed the tan line from that wedding ring you just slipped off and into your pocket. Watchers collect paintings, baseball cards, and comic books.

When rewarding a Watcher, give him a big wall plaque or a degree, something he can hang across from his desk and look at every day.

Listeners enjoy talking. Sometimes they talk, sing, or hum to themselves. They like music and often collect records. Like Watchers, Listeners remember faces well. Listeners enjoy listening activities, from music to poetry read aloud.

Listeners enjoy wordplay and verbal riddles. They are easily captivated by a good talker. Reward a Listener with concert tickets or a new CD.

Touchers like rewards they can (duh!) touch, trophies for example. A set of worry-beads will amuse them. A dead giveaway for spotting Touchers is their tendency to touch others when talking and to physically handle objects when working.

Touchers also use their hands when talking and unconsciously tap their pencils and bounce their feet while studying. They are poor spellers. They enjoy physically challenging—hands on—work, like taking engines apart and putting puzzles together.

Second, observe their breathing. Watchers breathe high in the chest. Listeners breathe evenly from mid-chest. Touchers breathe from their bellies. If you're a "Listener" yourself, you can hear them breathing—deeply for Touchers, more shallow for Watchers, mid-range for your fellow Listeners.

Third, note the angle of their head. Watchers keep their chins up, trying to see as much as possible. Listeners keep their heads balanced or cocked to one ear or the other. Head down with neck muscles relaxed usually indicates a Toucher.

Fourth, listen to the words they choose. The verbal imagery we choose to describe how we see and interact with the world betrays us as Watchers, Listeners, or Touchers:

Where a Watcher will tell you, "I *see* where you're coming from," a Listener says "I *hear* what you're *saying*," while a Toucher says, "I can get *behind you* on that" or "I'm sure I can *support* you on that."

The same newspaper headline that "screams" for the Listener, "jumps out" at the Toucher, and "blindsides" the Watcher.

Rather than making a decision based on only one or two descriptive words used by a person, instead look for *patterns* of speech that reveal a person favoring one form of verbal imagery over the others.

Watchers process the world through their eyes: "He was *short* with me," "That's certainly a *tall* order." For Watchers, a person is "positively glowing," "radiant," or a "shining" example to others. Words are "beautiful," the boss is in an "ugly" mood.

Listeners hear an office "buzzing" with gossip, a room "humming" with excitement. A name often "rings" a bell.

Touchers use direction (describing their mood as "up," "down," or "low") and temperature (describing people as "cold," receptions "chilly," and lovers "hot"). Touchers use tactile-oriented words describing others as "a hard nut to crack" or "a smooth operator." In dealing with others, touchers chide themselves for being too "soft," other times too "rough."

Using movement imagery, Touchers describe attitudes ("keeping one's head above water"), intent ("trying to sway the jury," "waiting for the other shoe to drop"), and actions ("give him the brush-off").

A dead giveaway is when Touchers get "vibes" and actually interject the word "feel" into their speech: "It just feels wrong to me," "We don't feel as close as we used to," "I have a feel for business," and "a feel for the game."

As already mentioned, the direction a person's eyes dance when you ask them questions can indicate whether they are being fully truthful or else have something to hide.

Sensory Mode Spotter Exercise

Use the following exercise as a score card to help you determine a person's sensory mode, then craft your approach to them accordingly. To accomplish this you first have to ask the person *questions you know they know the answer to* and are expected to answer truthfully to. Professional interrogators call this "establishing a baseline," a set of truthful body reactions that can later be used to trip up a liar. This same process works for initially determining a person's sensory modality.

Note where the person's eyes go to when they're searching for the answer. Accordingly, you'll want to ask him questions that engage his sense of sight, his sense of hearing, and then his senses of touch and taste. Any question designed to engage his senses will work. Remember, for ninety percent of people, looking to the left means they're actually remembering something. For example:

"Do you recall what the first car you owned *looked* like, what model it was?" Responding, he looks up and to the left, recalling the picture of the car in his mind.

"Do you remember what the radio *sounded* like?" Responding, he looks left and to the side, searching for a remembered sound.

"What kind of seats did it have, leather or fabric?" Responding, he looks left and down, remembering the feel (touch) of the seat.

Now you want to try and engage his right side (imagination) with questions like:

"Can you imagine what a car would be like if it didn't have wheels and instead flew?" Responding, he looks up and to the right, creating a picture in his mind.

"Did you ever wonder what a flying car's engine would sound like?" Responding, he looks to right side, trying to imagine the sound.

"Do you think a ride in such a car would be bumpy or smooth?" He looks right and down, trying to imagine what it would feel like.

Keep in mind that these directions are reversed for about ten percent of people, most often lefties. When encountering such a person, use the strategy, simply reversing directions. And, by the way, quick responses where a person immediately gives "right-side" responses to "imagination" questions often means they will be excellent subjects for hypnotism. Pegging a person's sensory mode as to whether your potential victim (uh, *subject*) is a Watcher, Listener, or a Toucher is vitally important in order to tailor an effective approach designed specifically to (1) catch their attention, (2) sway their opinion in your direction.

For example, when dealing with a Toucher, don't *talk* a mile a minute and don't waste your time describing how something *looks*. Instead, let the Toucher feel, smell, or taste the product. Even if you're trying to sell him a piece of land three states away, bring him a sample of the soil or a pinecone from the site to touch and smell.

When debating, arguing, or NO-gotiating, in order to fluster and frustrate your opponent, deliberately choose opposing sensory modes. If he's a Toucher, blind him with vivid visual descriptions, wall charts, and descriptive metaphors.

When confronted by two individuals with differing information-gathering styles, you can drive a wedge between them by choosing a style favored by one but not the other. Thus you kill two birds with one stone, freezing one of them out of the conversation, while praising the other for being smart enough to understand what you're saying.

Liar, Liar, Pants on Fire!

> *Falsehood is worse in kings than beggars.*
> —**William Shakespeare,** *Cymbeline*

Down through the ages, various techniques have been devised for testing truthfulness. Ancient Chinese placed rice powder in the mouths of suspected liars. The nervous liar's mouth would already be dry, thus a guilty person would be unable to speak. As dubious as some ancient lie-detection methods were, the accuracy of modern electronic lie-detection equipment is equally debatable. In the final analysis, even modern lie-detection equipment only does what we can learn to do by using (1) our eyes, (2) our ears, and (3) through our mastery of "Shadow Language."

As just covered, by learning to spot and "baseline" a person's sensory mode takes you a long way towards being able to tell when they're lying. In addition, we want to listen for any (1) verbal inconsistencies in his story, (2) slips of his tongue, and (3) other verbal clues, especially what's *not* being said. We do this by learning to listen to *how* something is said in addition to *what* is said. Often what *isn't* said reveals the most.

To do this, first slow down a fast-talker so as not to allow his lies to get buried in that ton of bullshit he's shoveling your way. It's a proven fact some "psychopaths" have a natural talent for lying, deceiving, and manipulation.[116] Some experts have even speculated that lying may be a survival skill determined by genetics to save your lives. Is it any surprise then that one study determined that 91 percent of Americans lie regularly, with twenty-two percent admitting they can't get through the day without telling "a few" premeditated "white" lies.[117]

The only thing people are better at than lying is coming up with excuses that justify their lying.[118]

Liar-Spotting 101: Look and listen for "leakage," those hesitations and hangers-on at the end of a person's sentences and at the end of their conversations. Leakage includes:

---

116. Robert D. Hare, *Without Conscience: the Disturbing World of the Psychopaths Among Us* (Pocket Books, 1993).

117. *New York Times* News Service, June 16, 1996.

118. See *The Truth about Lying* by Dr. Haha Lung. Publication pending.

- Changes in voice pitch
- Changes in breathing (e.g. from deeper to shallower)
- Inconsistencies in facts
- Slips of the tongue, Freudian and otherwise, especially those that appear at the end of a conversation
- Emotional leakage beneath the words. Disguising words is easy, disguising emotions is difficult. Fleeting facial expressions (aka "micro-expressions") often reveal genuine underlying emotion. On the other hand, strong shows of emotion (anger, feigned indignation) may be a defensive strategy designed to divert attention from a lie.

Don't forget to look for Body Language "tells" that a lying person is consciously unaware of:

- Compulsive swallowing
- Nervous gestures (e.g. brushing imaginary dust—guilt!—off their clothing)
- A subconscious initial nod a speaker unconsciously gives just before saying "no"
- An almost imperceptible shrug coming right before he agrees with you (a sign the speaker is uncertain and has second thoughts)

We often experience a vague feeling of unease, of "bad vibes," when listening to someone. This is because we subconsciously perceive their lying "tells," those words that don't match body language, warning us that we are being lied to.

To illustrate how important it is to match body language to words, try this experiment the next time a friend asks you a question: Nod "yes," but say "no." Watch the confusion on his face as his brain tries to reconcile two contradictory messages.

Use a variation of our Sensory Mode "baselining" to uncover another's lying:

First, ask three "control questions": (1) a question you *know* the person knows the answer to, (2) a question the person *might* know the answer to, and (3) a question you know the person *doesn't* know the answer to.

Second, as the person responds, watch for the speaker's tells. Spotting tells in response to these different questions provides clues to his truthfulness. You can also use his answers to help you determine whether he is a Watcher, Listener, or Toucher.

If you ever get a "vibe," "hunch," or just a "gut feeling" someone is lying to you, they probably are. What you may be "hearing" is your subconscious mind trying to warn the conscious part of your mind. Trust your "gut feelings." Keep in mind your gut evolved a few million years before your politically correct, "Wouldn't want to offend anyone with my suspicions" brain.

By the way, since we're being politically incorrect (yet scientifically accurate!): Lying techniques vary by gender. In general, men lie by *commission* (adding information), while women lie via *omission* (by leaving out important details). Therefore, when talking to a man, keep track of *what he says*, noting any inconsistencies, returning to contradictions and points needing clarifying at the end of his speaking. When talking to a woman, pay attention to *what she doesn't say*. Look for gaps in the continuity of her narrative. A quick "Body Language Busts Lying" headline: Men tend to lean forward, towards you, when lying. Women tend to lean away when lying.

Mirroring and Matching: Establishing Rapport

When you generate familiarity, trust, and comfort in others, they become more receptive to your ideas and are more willing to help you accomplish your goals. Doctors call establishing this kind of initial rapport their "bedside manner." Salesmen and Jehovah's Witnesses call it "getting a foot in the door." Unscrupulous mind manipulators call this "the beginning of the end"!

To establish rapport with another person, whether a potential customer or an enemy you are trying to "rock to sleep," pay close attention to him while you:

> Make direct eye contact
> Smile as much as possible. Beware! You can spot a fake smile
> > because it's (1) switched on more abruptly than a genuine
> > smile and (2) is generally held longer—about four to five
> > seconds.
> Watch how he moves, his body language, and how he sits.

> When sitting with him, adopt an "open posture" (elbows away from your body, your legs stretched out) rather than a "closed position" (your elbows close in to your body, and your knees together).
>
> Begin "mirroring" the person you are trying to persuade.
>
> Adjust your gestures, your voice (tempo and tone), and body positioning to mirror his. Subtly imitate his distinctive movements and body positioning (e.g. sitting upright versus lounging relaxed). Be careful not to appear mocking.
>
> Listen not only to what he says, but also to how he says it.
>
> Pepper your speech with Sensory Mode phrases ("I see . . . ," "I hear . . . ," "I feel . . ."), tailored towards his Watcher, Listener, or Toucher orientation.

"Mirroring" (aka "Matching") sense modality convinces the other person that you're just like him. Remember: We like those who are like us. Once you've convinced him of this, once you're "in synch" with the other person, you can then begin manipulating the pace, tone, and direction of your communication, gently leading the conversation where you want it to go.

Manipulators study both the speech styles and patterns of speech of potential victims in order to better mimic those styles and patterns. Other times, manipulators purposely choose contra-styles and patterns of speaking they know will confuse their victim:

Watchers tend to speak quickly (trying to describe the images they see in their mind's eye). Their minds stray during long lectures. When trying to win them over, be short and to the point.

Listeners are more selective about the words they use and tend to have more tone-rich voices. Their speech is slower, more rhythmic, and measured. Since words mean a lot to them, they are careful what they say. Listeners are quick to pick up on that intentional "slip of the tongue" and that influential name you intentionally drop.

Touchers are even slower in speech than watchers and listeners. They tend to have deeper voices and to speak smoothly.

Watch your tone. The tone of speech a person uses, as well as the type of words he employs, says more than the actual words spoken. Nearly forty percent of human communication comes not from the words spoken but from the tone used, e.g. quiet tones can indicate fear, conspiracy, or intimacy. Loud, forceful tones can indicate confidence, or false bravado. Terse speech is used for scolding others and indicates impatience. Soothing tones calm and heal.

When attempting to establish rapport with another person in order to induce a hypnotic state, professional hypnotists first identify the person's dominant speech patterns—tone and type. Then they tailor (i.e. "mirror and match") their own speech accordingly, using words and phrases of similar tone and type designed to make the subject feel at ease. Con men and cult leaders do the same.

MASTERING THE MUSASHI METHOD

All battles are first won in the mind.
—**Miyamoto Musashi**

It has been said "Musashi's Zen was godless."[119] "Godless" perhaps in that his "Way" (Jp. *Do*) of both action and thought were admittedly beyond the reach—and understanding—of average men. "Godless" also in that his means will be seen by most today, indeed by most even in his day, as ruthless approaching the level of a god striking down lesser mortals at his whim. Ruthless, yes, albeit *always* effective.

Yet Musashi devotees and detractors alike agree on one thing: In every life and death encounter, it was Musashi who exercised Ultimate Control—Ultimate Control over Self, over Foe, over Environment and situation. Rather than dance to circumstance and flux as did—as still do—lesser men, it was Musashi who called the tune!

During his violent life, Ben No Soke, better known as Miyamoto Musashi (1594–1645) killed well over a thousand men, sixty of those during personal duels, the rest while fighting in six different wars over the years. By the time of his death Musashi would be universally acknowledged as *Kensei* "Sword Saint," the greatest swordsman who ever lived in Japan.

Ironically, however, Musashi defeated his greatest opponents and foes not with his blade, but with his brain.

---

119. Bart Kosko *Fuzzy Thinking* (1993).

Ever on the alert for that one special trick[120] or technique that would give him the edge, Musashi first mastered the traditional Samurai long sword (*taishi-katana*), before going on to develop a style of fighting using two *katana*. Still not satisfied, Musashi continued to perfect his chosen art by mastering first Samurai weapons—the *jutte*, bow, spear, and so on–before then daring to study "forbidden" Ninja weapons: *manriki*-chain, *kusauri*-sickle, and *Kakushi-jutsu* (the Ninja art of fighting with small, easily concealed weapons, e.g. *shuriken*—throwing stars).[121] By the end of his bloody career, Musashi successfully killed opponents with every conventional Samurai weapon of his day, as well as having used unconventional "environmental weapons" (e.g., an empty scabbard, a tree limb, a kitchen ladle).

Still, no matter what the tool in his hand, Musashi defeated his foes first and foremost by using his power to "see" (*yuku mireba)*, to look into the heart of his enemy, and then playing on his enemies' emotional weaknesses: their bravado, confusion, and their susceptibility to "The Five Warning F.L.A.G.S."[122]

The truth in his ability and in his method comes in the fact that Musashi died of old age. Luckily for us, two years before his death Musashi wrote down his thoughts, tactics, and techniques into *Go Rin No Sho* ("A Book of Five Rings"). Though written 400 years ago, *A Book of Five Rings* remains one of the greatest classics on warfare even written, spoken of in the same breath as Sun Tzu's *Ping-Fa*. Far from being an "outdated" manual on medieval Japanese sword fighting, *A Book of Five Rings* is recognized for its application to every area and arena of endeavor. Even today, successful Japanese businessmen consult their copy of *A Book of Five Rings* on a daily basis.

Musashi was one of the original "think outside the box" guys. Unfortunately not everyone takes the time to develop this skill. Thus, while many may *appreciate* Musashi, just as many run into the problem of how to practically *apply* Musashi to our everyday—modern—battles. But, if we learn naught else from Musashi we must remember his cardinal observation that,

---

120. Tricks well-mastered are called "techniques." Techniques half-learned are merely "tricks."

121. See *Classical Budo* by Donn F. Draeger (Weatherhall Press, 1973).

122. Fear, Lust, Anger, Greed, Sympathy.

whether on the battlefield, in the board room, or even in the bedroom: "All battles are first won in the mind."

One of Musashi's rules was "Learn the ways[123] of all professions." Not only so we learn to respect such craftsmen and their skills, but also so we could "see" through the eyes of others.

In what is perhaps his most (in)famous duel, Musashi carried the day by using a boat oar to kill the man. Had Musashi suffered from "object fixedness"—seeing only one use for an object or tool—and had therefore been unable to "see" (*yuku mireba*) the possibility of using the oar as a weapon, then it is doubtful we would know the name "Musashi" today.

In order to develop *yuku mireba*, our "Power of Seeing," Musashi advises (nay! *warns*) that our overall attitude, our strategy for life in general and special endeavors in particular, must begin with our first concentrating on developing what he calls *senki*, our "war-spirit." Senki includes, but is not confined to:

1. *Focus*, i.e., where we look
2. *Concentration*, i.e., in what manner we look and, more importantly, "see"
3. *Determination*, what we are looking for

Thus whatever the task at hand, we must focus on it with the same intensity as we would if facing a Samurai in a life-and-death confrontation. As on the battlefield, so in the boardroom, so in the bedroom. Musashi thus gives us five ways of "moving an opponent's attitude," i.e., unbalancing him:

- **Attack where his spirit is lax** (e.g., exploit any sloth or lack of focus in your enemy). Create this condition when possible.
- **Throw him into confusion**. Create this condition when possible.[124]
- **Irritate him** (through the use of anger and frustration). Create this condition when possible.
- **Terrify him.** Fear, the first of the deadly "Warning F.L.A.G.S." Go out of your way to create this condition. Remember Machiavelli's advice that it is better (safer!) to be feared than loved.

---

123. Jp. *Do*, lit. "way," "discipline," "skills and crafts."
124. C.H.A.O.S. Theory ("Create Hazards/Hurdles/Hardships And Offer Solutions").

- **Take advantage of the enemy's disrupted rhythm** when he is unsettled; throwing him "off his game" and "out of kilter."

But, of course, before we can unbalance our opponent we must first learn to really "see" him—*yuku mireba!*—to understand his inner nature: what drives him, not only the "nature" he projects to the world, but the inner nature—beast—he was born with . . . and tries so desperately to keep caged.

II.

Junishi-do-jutsu:
Seeing with Your "Animal Eyes"

Don't judge me until you've walked a mile in my paws.
—Anonymous animal wit

DURING OUR DEVELOPMENT IN the womb, we pass through every stage of animal as we grow from gamete to zygote to fetus. Of course, no sooner are we birthed than we begin crying for more oxygen, the memory already fading of a time when we had gills.

We should not so soon divorce ourselves from our animal ancestors, as there is much they could teach us. Would it pain us so to be:

- As loyal as the dog?
- As faithful to our mate as the wolf?
- As filial and sane as the elephant?
- As adaptable as the chameleon?
- As pliable and versatile as the octopus?

Speaking of our "lowly" eight-armed cousin, did you know he can both camouflage himself and set booby-traps like the best Special Forces trooper? Mother Nature has also equipped him with specialized skin cells allowing him to change color, chameleon-like, helping him blend in with his background or else hide unnoticed on the sea floor. Disguising himself by hiding inside an abandoned clamshell, the octopus leaves one of his tentacles outside, wiggling it like a worm, to lure in unsuspecting fish. His body is so flexible he can wiggle his way into the tiniest of crevices in pursuit of prey. When threatened, he emits a cloud of ink that not only acts like a jet to propel him away from a predator, but also obscures his escape route by blinding his enemy. Of course, we do acknowledge other admirable qualities of some of our other animal relatives.

In his *Discourses*, Machiavelli advises an aspiring Prince that he must cultivate both the fierceness of the lion, while tempering it with the cunning of the fox. Conversely, in Japan the fox is considered an ill omen—analogous to a black cat crossing your path. Still, for good or ill, East or West, the "slyness" of the fox is renowned, at least in myth and metaphor.

And we all know, "Slow and steady wins the race" is the moral of "The Tortoise and the Hare." Perhaps that's why Black Science Master Robert J. Ringer chose the tortoise as his personal "totem."[125]

Unlike so many humans, all animals have admirable qualities. Whether psychically, or metaphorically, there is much we can learn from our animal friends. Conversely, we can also learn from an animal's short-comings. For example, drop a bumblebee into an open water glass and instead of simply escaping out the top, the bee will buzz around inside the glass, literally bouncing off the walls, until it dies. There's a lesson in there for us—maybe that we should practice thinking outside the box (or glass, as the case may be). Or how about the raccoon reaching inside a small opening to seize hold of a shiny object (which they are especially susceptible to) then refusing to let go of the object, trapping his clenched paw.

Western astrology honors some of our animal friends in its zodiac: there's a fish and a crab, a scorpion, the goat and the ram, a bull, and a "centaur" (*half* a horse, at least!).

Eastern astrology on the other hand assigns each person one of twelve noble animals as their birth sign. And, as in Western astrology, these birth signs are believed to influence a person's attitudes and actions throughout their lives. The human relationship and correspondences with these celestial

---

125. See *"Looking Out for Number One: Bring in the Ringer!"* next section.

beasts were catalogued over centuries of observation by Chinese astrologers—recording the tendencies of persons born in each year, discovering that the animal ruling the year we are born has a profound influence on our personality and potentiality.

The Chinese will tell you: "This is the animal which hides in your heart."

In other words, we see with "animal eyes." In much the same way, "mama, drama, and trauma" affect whether we see the world through rose-colored glasses or through black eyes; how we "see" the world is also distilled or else distorted by the animal "totem" controlling the time of our birth.

Your "birth beast" can exercise both positive and negative influences on your life. Keep in mind these are but *predispositions, not predestinations*, pointing only to innate tendencies that, once we become aware of them, we are free to embrace or reject. Understanding your birth beast gives you insight into yourself and helps you avoid disaster by advising you when best to act, when to refrain from acting.

And it also gives you insight into others—granting you unlimited access into the inner reaches of their Self—portions of their psyche they themselves may be blissfully—dangerously!—ignorant of.

In the East there have always been numerous various divination methods (e.g. *I-Ching*, geomancy, reading tea leaves, astrology) that allow an enemy to discover the hidden proclivities and vulnerabilities you possess. A wily enemy will also take the time to examine such influences on those close to you. Thus, when unable to attack an enemy directly, we can use this knowledge to attack an adversary by psychologically "cutting at the edges" of his world, undermining his confidence by eroding his comfort zone. This can include studying such arts as astrology.

Astrology, in one form or another, has always been popular throughout the world. Astrology was studied by soothsayers in ancient Babylon and Egypt, among the Druids of Europe and the Incan, Mayan, and Aztec high-priests of the pre-Columbian Americas, as well as in the kingdoms of the East, not the least of which was the Chinese imperial court.

Chinese legend tells how the Emperor of Heaven (later identified with the Buddha) sent invitations out to all animals inviting them to a great feast, but only twelve animals answered the summons. The Emperor subsequently rewarded these twelve beasts by naming one year of the traditional twelve-year celestial cycle after one of them: Rat, Ox, Tiger, Rabbit, Dragon, Snake, Horse, Sheep, Monkey, Cock, Dog, and Pig.[126]

Asian astrology is thus based on the longest chronological record in history, the Chinese lunar calendar, a cycle of which is completed every sixty years. This sixty-year period is further broken down into five sub-cycles of twelve years each. Our current sixty-year cycle began in 1984. Feb. 7, 2008 by Western calculation marked the Chinese New Year, opening the Year of the Rat, 4706.

This kind of astrology was practiced in China from ancient times, and was still thriving in the thirteenth century when Marco Polo recorded that the city of *Kanbalu* had more than 5,000 astrologers under the protection and patronage of the emperor. According to Marco Polo these "wizards" used a variety of fortune-telling methods to forecast weather and prophesy floods, epidemics, war, and conspiracy. But by far the most popular was their casting of horoscopes.

When Chinese astrology was first introduced to Japan—no one's sure exactly when—*Shinobi* Ninja sennin immediately recognized it as both a valuable tool and a weapon. From these sennin's mastery of Chinese astrology came the art of *Junishi-do-jutsu*, a vast catalogue of valuable clues to an enemy's vulnerability. Simply put, an enemy's birth date reveals valuable information about his personality—insights that can be used when plotting strategy: inherent strengths, as well as indications of when an enemy is the weakest and thus most vulnerable to attack.

According to *Junishi-do-jutsu*, each yearly animal totem has a strongest and a weakest time of the day (corresponding to a period of two Western hours). For example, for a person born under the sign of the Cock, the strongest period of the day is from 5 P.M. to 7 P.M. Ascending toward this time period, the Cock steadily gains in strength. Moving away from this prime time, toward its 11 A.M. to 1 P.M. latency period, the Cock becomes weaker and more vulnerable to both physical and mental assault.

Employing *Junishi-do-jutsu*, we take into consideration our enemy's weakest time of day in order to determine when that target will be most susceptible to our power of Suggestology.

---

126. Sadly, our cousin the amazing octopus was not on the guest list . . . although he might have been on the menu!

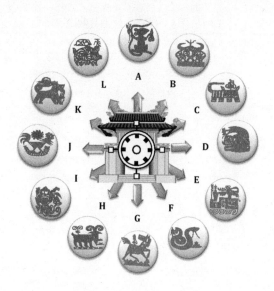

JUNISHI-DO-JUTSU BIRTH DATES

A	Rat	1936	1948	1960	1972	1984	1996	2008
B	Ox	1937	1949	1961	1973	1985	1997	2009
C	Tiger	1938	1950	1962	1974	1986	1998	2010
D	Rabbit	1939	1951	1963	1975	1987	1999	2011
E	Dragon	1940	1952	1964	1976	1988	2000	2012
F	Snake	1941	1953	1965	1977	1989	2001	2013
G	Horse	1942	1954	1966	1978	1990	2002	2014
H	Sheep	1943	1955	1967	1979	1991	2003	2015
I	Monkey	1944	1956	1968	1980	1992	2004	2016
J	Cock	1945	1957	1969	1981	1993	2005	2017
K	Dog	1946	1958	1970	1982	1994	2006	2018
L	Pig	1947	1959	1971	1983	1995	2007	2019

Figure 13.

THE 12 NOBLE BEASTS

Beast	Strength	Strongest Time	Weakest Time	Enemy	Weakness to Exploit
Rat (Jp. Ne)	Smart, quick-witted	11 P.M. to 1 A.M.	5 P.M. to 7 P.M.	Cock	Play to Rat's vanity. Trap him with a mystery. Rat is a social animal—draw him in by making him your guest of honor.
Ox (Jp. Ushi)	Big-hearted, long-suffering	1 A.M. to 3 A.M.	7 P.M. to 9 P.M.	Dog	Trap Ox with sympathy ploys. Ox tries to live up to the expectations of others. Offer to show him how to do this.
Tiger (Jp. Tora)	Keeps promises	3 A.M. to 5 A.M.	9 P.M. to 11 A.M.	Pig	Suspicious by nature, feed his paranoia.
Rabbit (Jp. U)	Clever, talented	5 A.M. to 7 A.M.	11 P.M. to 1 A.M.	Rat	Self-indulgent. Trap him by praising his talent. Play to his "lucky streak."
Dragon (Jp. Tatsu)	Energetic, direct	7 A.M. to 9 A.M.	1 A.M. to 3 A.M.	Ox	Use the judo principle. Support his plans until he overloads, and then turn his energy against him.
Snake (Jp. Mi)	Quick to seize an opportunity	9 A.M. to 11 A.M.	3 A.M. to 5 A.M.	Tiger	Trap Snake with an offer he can't refuse, an opportunity "too good to be true."
Horse (Jp. Uma)	Hardworking	11 A.M. to 1 P.M.	5 A.M. to 7 A.M.	Rabbit	A workaholic, quick to anger. Help him work himself to death.
Sheep (Jp. Hitsuji)	Respectful, peaceful	1 P.M. to 3 P.M.	7 A.M. to 9 A.M.	Dragon	A homebody. Panics when home life is threatened. Use cutting-at-the-edges ploy.
Monkey (Jp. Saru)	Energetic, full of plans; An inventor	3 P.M. to 5 P.M.	9 A.M. to 11 A.M.	Snake	Trap Monkey by making all his schemes and dreams seem possible. Has a short attention span.
Cock (Jp. Tori)	Punctual	5 P.M. to 7 P.M.	11 A.M. to 1 P.M.	Horse	Predictable, his routine can be the death of him. Never admits he's wrong, tries to cover up mistakes, which leaves him open to blackmail.
Dog (Jp. Imu)	Loyal, keeps secrets well	7 P.M. to 9 P.M.	1 P.M. to 3 P.M.	Sheep	Bureaucrat. Easily led. Doesn't like phonies. Make him think he's been betrayed.
Pig (Jp. I)	Home-loving; Likes comfort, has faith in others	9 P.M. to 11 P.M.	3 P.M. to 5 P.M.	Monkey	Prone to laziness. Entice Pig with promises of increased comfort. Undermine his faith in those around him by cutting at the edges.

Figure 14.

Another factor is whether or not our enemy is surrounded by conflict-ing (adverse and toxic) birth beasts that draw off his energy, rather than com-plementing birth beasts that strengthen him. A Cock, for example, will have trouble working with or marrying someone born under a Horse sign.

When infiltrating female agents (e.g., Chinese "Black Lotus" or Ninja *kuniochi*) into an enemy court, Asian strategists employing Junishi-do-jutsu type technique were careful to pick a female whose birth beast made her "compatible" (i.e., more attractive, less suspicious) to the targeted foe.

Let's take a look at the pluses and minuses of these "Birth Beasts":

- **The Rat** is an ambitious hard worker who refuses to ask for help or take charity. Thus his pride cometh before his fall. The Rat seldom makes lasting friendships. He (or she) has a small circle of friends. Manipulate and otherwise undermine the Rat by targeting his small circle of friends. In the east the Rat symbolizes wit and imagination and curiosity. Those born into a year of the Rat can be extremely perceptive and wise, and possess keen observation skills. They are full of energy and often charming. Rats make good bosses but too strict a routine can stifle their natural creativity. On the negative side, they can become aggressive and overly-talkative. A Rat enemy is no "push-over," because Rats are natural survivors.

- **The Ox** is a complainer. Pretending to sympathize with him gets you closer to him. The Ox tries to live up to the expectations of others. Show him a way to do this (building up his confidence), or make him doubt that he is accomplishing this (undermining his confi-dence), and you'll have the Ox's undivided attention.

- **The Tiger** is candid to the point of being rude. Restless, rebellious, and suspicious describes him to a "T." The Tiger keeps his promises and becomes angry with those who do not. Feeling betrayed, he may react violently. We can imagine the title character in *Othello* being a Tiger.

- **The Rabbit** is kind and sensitive, making him the perfect patsy for sympathy ploys. The Rabbit becomes frustrated and doesn't think straight when inconvenienced. He hates to fight, and is thus too soon prone to compromise.[127] Rabbits are shy, yet are surprisingly good

---

127. A "Rabbit?" Review the section on "The Six Rules of NO-gotiation" (p. 62).

in business and handle money well. A business venture that "needs" his expertise will get the Rabbit to open his door every time. For all their business savvy, however, the Rabbit believes in luck. Take off his foot and make his luck your own. A windfall becomes the Rabbit's downfall.

- **The Dragon** thinks he's above the law. Eccentric (like the Cock) the Dragon expects admiration. The Dragon has an explosive temper, and is passionate about nature and his health. The Dragon is so energetic that, like a fire which is continuously fanned higher and higher, Dragons often burn out early in life and are consumed on a pyre of their own energies.

FYI: Martial arts great Bruce Lee was born in 1940, year of the Dragon at the hour of the Dragon, making him a "Double Dragon," a very powerful celestial sign in the East. A restless, noisy, and temperamental child, the Bruce Lee the world came to admire was in every way a Dragon personality: passionate about health (to the point of being eccentric, possibly obsessive), in many ways he felt himself above the law in the way he casually revealed many *"forbidden"* Eastern martial arts secrets to the West (for which, many believe, he was assassinated).

- **The Snake** is attracted by physical beauty. Susceptible to "the finer things" in life, vain and high-tempered, a Snake-dominated personality is a prime candidate for lust and seduction ploys. As a result, a Snake (male or female or somewhere in the middle) will be putty in the hands of a *kuniochi*. A vain Snake (male or female or somewhere in the middle) can be trapped with promises of the fountain of youth. Snakes look for love in all the wrong places and, as a result often end up with . . . egg on their face. Don't underestimate the Snake. Snakes can be calculating and ruthless. A Snake's weaknesses are that they make poor gamblers and they are superstitious. But the Snake's biggest failing is that he can't let an opportunity pass.
- **The Horse** likes to be the center of attention and needs people. Like the rest of us, a Horse-personality likes people to like him and likes people who like him. But, unlike the rest of us, Horse takes it

to extremes, often to the point of being "needy." Get close to the Horse by posing as an adoring fan. Ostentatious and impatient, chomping at the bit Horse often suffers from restlessness and insomnia. They don't take to the bridle and saddle well, but, once "broken," serve loyally.

- **The Sheep** is timid and prefers anonymity. They are quick to defend the underdog, making them suckers to "sympathy" ploys. The Sheep doesn't take personal criticism well. As a result, Sheep let pressure build up until, when the Sheep finally does explode, it is with inappropriate anger (remember *Rams* are sheep too!). Rather than arranging and rearranging major trauma stressors in a Sheep's life, attack him in small increments ("molehills"), increasing the pressure little by little until the Sheep explodes and, in a rage, makes a fatal mistake. Sheep-dominated people are not cut out to be postal workers! To seduce a Sheep: tease them in order to pull the wool over their eyes.

- **The Monkey** is always full of plans, and always looking for someone (like a pretend friend) to tell those plans to. Give the Monkey your ear. Innovators and inventors, Monkeys are nonetheless easily discouraged and confused, and thus open to anyone (such as that pretend friend) who acts like he knows the answer.

- **The Cock** has a strong point when it comes to being punctual. However, that same punctuality—read *predictability*—makes a Cock more vulnerable to anyone spying at his path through life.[128] On the battlefield nothing is more welcome than a predictable enemy. Musashi warns against being predictable, even to the point of never having a favorite weapon or even footwork one favors. Combative, eccentric, and often selfish, Cocks like the public eye. Still, they can be secretly insecure and in need of constant bolstering—opening the door for the insincere praise of a "sympathetic" (i.e. manipulative) ear. The Cock is a perfectionist who can't admit to being wrong and is thus easily trapped by the C.H.A.O.S. ploy, whereby a manipulator who first makes the Cock appear wrong then provides him a way out of being wrong. This two-pronged ploy follows classic Chinese strategy: Says Tu Mu:

---

128. "Nature punishes the predictable." (Lung, 2006:138)

> Trap an already trapped foe twice by offering him a clear road to safety, creating the possibility for life where before there was only the determination of death. Having done so, strike!
> —Tu Mu

- **The Dog** is loyal to a fault. That's the positive. The negative is that Dog-people are born followers, easily led astray. Dogs are generous to a fault, making them prime targets for donation scams, especially from religious hucksters who use "plain talk."
- **The Pig** lives for today and has a (dangerous) "fatalistic" streak. Home-loving (which can lead to laziness) and family-oriented, Pigs marry early and, as a result, are prone to marital strife. Get to the Pig through his spouse.

It's important to realize that the Asian birth beasts who influence us are, in turn, influenced by "The Five Elements": Earth, Air,[129] Fire, Water and Void (See Figure 15, opposite). A little math: 12 Beasts × 5 Elements = "cycles" every 60 years. This produced subtleties within each sign. Take the Rat, for example:

- If you were born into the Year of the Rat 1960 makes you a "Metal Rat," an admirably strong-willed and determined individual, who is nonetheless prone to being overly-emotional to the point of dangerous rage—dangerous not only for others but for yourself as well.
- Born twelve years later in 1972 makes you a "Water Rat." You get along well with others because you're confident, smart and insightful.
- The "Wood Rat" (1924, 1984) appears confident on the surface but underneath hides a secret insecurity. Despite this inner fear, Wood Rats are generally successful in life, often due to their devotion to friends and family.
- Always enthusiastic,[130] "Fire Rats" (1936, 1996) are quick to take

---

129. Also called "*metal*" and sometimes "wind" in Chinese *wu-hsing* zodiac. Likewise, "Void" is often referred to as "*Wood*."

130. Aside, the term "rat race" originated as Jazz slang for a particular type of enthusiastic dance.

ELEMENTS CORRESPONDENCE

ELEMENT	WOOD	FIRE	EARTH	METAL	WATER
YIN ORGAN	Liver	Heart	Spleen	Lungs	Kidney
YANG ORGAN	Gall bladder	Small intestine	Stomach	Large intestine	Prostate
SENSE COMMANDED	Sight	Words	Taste	Smell	Hearing
NOURISHES THE	Muscles	Blood vessels	Fat	Skin	Bones
EXPANDS INTO THE	Nails	Color	Lips	Body hair	Hair on head
LIQUID EMITTED	Tears	Sweat	Saliva	Mucus	Urine
BODILY SMELL	Rancid	Scorched	Fragrant	Fleshy	Putrid
ASSOCIATED TEMPERAMENT	Depressed, Anger	Emotions up & down, Joy	Obsession, Sympathy	Anguish, Grief	Fear
FLAVOR[1]	Sour	Bitter	Sweet	Pungent	Salt
SOUND	Shout	Laugh	Sing	Weep	Groan
DANGEROUS TYPE	Wind	Heat	Humanity	Dryness	Cold
OF WEATHER SEASON	Spring	Summer	Mid-summer	Autumn	Winter
COLOR	Blue/Green	Red	Yellow	White	Black
DIRECTION	East	South	Centre	West	North
DEVELOPMENT	Birth	Growth	Transformation	Harvest	Store
BENEFICIAL CEREAL	Wheat	Millet	Rye	Rice	Beans
BENEFICIAL MEAT	Chicken	Mutton	Beef	Horse	Pork
MUSICAL NOTE	Chio	Chih	Kung	Shang	Yu
DIRECTION	East	South	Centre	West	North
COLOR	Blue/Green	Red	Yellow	White	Black
NUMBERS	8 and 3	2 and 7	10 and 15	4 and 9	6 and 1
CLIMATE	Windy	Hot	Wet	Dry	Cold
PLANET	Jupiter	Mars	Saturn	Venus	Mercury
SOUND	Shouting	Laughing	Singing	Weeping	Groaning
VIRTUE	Benevolence	Propriety	Faith	Rectitude	Wisdom
EMOTION	Anger	Joy	Sympathy	Grief	Fear
HOUR	3-7 a.m.	9 a.m.-1 p.m.	1-3, 7-9 a.m. 1-3, 7-9 p.m.	3-7 p.m.	9 p.m.-1 a.m.
ANIMAL	Dragon	Phoenix	Ox	Tiger	Snake, Tortoise
CELESTIAL STEM					
(YIN)	i	ting	chi	hsin	kuei
(YANG)	chia	ping	wu	kéng	jen
TERRESTRIAL BRANCHES	yin, mao	ssû, wu	ch'ou, wei, ch'én, hsü	shén, yu	tzù, hai
ZODIAC	Gemini, Cancer	Virgo, Libra	Taurus, Leo Scorpio, Aquarius	Sagittarius, Capricorn	Ares, Pisces

[1]Sour like vinegar, bitter like bitter lemon, sweet like sugar, pungent like ginger, salt like common salt.

Figure 15.

on new projects. The downside of this is that they do so because they hate routine and are easily bored (hence easily distracted).

- "Earth Rats" (1948, 2008) are stable and dependable. Beware becoming *sedentary*! Well-liked, they are correspondingly successful. Earth Rats' mantra is (or should be) the universal salesman's adage: "First sell yourself, then sell your product." In other words, if people like *you*, they'll probably like what you're selling.[131]

What's that you say? You're still not buying into some "Far-Eastern astrology crap?" Fine. But perhaps your enemy and/or future *Asian* business partners do, so it might be a good idea to at least get an understanding of this ancient belief-cum-art. So, whether you think astrology is valid or not matters only so far as you can make it work to your advantage—to give you insight into yourself, and/or insight into your enemy's way of thinking.

During World War II, the British Intelligence maintained a special division known as the "Occult Bureau" replete with astrologers on staff. Why "waste" valuable man-power on such a project? Because it was well known that Hitler and many other Nazi big-wigs believed in astrology. This Occult Bureau used their astrologers to figure out what Hitler's astrologers were telling him on any given day, hence, how the German dictator might be expected to act or react on any given day. That worked out pretty good in the long run, right?

To repeat: It doesn't matter if we don't believe in astrology, but it helps to know if our foe—or that babe at the bar—does. Whether we think astrology is a crock or not matters only so far as it can be made to work to our advantage. The same holds true for "the power of color."

---

131. For a more detailed reading of your Chinese zodiac animal influence, go to chinese-zodiac.com. Don't forget to tell 'em Dr. Lung sent you.

12.

The Power of Color

THE COLORS WE FIND ourselves surrounded with can affect our mood, our health, and our overall well-being. It is believed the ancient Egyptians actually used color therapy to heal various ailments.[132]

According to Chinese philosophy/art of *Feng Shui*, colors carry their own *chi*.[133] Thus, someone's "favorite color" can provide both clue and crowbar to controlling what they *consciously* want to attain in life and/or what they secretly—*subconsciously*—desire.

In India, and later in Tibet, China, and Japan, *mandalas*[134] were deliberately painted with specific colors designed to subconsciously influence the meditator concentrating on them, gently "leading" the student in a deliberate visual spiral as they concentrated on each "station" (aspect) of the complex image, in effect leading the observer mentally (and spiritually?) inward through various stages of "emotional cleansing" to enlightenment. For example the initial colors encountered might be *pinks* and *violet*, relaxing the student. Next would come *white*, designed to invoke a feeling of both clarity of thought and purity of purpose, helping the meditator better focus. As his/her

---

132. *The Doctors*, syndicated/NBC-TV June 17, 2009.

133. For a complete study of Feng Shui, and especially how it applies to Sexual Feng Shui, See *Mental Domination* by Lung and Prowant (Citadel, 2009).

134. Designs of concentric and geometric patterns depicting various hierarchies of gods and Buddhas used as a meditation tool.

eyes traveled around the edges of the mandala, on a slow (usually counter-clockwise spiral), depending on the desired purpose, *red* might then dominate their vision field, strengthening them, *indigo* to inspire new ideas, perhaps *brown* to "ground" (i.e., center) them.

Easterners not only use color in their spiritual practices, but in such pseudo-sciences as *Feng Shui*, resulting in their having compiled extensive lists of correspondences wherein the value of color, as both a curative and corruptor, is highly touted.

In the west we also use color to express attitudes and emotions, praise and scorn, from saluting "The Ol' Red, White, and Blue" to cheering on our school colors.

- A *black* flag signals "No mercy!" A *red* flag, anarchy. The *rainbow* flag . . . Don't ask, don't tell. Islam Jihadists fly a black flag.
- We show the *white* flag of surrender. A disgraced soldier is given the *white* feather when drummed out of the corps for cowardice, for turning *"white* as a sheet," for having "a *yellow* streak" up his back (and perhaps a *brown* streak in his shorts!).
- Beware crossing the seasoned politician. He's a *"gray* eminence," the man behind the scenes pulling the strings. Maybe he got that way by *"brown*-nosing." No doubt about it, he's a dastardly *"black*heart," *green* with envy (coincidentally the color of money . . .). Conversely, his brother's "true *blue*" faithful, a *"red, white, and blue"* patriot with a heart of *gold*.
- The bride wears *white* to prove she's . . . well, you know. But then, with Procol Harum playing "Here Comes the Bride" in the background, her face turns "a *whiter* shade of pale" as someone doesn't forever hold their peace, and instead stands up to brand her a *scarlet* woman who turns on the *red* light every night.

Thus, from noticing the color of the car your rival drives, to the color of your new girlfriend's teddy-bear, the choice of color a person favors, can give us potentially valuable information about them: their likes and dislikes, what color we might need to (literally) clothe ourselves in, in order to obtain the upper hand over them.

Likewise, even the color of the meeting room where you'll be giving your big presentation can have a positive effect on your audience—and on

COLOR	CORRESPONDENCES
White	Clarity of thought and purity. The season of fall and the direction west. The *mantra* SEE-AHH. Stimulates health and healing in the lungs and small intestine.
Red	Associated with the heart and the blood, hence often with danger. Vitality and increasing your sex-drive. Summer. South. Easterners assign red to the Base or Root chakra, which in turn is associated, in the West, with the adrenal glands. The mantra HO is believed to stimulate the heart, hence blood circulation.
Pink	Takes a little from white (purity) and a little from red (vitality) and creates love . . . and boundaries.
Orange	Physical strength. Stimulates creativity, our sense of adventure and is thus also associated with charm and extroversion. In the East, orange is associated with the Belly chakra, hence with the reproductive glands (testes and ovaries).
Green	Represents skill. Green lightens mood, relaxing the heart, helping you breathe more smoothly. In the East green is linked to the health of both the gall bladder and the liver. Mantra: SHUU. Rules the Heart chakra, controlling the thymus gland.
Blue	The most popular color, is associated with growth and nurturing in both East and West. Has been shown to lower the pulse rate, decrease body temperature, and increase appetite. Blue, especially sky-blue, has a calming effect. Spring, East. Influences the liver and is associated with the Throat chakra, hence with the thyroid gland
Violet	Calms and relaxes. Crown chakra, corresponding to the pineal gland in Western medicine.
Yellow	Like violet, engenders a calming effect. Associated with the spleen (which in turn was believed to control emotion). Yellow's favored time of year is Indian summer/autumn. The Solar Plexus chakra. Mantra HOOO.
Turquoise	Represents adaptation to changing circumstance.
Purple	Authority, nobility.
Indigo	Inspires new ideas and innovation. "Third Eye" chakra, equal in Western medicine to the pituitary gland.
Brown	"Grounding" and "centering." A person whose favorite color is brown is dependable.
Tan	Internal control, helping us (re)establish internal balance and self-control.
Black	Positive side: accepts, absorbs and integrates. Negative side: associated with all things sinister. In the East also has the art of Feng Shui which generously credits black with the quality to absorb and counteract negative influence. Winter, hence the direction north. Body wise, black influences the kidneys and its curative mantra is SHE-ROW-EE.

Figure 16.

how well you perform. And speaking of color helping you "perform"—what color are the walls in your bedroom?

Do you see now why, even if you're not planning on becoming the next Picasso, you still might want to get to know your basic colors a little better, comparing their influence, in the East and West:

> **WHITE** in the West is associated with both clarity of thought and with purity. However, in the East, white is often worn at funerals and is associated with death in some Asian cultures. Easterners associate white with the season of fall and the direction west. Reciting the *mantra* SEE-AHH while swaddled in clean white cloth is believed to stimulate health and healing in the lungs and small intestine.
>
> **RED** in the West is associated with the heart and the blood, hence often with danger. Red is also associated with vitality and with increasing your sex drive. That's because red has been proven to make the heart beat faster (and sex is all about how—and where to!—the blood flows, increasing both your taste buds and your sense of smell. However, despite stereotypes, red is *not* a good color for seduction even though red (1) makes you stand out in a crowd and (2) has also been proven to speed up the heart rate of those who see red. Wearing red can give you a competitive edge according to a recent study from Durham University in England where test subjects performed worse in red rooms than they did in blue-colored rooms. In addition, athletes wearing red uniforms performed better than those wearing blue uniforms in combat sports. The key seems to be that wearing red doesn't necessarily make *you* play better, but it can make *your opponent* play worse. This is because we tend to associate—both consciously and subconsciously—the color red with danger and with making mistakes.[135]

In the East, red is also associated with vitality, hence with the season of summer (when folks are more active), and with the direction south.

---

135. *"Seeing Red"* by Rachel Mahan, *Psychology Today*, Sept/Oct, 2008:53.

Easterners assign red to the Base or Root *chakra*,[136] which in turn is associated, in the West, with the adrenal glands—source of vitality. Chanting the mantra HO is believed to stimulate the heart, hence blood circulation.

According to Nitya Lacroix and Sharon Seager in their highly-informative *The Book of Massage and Aromatherapy* (1994), scents and oils can also be used to positively affect the body. In conjunction with the color red to stimulate the body, use Frankincense, black pepper, clary sage. An *aphrodisiac* blend believed to help stimulate the Base chakra (which controls sex) is composed of black pepper, cedar wood, clary sage, fennel, frankincense, ginger, jasmine, rose, and sandalwood.

> **PINK** takes a little from white (purity) and a little from red (vitality) and creates love . . . and boundaries.

> **ORANGE** in the West represents physical strength, perhaps in part due to the health benefits of the same-named fruit. (This is somewhat ironic, in the West at least, since prisoners are now dressed in orange jumpsuits!). Orange stimulates creativity, and our sense of adventure, and is thus also associated with charm and extroversion. In the East, orange is associated with the Belly chakra, hence with the reproductive glands (testes and ovaries). Scents and oils used in connection with orange to stimulate the body include chamomile, fennel, marjoram, orange (duh), peppermint, rose, and sandalwood.

> **GREEN** epitomizes "skill" in the West, perhaps because we associate it with farmers and gardeners and the skill required to tend to things "green"? Green lightens the mood, relaxing the heart, helping you breathe more smoothly. In the East green is linked to the health of both the gall bladder and the

---

136. In India, *chakras* (Skt. "wheels") are believed to be seven "power centers" situated along the spine. Once "activated" through various practices, from meditation to severe asceticisms, an energy residing at the base of the spine called "*kundalini*" is released up the spine, "opening" these chakras, infusing the practitioner with health and—some believe—higher powers called siddhas (e.g. ESP). Chakras have since been identified with the modern endocrine glands in the body.

liver. Chanting the mantra: SHUU is believed to keep both functioning well. East Indians believe green rules the Heart chakra, controlling the thymus gland. Scents & oils such as benzoin, bergamot, geranium, mandarin, peppermint, rose, sandalwood, and *ylang ylang* can all be used in harmony with green to stimulate this chakra, especially while meditating.

FYI: Replace red with green—a much more user friendly color—when trying to score with the babes.

BLUE, the most popular color, is associated with growth and nurturing in both East and West. Blue has been shown to lower the pulse rate, decrease body temperature, and increase appetite. Blue, especially sky-blue, has a calming effect (this is why all those sleeping-pill TV commercials are dominated by blue). In the East, the season of spring and the direction east both belong to blue. Blue influences the liver and is associated with the Throat chakra, hence with the thyroid gland (which Western medicine tells us controls growth!). Blue scents and oils used to stimulate this aspect of self and health include chamomile, clary sage, and sandalwood.

VIOLET calms and relaxes. In the East violet is the color of the Crown chakra (corresponding to the pineal gland in Western medicine). Violet-linked scents and oils used to stimulate this area of activity include cedarwood, cypress, eucalyptus, frankincense, juniper, lavender, mandarin, neroli, rose, rosewood, and sandalwood.

YELLOW, like violet, engenders a calming effect—cue "They call me Mellow Yellow . . ." Not surprising considering that in ancient times yellow was associated with the spleen (which in turn was believed to control emotion). Yellow's favored time of year is Indian summer/autumn (perhaps due to the changing color of leaves). In the East yellow represents the Solar Plexus chakra (corresponding to the pancreas and spleen) and is the official color of the Chinese Emperor who sits at the "center" of the world, hence, yellow's direction is likewise "center." The mantra HOOO (who) can be used in conjunctions with scents and oils such as frankincense, fennel, juniper, lavender, peppermint, neroli, rosemary, and rosewood to stimulate this area of concern.

TURQUOISE represents adaptation to changing circumstance.

PURPLE is the color of authority, inspiring thoughts of nobility. The ancient traders who we call the Phoenicians[137] were so named by the Greeks because they sold a special dyed purple cloth favored by kings and royalty—by *authority, nobility.*

INDIGO inspires new ideas and innovation. In India indigo is associated with the mystical "Third Eye" chakra, equal in Western medicine to the pituitary gland. Use indigo-friendly scents and oils like benzoin, clary sage, jasmine, juniper, orange, and rosemary to stimulate this gland.

BROWN is an "earthy" color, literally "grounding" and "centering" you. A person whose favorite color is brown is probably pretty dependable.

TAN, a more subtle brown, symbolizes internal control, helping us (re)establish internal balance and self-control.

BLACK, on the positive side, accepts, absorbs, and integrates. Negatively, in the "wild" West at least, black is associated with all things sinister—from the western outlaw sporting a black Stetson, to the Old Gray Mower's flowing black robe. Of course, the East has black-clad *ninja* who are also nothin' nice! But the East also has the art of Feng Shui which generously credits black with the quality to absorb and counteract negative influence. The season winter, hence the direction north (with its long, dark winters) belong to black. Bodywise, black influences the kidneys and its curative mantra is SHE-ROW-EE.

A **Quick Color-Power Meditation**: When doing slow, deep meditative breaths, close your eyes and imagine the air coming into your body is tinted with the color of whatever physical or mental color-lined benefit you

---

137. They called themselves "Sidonians" after their main city Sidon in Canaan-Palestine.

desire. This meditation is further aided by employing candles (etc.) scented with the scents and oils corresponding to and complimenting the desired color-effect.

You can choose to augment this meditation by sitting in a tranquil space dominated by the color(s) you are invoking (e.g., wall color, soft-pulsing lights, a prayer-rug and/or shawl of the same color).

III.
Commanding
Ultimate Control

A page of history is worth a volume of logic.
—Oliver Wendell Holmes

INTRODUCTION

Ruthlessness for
the Rest of Us

HOW 'BOUT SOME RUTHLESSNESS for the rest of us?

Why should criminal curs, serpentine cult leaders, and the fat cats of corrupt government *realpolitik*—bastards all!—possess an advantage they can—and do use routinely—against us? That advantage is *ruthlessness*.

So how about some of that ruthlessness for the rest of us, some tried and true ways of protecting ourselves against mind-rape and ravishment from low-lifes and liars-in-wait?

As in the East so too in the West, we've plenty of master manipulators to choose from—bold men of free thought and unfettered conscience from whom we can learn; pioneering masterminds who instinctively understood that, even in the honest man's arsenal, there is a place for poniard-pointed ruthlessness . . . and that "place" is thrust six inches deep into the heart of our enemy!

In choosing which of these masters with whom to study, we ultimately decide on those who themselves progressed from naïve *awe*, through *appreciation*, to finally arrive at ruthless *application*.

There, then, is the formula for Ultimate Control: First comes awe, then comes appreciation, finally comes application.

In this way we too will be inspired to strike a working balance between appreciation for the innovative methods of these past masters, and practically applying their always succinct—and often sinister!—seeds to our needs.

Ruthlessness comes to us from the root "rue"—to dread, to regret, as surely our enemies will!

Machiavelli followed this path, learning first an appreciation for the treachery and tactics of yore—especially Roman times—before finding useful application in his own time. Sure, for a while it wound him up in prison being tortured, but he knew enough about fate (whom he more than once likened to a "fickle whore"!) not to waste precious time with his anger pressed to the regret-stone, and instead to spend more attention to keeping his nose pressed against the Universe's grindstone.

Watching the prince and potentate you've backed suddenly go belly up; subsequent shackling in prison; sundry tortures; before the ultimate disgrace—being judged "no longer a threat" and summarily released by the new regime—Machiavelli took it all in stride. "Overhead," just the cost of doing business in Machiavelli's world.

Stalin too first learned to appreciate the covetousness and covertness of those around him—the practical principles of unprincipled politicians-in-waiting. And, like many ruthless men, Stalin got his the hard way—he paid his dues: first learning to appreciate, then to apply the skills of subterfuge and skullduggery. And then, after ruthlessly using those skills to outwit, outlast, and out-fight any and all who stood in his way . . . *everybody paid!*

Like Machiavelli, Stalin spent scant time sniveling at the regret-stone, and more time honing both blade and brain with the whet-stone of patience . . . and long memory. *Really* long memory—just ask Trotsky.

Likewise, American Revolutionary War guerrilla commander Major Robert Rogers first learned to appreciate the tenacity and tactics of his shadowy woodland foes, before taking those ruthless tactics as his own. Teaching those same tactics to his men, he then ruthlessly applied those same tactics against their originators. Turnabout's fair play.

And how is this any different from the craft and charisma of Robert J. Ringer, a modern-day Machiavelli, for whom appreciation and application became the twin sisters of success with whom only the most ruthless men then willingly, thrillingly, and—Ah!— "spillingly" bed down.

We must surely study such men . . . for surely they are studying us!

The serious study of the past provides the
raw material for wise decisions
today and tomorrow.
—Michael A. Ledeen[138]

138. Michael A. Ledeen, *Machiavelli on Modern Leadership* (Truman Talley Books/St. Martins, 1995), xiv.

13.

Chun-tzu: Men of Worth

Clarity of the mind opens the way to knowledge. Knowledge opens the way to wealth. Wealth opens the way to the allegiance of people. With the allegiance of the people you will attract true Men of Worth to your cause. With the allegiance of such Men of Worth a man can become King of all the world.
—the T'ai Kung

DOWN THROUGH THE CENTURIES many well-qualified generals have weighed in on exactly what it takes to command and control. For with control comes command, with ultimate command comes Ultimate Control. This only comes through *discipline*—measured by what we can do without. General William Westmoreland praised discipline above all else:

> It is certain, only with either fortune or discipline can catastrophe be avoided. Of the two, the only one you can never run out of is discipline.

Another battlefield commander who knew what it took to command and control was Confederate Civil General Nathan Bedford Forrest, who, when pestered by reporters to reveal "the secret" of his battlefield successes, snapped, *"It's whoever simply arrives first with the most!"*

Around the same time up north, politicians were complaining to President Abraham Lincoln demanding to know what he intended to do about

Ulysses S. Grant's excessive drinking. Pointing out Grant's recent string of victories, Lincoln replied that he intended to find out what brand of liquor Grant favored and then send all his generals a case!

Down through the centuries Asian masters have also pondered the same question. What are the qualities that make a man fit to command others?

For the great Chinese strategist Cao Cao (aka T'sao T'sao), there were five "virtues" a commander had to exhibit: wisdom, integrity, compassion, courage, and severity (discipline). Compare these with Sun Tzu's list: wisdom, sincerity, benevolence, courage, and strictness.[139]

If these are The Five *Virtues*, then the negative attributes we want to look for (and eventually find a way to exploit!) in others in order to exercise Ultimate Control over others/our enemies must be their *opposites* (see Figure 17, p. 208).

Thus, when studying the great masters—both East and West—we look for these characteristics, both notable and noble,[140] virtues we should strive to acquire if we are to learn to command, and by commanding exercise Ultimate Control, thus becoming what the Chinese call *Chun-tzu,* literally, "A True Man of Worth."[141]

Similar in many ways to the Japanese *Shibumi,*[142] Chun-tzu is also similar to Machiavelli's man of "virtu."[143] This concept was first championed by the great Chou Dynasty commander the T'ai Kung, a man who not only "talked the talk" but also "walked the walk" when it came to living up to the ideal of chun-tzu.

Chang Lu Shang, called the "T'ai Kung," rose to prominence by helping the emerging *Chou*[144] Dynasty succeed in overthrowing the *Shang* at the decisive Battle of *Mu-yeh* in 1045 B.C.

Also known as "Lu Wang," the "T'ai Kung" is sometimes referred to as "*T'ai Shih Shang-fu,*" with *Shih* meaning "Commander." He originally served the Shang for many years, before defecting to the Chou, serving first King Wen of Chou and then his successor, King Wu.

Thanks to the T'ai Kung, the end came swiftly for the Shang at the Battle

---

139. Sun Tzu's *Ping-Fa*, 1:7.
140. That's not to say we can't learn from the more *ruthless* bastards as well!
141. Sometimes rendered "Perfected Men."
142. Literally, man of honor, style, and impeccable taste.
143. More on this in the chapter *The Machiavelli Method*.
144. Often spelled *Zhou*.

FIVE VIRTUES

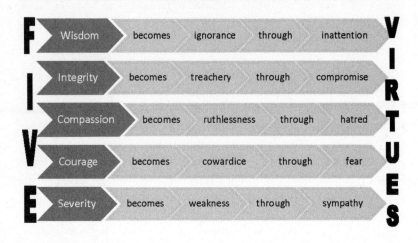

Figure 17.

of Mu-yeh. Experts all agree it was the T'ai Kung's innovative strategy and tactics (including the use of pre-war propaganda,[145] spies, and the deployment of "Special Forces") that carried the day.

Following the Chou victory over the Shang, the T'ai Kung went on to faithfully serve the Chou court for another twenty years. In recognition of his service the T'ai Kung was made King of the nascent and restless state of Ch'i. He died at well over 100 years of age, his longevity attributed to his mastery of Taoist alchemy.[146]

In later centuries, Confucian "moralists" sought to vilify the T'ai Kung for his tactics, for what they called "despicable machinations," painting him as ruthless and even cruel for advocating the liberal use of artifice, deception, sex, and bribes to achieve victory. Guilty as charged, the T'ai Kung was no stranger to using any and all available avenues to achieve victory.

Shortly before his death, the T'ai Kung wrote the *Liu t'sao* ("Six Secret

---

145. The T'ai Kung had spread the word long before the battle that the Chou people had nothing personal against the Shang people, only against their "evil" leaders. Read "Secret Civil Teachings" in *Mind Assassins*, Citadel 2010.

146. For a full discussion of Chinese alchemy, sex and longevity techniques read *Mental Domination* by Dr. Haha Lung and Christopher B. Prowant (Citadel 2009).

Teachings") a *ping-fa* ("war manual") preserving Chun-tzu's political advice and tactical instructions to Kings Wen and Wu that helped them, first, gain Ultimate Control and then, maintain Ultimate Control.

Preserved by the T'ai Kung's descendants in the state Ch'i, *The Six Secrets* became the foundation for Ch'i military studies and went on to influence later Chinese strategists such as K'ung Ming, T'sao T'sao, and of course Sun Tzu, as well as strategists outside China, most notably in Japan.

Six Secret Teachings was subsequently passed down orally through the centuries until (re)written into its present form hundreds of years after Chou actually overthrew the Shang, in the third century B.C. during the Warring States period when such works were especially prized—and used!

The T'ai Kung is still honored in China as "The First of Generals." So acclaimed was he that, during the Tang Dynasty, he was given his own temple and declared the living incarnation of the god of war! Military innovations attributed to him include the first strategic use of chariots in battle, the use of pre-war espionage (i.e., PsyOps, including propaganda) to "soften up" an enemy population before open warfare, and the creation and successful deployment of "special forces" of elite troops.

The T'ai Kung's observations on both the nature of men and on how to best "move" men (in accordance with their particular nature) still hold true today. These include understanding and employing "The Five Virtues," to first attract, and then focus such men to your cause; "Eight Ways" in which to gain (and then maintain) Ultimate Control by (1) gaining mastery over time and place, circumstance and flux, which means recognizing "The Eight Strikes that Lead to Victory," (2) using the "unorthodox" to confuse and confound, while (3) always remaining alert to the "Nine Situations" that can spell our downfall.

As with all such master strategists, with only the most basic of imagination we can easily apply the T'ai Kung's ancient strategies, tactics, and techniques to our modern needs . . . and greeds.

PUSHING AND PULLING WITH "THE FIVE VIRTUES"

The T'ai Kung had his own version of the Five Virtues, which both Sun Tzu and Cao Cao may have later "borrowed" from him.

Why "five" virtues and not more, or less? In Asia the number five is linked to the ancient art of Wu-hsing (lit. "The Five Movers") which teaches that all creation is composed of, and are the result of, interaction between *yin* (negative) and *yang* (positive). Yin-yang are then further distilled into five base elements: Earth, Air (aka Wind, Metal), Fire, Water, and Void (aka Wood).

Each person's overall disposition (hence their emotions) is linked to one of these five elements. By figuring out which of the five virtues dominates a person, we can then apply either *yin* "pull" (complimenting/attracting) or *yang* "push" (opposing/repelling) strategies to gain Ultimate Control over them.

THE EIGHT WAYS TO GAIN (AND MAINTAIN!) CONTROL

The T'ai Kung's overall strategy falls into what are (now) easily recognized, easily acquired skills, easily accomplished goals: anticipating and preventing trouble in your own "camp" while encouraging trouble (confusion and discord) in the enemy camp:

- **Anticipate the possibility of hostilities.** Forewarned is forearmed. This necessitates a constant source for *real time* awareness and intelligence. For any commander, the best battle is the one you avoid fighting—by nipping trouble in the bud. Sun Tzu's ideal.
- **Use camouflage and subterfuge wherever possible.** Distract, deceive, turn aside an enemy's suspicions. If they never see you coming . . . they'll never know what hit 'em! Don't forewarn an enemy to build up, instead make him play catch up. Before the Chou made their move against the vastly superior Shang, they spent years cementing alliances and building up their forces in secret. Perhaps you've heard of a place called Pearl Harbor? How about the World Trade Center?
- **Sow confusion, chaos, and consternation in enemy camp and court.** The brightest fruit rots from within.
- **Bribe the disloyal, dissatisfied, and disaffected in enemy camp and court.** "Loins and coins"—Sun Tzu, Chapter XIII.
- **Encourage dishonesty, debauchery, decadence, and depravity**

T'AI KUNG'S FIVE VIRTUES

	PUSH	PULL			
LOYALTY	Betrayal (of trust, ideals, etc.)	Mindless fan, dangerous fanatic	T'u (Earth)	Yellow	Faith
JUSTICE	Injustice and corruption	Revenge	Chi (Metal)	White	Righteousness
BENEVOLENCE	Greed	Sympathy	Mu (Wood)	Green	Benevolence
WISDOM	Ignorance ("to ignore")	Arrogance, hubris	Huo (fire)	Red	Wisdom
PROPRIETY (DECORUM)	Impropriety, "sin"	Outdated tradition, ritual, caste	Shui (Water)	Black	Decorum

Figure 18.

wherever possible within the enemy's ranks. Dishonest, drunk, decadent, and depraved men have little time to tend to business, neither the king's nor their own.

- **Constantly probe enemy lines.** The smallest gap in a general's concentration is large enough for an entire army to rush in!
- **Enforce secrecy and security within your own camp—ruthlessly!**
- **Assign the proper men to the proper task**, and then allow them free reign. Once he has assumed command, the king cannot interfere with the commander's actions or decisions. Having assigned your lieutenants to lead, allow them to lead.

THE EIGHT STRIKES THAT LEAD TO VICTORY

Time and place, circumstance and flux, all these factor into when to strike an enemy in order to ensure victory. Just as important is being able to perceive whether an enemy is "settled" or "unsettled." In ancient times, much notice was taken of whether or not an enemy camp was noisy (a sign of anxiety and fear), whether or not an enemy camp was already well-established and orderly, or still in the chaos of a disorganized army attempting to set up for the night.

Nothing has changed. Disorganization in your enemy's camp (his place of business, his friends and family) provides all the opening in his defenses a wily manipulator needs to rush in.

When does the T'ai Kung advise as the best time(s) to attack?

- **"Before the enemy is settled—strike!"**

  Translation: Strike while he is still disorganized, before his camp has settled in for the night, even before his plans and course of action have been decided upon, before he is "settled." Often it will be necessary for us to "unsettle" him ourselves.

- **"When his men and horses are still shifting about—strike!"**

  Translation: Look for signs of chaos in the enemy "camp." When none can be found, it will be necessary to create them.

- **"When some of his men advance while others retreat, when some move left while others move right—strike!"**

  Translation: Take advantage of any indecision, confusion, and lack of communication in the enemy camp. Incite same.

- **"When the form and focus of his force is not yet firm, when his officers and men look at one another dumbfounded—strike!**

  Translation: An unfocused enemy can't possibly be focused on what you're up to.

- **"When he advances he appears doubtful . . . when retreating he appears fearful—strike!"**

  Translation: An enemy who hesitates does half your job for you. Ross Perot Syndrome.

- **"When his fear is evident, his confusion all too apparent—strike!"**

  Translation: Fear and confusion . . . two strikes against him already. Add the third.

- **"When fighting on easy terrain to your advantage and twilight approaches without your being able to disengage from the battle—strike!"**

  Translation: Don't get too cocky just because you have him on the ropes. Most accidents happen on the way *home*.

• **"An enemy traveling far from home is fearful at dusk—strike!"**
Translation: What my enemy doesn't know *will* hurt him!

THE USES OF CH'I: MASTERING THE "UNORTHODOX"

Ancient Chinese military strategy divided tactics into *Cheng* and *Ch'i*, conventional tactics and "unconventional" tactics. Today we know Ch'i tactics as "guerrilla warfare," terrorism, and the type of no-holds-barred kick 'em in the nuts down-and-dirty fighting we might expect should we be stupid enough to try going toe-to-toe with Special Forces or Navy SEALs.

When attacking, noted Chinese strategist T'sao T'sao (pronounced "sow-sow") used what he referred to as his "two-headed snake," employing both regular troops in conventional direct formations (*Cheng*), as well as unorthodox and indirect (*Ch'i*) "special forces" and operatives. For example, his "Dragon-wings" warriors were specially-trained and equipped shock troops with much in common with modern Special Forces: travelling great distances in short periods by unexpected routes through hostile terrain to surprise the enemy (by arriving "early" at a battle site in order to lay in ambush) and/or to relieve beleaguered allies.

As part of his "two-headed snake" strategy T'sao T'sao made liberal use of spies and, when prudent, *Lin Kuei* assassins. This "two-headed snake" strategy allowed T'sao T'sao to attack with direct attack on the one hand, surprise attack on the other.

As already mentioned, the T'ai Kung was a big fan of Ch'i strategy and tactics. His genius is cited as the telling factor of how a relatively small border kingdom like the Chou could succeed in overthrowing the Shang, a powerful dynasty that had ruled China for over 600 years. The T'ai Kung accomplished this by convincing Wen and Wu that the use of Ch'i (unconventional warfare) tactics was called for if the smaller Chou army was going to have a chance overthrowing the larger Shang force.

Going against convention, (1) the T'ai Kung mounted his attack in the winter, (2) advancing swiftly on the unsuspecting Shang capital (3) by an indirect route he had previously mapped out while traveling through the area disguised as a rice salesman. (4) Skirting the larger main force of the Shang army, the Chou forces (5) forded a frozen river and attacked the Shang capital

(6) before the surprised Shang king had time to rally his forces and recall the bulk of his army.

The T'ai Kung's campaign against the Shang reads like the Table of Contents of every realistic guerrilla warfare manual ever written:

1. **Attack at unexpected times** (e.g. inclement weather).
2. **Advance swiftly.** Out of necessity, the hare must move faster than the fox!
3. **Move by indirect routes.**[147]
4. **Avoid contact with larger enemy forces.**
5. **Enter enemy territory by means of, and where, least expected.**
6. **Surprise the enemy before he has time to rally his forces.**

Compare this classic scenario with Major Robert Rogers' "19 Rules of War" in the chapter that follows.

---

147. Major Robert Rogers' 16th Rule of War: *"Don't cross a river by a regular ford."*

14.

Hannibal's Ninety-nine Truths

Adapting Hannibal's methods to your own daily battles will bring you untold power.
—*The 33 Strategies of War*, **Robert Greene**

HANNIBAL BARCA (247–183 B.C.), better known as "Hannibal the Conqueror," has been called "The Sun Tzu of the West," and rightly so. It has been said that no other single man was more responsible for building the Roman Empire than Hannibal—its most intractable *enemy*.

In the second and third century B.C., three "Punic"[148] wars were fought between the emerging empire of Rome and its chief rival, the North African city-state of Carthage. By far the greatest military strategist to emerge from more than a century of slaughter was the Carthaginian general Hannibal.

Considered Rome's "public enemy number one,"[149] during the second Punic War (218–201) Hannibal literally took the fight to the enemy, crossing what was then believed to be "impassable" Alps from Spain with an international mercenary force of over 26,000 men replete with elephants, surprising Rome's lightly-defended northern border. For the next sixteen years, Hannibal and army campaigned up and down the Italian peninsula,

---

148. The Roman name for Carthage.

149. Brian Sobel with Jerry D. Morelock, "100 Greatest Generals," *Armchair General*, March 2008.

subverting many of Rome's allies, and handing Rome its most devastating defeat ever at Cannae in 216 B.C.

Unfortunately, like so many accomplished military commanders before and after, in the end Hannibal was defeated more by bureaucracy at home than by bullets (or, to be more precise, sword blades) abroad.

Hannibal lived roughly 100 years after Alexander the Great (355–323) and 100 years before Julius Caesar (100–44). We can speak with certainty of the influence that tales of Alexander's conquests must have had on the boy Hannibal. Closer to home, his father Hamilcar Barca was himself a much-heralded military commander, having led Carthage against Rome in the first Punic War—a war that ended in a needless, "bureaucratic" defeat for Carthage, paired with humiliating terms for perpetual reparations to be paid Rome.

The story goes that, the bitter taste of defeat still in his mouth, Hamilcar took young Hannibal to Carthage's main temple where he made the boy swear on his father's sword his undying enmity with Rome. Hannibal kept that vow till his last day.

Beyond just the influence of his father—considerable!—and the near-mythical tales told to the young boy of Alexander's adventures—inspirational!—we can only speculate on young Hannibal's overall education. Certainly he studied the Greek classics. Like his fellow Carthaginians who made their living on the sea, he knew the Earth was not flat.[150] He was undoubtedly familiar with Phoenician and other Middle Eastern and further Eastern writings of the time. How *far* to the East?

No one can be certain whether Hannibal—a lifelong student—ever had a chance to actually study the writings of such Far Eastern masters as the T'ai Kung, Sun Tzu, and Cao Cao of China, or even Kautilya of India. That such writings were already available in Hannibal's time we know to be a fact. But whether any of these Masters' words actually found their way to Hannibal directly—through translated texts brought to Carthage by ship, or else passed along by word of mouth—we will probably never know. What we

---

150. The first person to suggest that the Earth was not flat but round was the Greek philosopher Philolaus around 450 B.C. During his 16-year "Roman holiday," Hannibal and his army spent considerable time in Philolaus's home town of Tarentum, situated on the "boot" of the Italian peninsula.

do know, and what is universally acknowledged is that, given his bold strategies and string of lifelong successes against what was then the most formidable force on Earth—Rome—when his time finally came, Hannibal was undoubtedly welcomed at that great round table of warrior-strategists in Valhalla, the respected equal of the T'ai Kung, Sun Tzu, Musashi, Patton, and the others.

Thus, to better understand the strategy of Hannibal, and most importantly to learn to better apply the "99 Truths" he left us, it behooves us to make a careful comparison of Hannibal's hard-won "Truths" with the thoughts of those great Masters of strategy living before and after his time.

Like Sun Tzu, Hannibal's "Ninety-nine Truths" are universal, capable of fitting into any time and place. Thus we further our own education by comparing his Truths with these insights of other masterminds and master commanders. For example, Hannibal's beloved city of Carthage in North Africa began as a trading outpost of the Sidonians, better known to history as the "Phoenicians." Thus we are obliged to compare the Carthaginian Hannibal's struggles and strategies of life with those of another philosopher from the same Canaan-Palestine area from roughly the same era, Jesus son of Sirach, writing from his academy in Jerusalem around 180 B.C.[151]

We can also benefit from the interpretations of Hannibal's life and his "99 Truths" by such later notable (or is that "notorious"?) wits as Machiavelli.

What sorts of things occupied the mind and manner of such a man as Hannibal? We discover thirteen distinct areas of concentration that we know of: *Enemies, Intelligence, Strategy, the Nature of War, Peace, the Gods, Vengeance, Honor, The Nature of Man, Struggle and Strength, Family and Friends, Wit and Wisdom*, and *Death*. For the sake of convenience, we have so labeled and arranged his "Ninety-nine Truths."

And if, to your oh-so-sophisticated—and perhaps jaded—modern ear, some of Hannibal's "Ninety-nine Truths" seem quite familiar—perhaps even *clichéd*, keep in mind that Hannibal said it first. And Hannibal *did* it first!

---

151. Being contemporaries, it's possible Jesus son of Sirach and Hannibal may have met face-to-face while the latter was a "guest" of Antiochus III of Syria after fleeing Carthage in 195 B.C. just ahead of a Roman hit-squad.

ENEMIES[152]

I. Enemy! When you look at me don't see something you hate . . . see the very thing you love the most. For that is what I will surely rip from you if you ever rise against me!

Machiavelli, in his *Discourses*, relates a conversation between Hannibal and Antiochus (when the former had fled Carthage with a price on his head following the second Punic War and was attempting to give Antiochus advice on how best to challenge Rome). From experience, Hannibal argued that the Romans could only be beaten *in* Italy. His reasoning being that an invading force would be able to gain both resources and allies in Italy—while denying the same to the Romans. Whereas, if Antiochus fought Rome *outside* of Italy, leaving the Roman homeland unmolested, the Romans would have an inexhaustible source from which to draw men and material.[153]

Machiavelli understood both views, first pointing out that if one wants an enemy to "succeed ill" you should get him as far away from his home (i.e. comfort zone and supply lines) as possible. Machiavelli concludes, "Nor does anything impede you so much as does war in your own domains."[154]

Scipio Africanus, Hannibal's Roman nemesis, soon bowed to Hannibal's wisdom in this matter. Countering Hannibal's invasion of Italy, Scipio first counter-invaded the Barca "kingdom" in Spain in an effort to dislodge Hannibal from Italy, before finally invading North Africa to threaten Carthage proper with invasion. As Chinese strategist Cao Cao put it:

> Attack what he holds dear. Go where he must go and he will have to come to the rescue.

II. We are made as much by our enemies as by our ambitions.

> *For a man who is accustomed to act in one particular way,*
> *never changes. . . . Hence when times change and no longer*
> *suit his ways, he is inevitably ruined.*
> *—Machiavelli[155]*

---

152. What's that you say, you don't have any "enemies"? That's exactly what your enemies *want* you to think!

153. FYI: Antiochus failed to take Hannibal's advice. Which may explain why you've probably never heard of Antiochus!

154. *Discourses* II:12.

155. *Discourses* III:9.

Truth VI expands on this thought.

III. We sometimes win simply because our enemy chooses to lose.

Hannibal was quick to profit by the mistakes of his enemies. Chance favors the prepared mind.

IV. What a man loves, what he hates, what he needs, what he desires: These are the four pillars that support his house.

The Four Humors, originated by Sicilian philosopher Empedocles (490–430 B.C.) theorized that man is composed of and dominated by the "Four Humors": Earth, Air, Fire, and Water. This combination of philosophy, psychology, and medicine would hold sway for the next 1500 years, till the rise of more modern thinking during the Renaissance.

Hannibal was undoubtedly familiar with Empedocles' four humors, as were learned men of his day; however, for his part, Hannibal's psychology for "moving" men was much simpler:

- Discover what he *loves* and threaten to take it away from him.
- Discover what (and who) he *hates* (and fears) and join with it. The enemy of my enemy is my friend.
- Discover what he *needs* and withhold it from him.
- Discover what he *desires* and dangle it in front of him . . . with strings attached. (See Truth XCII.)

V. Distinguish between gain and loss. Nothing you can hold in your hand can ever truly be held for long.

Distinguish between need and desire.[156]

I desire many things. I need few. My enemy can entice me with both of these—drawing me here, sending me running there.

All I truly need beats within my breast. All I desire can all too easily fall into my enemy's coarse hand. The more a man possesses, the more easily he can be possessed.

---

156. Basic Buddhism: "All suffering is caused by desire." Could Hannibal have been exposed to the teachings of Buddha, who lived roughly 300 years earlier? It's possible. We do know Buddhist missionaries at one point liaisoned with the Essenes, the "cult" Jesus of Nazareth is believed to have belonged to. For those who see Buddha's non-violent philosophy at odds with Hannibal's "violent" life . . . consider the Buddhist Samurai.

Or, as the hippies of the '60s used to warn, "The more things you have, the more things have you."

VI. *A warrior is known by his enemies, even as a fat man is known by his appetites, a lean man by his fears.*

I give thanks for my enemy.[157] *Were it not for my enemy I would sleep past dawn, I would eat too much, I would become loud and over-proud, and both my arm and eye would grow lax.*

My enemy determines when I rise, when and where I sleep tonight, what I eat and when and whether I will ever see my home again.

I thank my enemy for making me strong and look forward to repaying him in kind!

> *Love your enemies; for they shall tell you all your faults.*
> —Ben Franklin

> *There is nothing so disorienting as the loss of a good friend, except perhaps, the loss of a good enemy.*
> —Barash, *Beloved Enemies*

VII. *Give freely to your enemy. Give him a clear and straight path to go down, wish for him a soft bed to sleep in tonight. Pray all his ships find the calmest of seas.*

At the battle of Cannae Hannibal gave the Romans just such a "gift," leading to the greatest single defeat in Roman history.

Facing a Roman force of over 50,000 men, in order to draw the Romans into his trap, Hannibal offered "proffered meat,"[158] or as Cary and Sullard recount the battle in their 1975 *A History of Rome*:

> Against this force Hannibal could put no more than 40,000 men into line, yet he humored his opponents by offering them battle in a bare plain near the Apulian town of Cannae, where the Romans had nothing to fear from hidden reserves. In this open position the Romans made no other use of their superior numbers than to deepen their infantry line so as to

---

157. Compare this with Truth LXXVII.
158. "Offer your enemy proffered meat to draw him out." —Cao Cao

increase the weight of its impact upon Hannibal's front. Hannibal, on the other hand, starved his centre of troops and instructed it to fall back before the enemy's charge. While the retreat of the Punic center drew on the enemy infantry and shepherded it, as it were, into the slaughtering pen, the light troops on the Carthaginian wings took it in flank, and the cavalry, which had driven the Roman horse off the field, closed in on the rear of the Roman center. At the cost of barely 6000 men Hannibal virtually annihilated the Roman forces compressed within this ring of steel. The battle of Cannae was a unique instance of a complete encirclement of a numerically stronger army by a weaker one.

In simplest terms, Hannibal dangled the "proffered bait" of an easy victory in front of the Romans, all too eager to gobble it down. As they collided with Hannibal's troops, as planned, his troops fell back and around on both sides ("flanks") until the Romans were entirely surrounded and unable to escape . . . and then the slaughter began in earnest.

Let's try putting this in images a modern audience might understand:

Remember the final confrontation at the tournament in the movie *The Karate Kid* (1984)? Daniel-san goes into that funny "Crane" stance with both arms wide open—inviting, seemingly defenseless; his leading-foot dangling in the air, seemingly easy to block once his evil Cobra-Kai opponent decides to rush in. Ah! But no sooner does his opponent "take the bait" than Daniel-san suddenly switches legs (his dangling leg was but a feint!) catching his attacker full-on with his other leg. Point and match!

So too the ever-elusive Hannibal pretends to finally be willing to face the Romans the way they like—"Roman style," out in the open on a wide plain, where they hold the advantage—before suddenly trapping them!

VIII. *The hand guides the blade but the eye guides the hand. The sword is nothing without the hand, the hand nothing without the eye.*

By "the eye" Hannibal means the mind. The best of all armies (the sword), though rarin' to go, is useless unless it has a good general (mind) to guide them. Conversely, the greatest of ideas, deepest of thoughts, best of noble intentions means nothing unless put into action.

IX. *Enemy! My generals keep me awake at night. Your generals keep me laughing during the day!*

Your Lord may be flanked by sycophants, who when facing him feign an air of morality, but who when looking down at the ruled give an angry glance. Such men, unless you lie low before them, will speak ill of you for something good you have done. As a result, the innocent suffer and the sinful thrive. Understanding this is more important than the ability to judge your opponent's stratagems in a sword fight.

—Yagu Munenori[159]

INTELLIGENCE[160]

X. Enemy! I watch your every move as if you were the most beautiful of dancing girls: I watch your every step forward and back and to the side, each bend of your knee, every sway of your ample hips. I study every gesture of your hand—closing, opening; the practiced smile of your brightly-colored lips, the wide and the narrow of your painted eye. Soon enough we dance!

Precision personal intelligence can be more critical that precision-guided munitions.

—Count de Marencnes, former Chief of French Intelligence

Do not engage in speculative enterprises. Get the facts and then act on the facts.

—Yataro Iwasaki, Samurai and founder of The Mitsubishi ("Three Diamonds") Corporation, 1870[161]

Any prejudice can cause us to dismiss potential teachers out of hand because of their race, religion, gender, or culture. A truly wise man learns from both friend and foe.

—Lung and Prowant, *Mind Control*, 2006

---

159. Samurai strategist (1571–1646). See "Munenori's War to the Mind" in *Mind Assassins!* (Citadel, 2010).

160. Recall there are two types of intelligence: *innate intelligence*, the kind we're born with, and *gathered intelligence* (e.g., information, espionage).

161. See Lung and Prowant, *Mind Control* (2006), 250.

XI. To see only what the enemy shows you makes you his fool! To hear only what your enemy wants you to hear places you in grave danger.

To look but not to see, to listen but not to hear, this is the beginning of your doom!

Once, trapped on a mountain at night, surrounded by Roman armies, Hannibal had his men tie torches to the horns of a herd of cattle before stampeding the beasts down the hill straight towards the Roman lines. Seeing the "herd" of torches fast approaching, the Romans broke and ran, mistaking the cattle for a large(r) force of Hannibal's men.

> *All warfare is based on deception. When strong, appear to be no threat. When on the march, make it appear you are still encamped. When drawing close, make him think you are still far away. And when still far distant, make him feel you are breathing down his neck!*
> —Sun Tzu

> *Like a thirsty man stumbling across the desert, how many times have you mistaken a mirage for a miracle, optical illusions for opportunities. . . . Perception, no matter how screwed-up, is reality. If your enemies "see" you as a force to be reckoned with, they will act (cower!) accordingly.*
> —Lung and Prowant, *Mind Control,* 2006

Truth XXXI, "The Drunken Man," expands on this.

XII. One eye is all you need to see clearly . . . if you are truly looking. A three-legged dog still bites!

Ironic, if this was written *before* the fact of Hannibal losing an eye during his campaigning in Italy. This also brings to mind the old adage about "a one-eyed man being king in a blind kingdom." We are also reminded of the Egyptian all-seeing "Eye of Horus,"[162] and the eye that the Norse God Odin gave up in order to gain wisdom. Compare with Truth XX.

---

162. Yeah, the one on top of the pyramid on the back of the dollar bill.

"All Masters agree": To see with senses alone is not to "see."
—Lung and Prowant, *Mind Control*, 2006

XIII. Do not fear those things you can see, do not be troubled by rumors and loud noises you hear. Fear instead those things you neither see nor hear but that lurk in your enemy's breast!

An enemy will speak sweetly with his lips, but in his mind he has plans to throw you into a pit. He weeps with his eyes, but when he finds his opportunity, his thirst for blood will not be satisfied.
—Jesus, son of Sirach 12:16-18

When you cannot be deceived by men you will realize the wisdom of strategy.
—Miyamoto Musashi, 1645

XIV. Secrets bleed like blood.

It is widely held that the Romans successfully built their own novice navy into a formidable fighting force after capturing and "reverse-engineering" a Carthaginian warship that had run aground. This would be not only yet another example of how "chance favors the prepared mind," but also of how easily "intelligence" secrets can get away from you.

Hannibal knew well the importance of both kinds of intelligence. Gifted with *Innate Intelligence*, the first type, he took pains throughout his whole life to acquire the second type, *Gathered Intelligence*.

One tale has Hannibal secretly visiting Italy and actually walking the streets of Rome prior to his invasion. While unverifiable, it would not have been outside his character to do so.

Having inherited a respect for espionage from his father, throughout his life Hannibal maintained a vast network of spies who aided him several times during his campaigning in Italy. For example, Hannibal took the heavily-fortified southern Italian city of Tarentum in 212 through use of a classic Sun Tzu Chapter XIII ploy—bribing guards at the gate.

Ironically, it was just such a singular "bleeding" secret that finally tipped the scales in favor of the Romans when they intercepted a secret message to Hannibal in southern Italy from his brother Hasdrubal (who, unbeknownst to Hannibal, had just recently arrived in northern Italy with a relief force).

This allowed the Romans to trap and massacre Hasdrubal's army at the Metaurus River in 207, before Hannibal was even aware his brother was in Italy. The death of Hasdrubal marked the beginning of the end of Hannibal's campaign in Italy.

> *Observation and prediction: Gunpowder changed warfare forever by substituting chemical energy for physical strength. So too, today we find ourselves in a rapidly changing world where information is slowly replacing all other forms of "persuasion."*
> —Lung and Prowant, *Mind Control*, 2006

XV. Mysteries call out to be understood. Every lock longs for a key, every empty cup thirsts for wine.

Every problem has a solution, no matter how formidable it might at first appear. Though others thought it impossible, Hannibal succeeded in going toe-to-toe with the best Rome had to offer for nearly two decades, most of that while on Roman soil! Keep that in mind—keeping problems in perspective—next time you're thinking how "impossible" it's going to be to talk your boss into a raise.

Nine-eleven put a lot of things in perspective.

XVI. A mystery begins where light ends.

For every mystery laid to rest, another mystery rises. Better the mystery familiar.

For every enemy laid to rest, another enemy rises. Better the enemy familiar![163]

> *Ignorant of the familiar, you seek after the unfamiliar.*
> —Jesus of Nazareth, *The Gospel of Thomas*

XVII. What I know today, my enemy knows tomorrow.
What my enemy knows tomorrow is what I teach him today!

> *Today is victory over yourself of yesterday,*
> *tomorrow is your victory over lesser men.*
> —Miyamoto Musashi

---

163. Read *Beloved Enemies: Our Need for Opponents* by David Barash. (Prometheus Books, 1994).

XVIII. A secret is useless unless someone knows it.

Epaminondas, the Theban, used to say that nothing is more
essential or more useful than a general to discover what the enemy
has decided and is planning to do. And since it is difficult to
discover this, the more praiseworthy does he become who
conjectures it aright.
—Machiavelli[164]

Read *Sun Tzu's Art of War*, Chapter 13. And then, read it again.
XIX. The darkest secrets bury themselves.

Hannibal is saying "You're only as sick as the secrets you keep," that
the secrets we try to hide the hardest are the secrets that try the hardest to
come to light and do us in. Any policeman will tell you every criminal
secretly wants to confess . . . It's called "bragging."

A slip on the pavement is better than a slip of the tongue.
—Jesus, son of Sirach 20:18

In the dungeon of your mind, who do you keep chained to the wall?
—Kenny Rogers

XX. A fool begins by telling you what he knows and ends by telling
you what he doesn't know.

The best place to get information about the other side
is from the other side.
—Ronald Shapiro[165]

XXI. The wise feed off the foolish, but are all too soon hungry again.

According to Soren (1990) one of Hannibal's main problems while campaigning in Italy in resupplying his army was poor management by the
Carthage fleet. Realizing this, the Roman Fabius consul commander tasked
with stopping Hannibal made special effort to cut off Hannibal's supply lines,
forcing Hannibal's army to forage (i.e., *loot*) what they needed from the Italian

---

164. *Discourses*, III:18
165. Ronald M. Shapiro, "How to Negotiate So Everybody Wins," *Bottom Line/Personal.*
October 1, 2001.

countryside, alienating many farmers and peasants who might have otherwise joined Hannibal against Rome.

STRATEGY

XXII. A wise general must fill his head before he fills his belly. A wise general must fill the belly of his army before he fills their hand.

Hungry soldiers pay more attention to the cook than to the commander. Tired men look more towards the night's sleep than to the day's task.

While the first part of this Truth can be seen as a reminder that a wise general must first and foremost gather good intelligence, the second part of this Truth is surely the universal commandment for all generals, indeed, for leaders of all sorts: *Tend to your own before you tend to the enemy.* In other words, charity—and safety!—begins at home.

XXIII. The weather changes freely to please the gods.
My enemy's mind changes as it pleases me!

> *The thing to do is to force your opponent to follow your changes and by following his resultant changes to win.*
> —Yagu Munenori

XXIV. Nature commands me, "Play the actor." So I play the wave. I don the mask of the wind:

Slowly wearing away my enemy's shore, lazy lapping waves suddenly surge, seizing up and drowning all within reach!

Felt but never seen, the wind gently sways the palms . . . before suddenly snapping the trunk in two!

> *Diligence is the mother of good luck.*
> —Ben Franklin

XXV. Nature commands me, "Take this gift of strategy."[166]

So, I study the tracks and droppings of a great beast, I perceive my enemy's passing.

As one beast preys upon another and is in turn preyed upon:

---

166. "Take advantage of the shelter provided by the mountains, rivers, and other natural features. Take advantage of changing weather."—Cao Cao

Alert below for food, the kite does not see the threat from above. Like-
wise, feeling himself general of the sky, the hawk does not see the lowly
threat. In this manner, the striking hawk takes the kite from above while,
unseen and unexpected, my arrow takes the hawk from below!

In any endeavor, from striking a blow against a foe to snatching up a
hot stock commodity, ever the rule is "Strike while the iron is hot!" Timing
is the key:

> For a commander who has an army massed together and sees
> that for lack of funds or of allies he cannot keep it long on the
> field, is quite mad if he does not put his fortune to the test
> before his army has to be disbanded; because, if he waits, he
> is surely lost; but if he tries, he may succeed. —Machiavelli[167]

> Long ago warriors knew to make themselves invulnerable
> while patiently anticipating their enemy's moment of vulnera-
> bility. —Sun Tzu

> Adapt or die is the most unforgiving rule of nature. We adjust
> ourselves to changing realities . . . or those changing realities
> "adjust" us. —Lung and Prowant, *Mind Control,* 2006

The Romans believed the Alps impassable and their northern border
secure. Hannibal taught them different.

XXVI. Better an enemy over-bold than a timid one. The former tests my
mettle, the latter tests my patience!

> *I have often thought that the reason why men are sometimes*
> *unfortunate, sometimes fortunate, depends upon whether their behavior*
> *is in conformity with the times.[168] For one sees that in what they do*
> *some men are impetuous, others look about them and are cautious;*
> *and that, since in both cases they go to extremes and are unable to*
> *go about things in the right way, in both cases they make mistakes.*
> *—Machiavelli[169]*

---

167. *Discourses* III:10.

168. The word used here by Machiavelli is "*i tempi*" which can mean both "time" and "circumstances."

169. *Discourses* III:9

Before Scipio Africanus, Hannibal's' most formidable—most frustrating!—opponent, there was Roman counsul commander Fabius Maximus who positively refused to meet Hannibal in pitched combat.[170] But, as Machiavelli points out, this was again the case of Fabius taking a page from the play book of "The Carthaginian Master":

> Nor can it be said that Fabius avoided battle, but rather that he preferred to fight when he had the advantage. For if Hannibal had gone to seek him out, he would have awaited him and made a day of it. But Hannibal did not dare to fight with him on these terms. So that it was as much Hannibal who avoided battle as Fabius . . .[171]

So successful was Fabius Maximus' tactic in stifling Hannibal's advance that, still today, any purposeful delaying tactic is rightly dubbed "Fabian."

Compare this Truth with Truth XXX.

XXVII. Impatience has slain more men than even the best of bowmen.

To quote Ben Franklin, "He that can have patience can have what he will, for little strokes fell great oaks."

He who is prudent and lies in wait for an enemy who is not likewise prudent, that man will know victory.
—Sun Tzu

Do nothing without deliberation and when you have acted, do not regret it.
—Jesus, son of Sirach

XXVIII. Brick-by-brick the patient thief carries away the rich man's house in a single night.

This is Hannibal's way of saying "Slow and steady wins the race," that patience—and a little pre-planning—will always carry the day.

Compare this with Truth XXX, and with the following story that, ironically comes to us, not from Hannibal's North African desert, but from a desert of a different sort yet one just as unforgiving, the frozen Arctic, where

---

170. Understandable, given Hannibal's victories over larger Roman forces at Lake Trasimene and Cannae.

171. *Discourses* III:10

they still tell the tale of the brave little Native American Inuit boy known as "Little Spear" who saved his tribe:

> *A fierce polar bear was stalking the little Inuit boy's tribe. Time and again the brave hunters of the tribe all took their large spears and went in search of this rogue beast but the bear was cunning, hiding from large hunting parties, picking off stragglers. The boy watched from the sidelines, still too young to hunt with the men. Time and again he tried to talk to the older hunters, trying to explain that* he *knew how little spears could be used to kill the bear. At best, the older men would only look at the little, stone-tipped spear in the little boy's hand and shoo the child away.*
>
> *Finally, the tribal elders decided too many of their young men had been killed by the bear and that they had no other choice but to pack up and move the village, far away from the fierce bear's hunting ground. But it was the dead of winter, and some of the old folk, including the boy's grandfather, were too sick to survive such a trek. That night, while the others slept, armed only with his small stone-tipped spear and carrying a food sack he'd spent all day preparing, the little boy snuck out of the village.*
>
> *When the sun finally came up, far across the flat snowscape, the little boy spotted the great bear. And the bear had spotted him as well. Knowing the beast now had his scent, the boy moved away as fast as he could, outrunning the bear as best he could, knowing it was a race he was doomed to lose.*
>
> *As he ran, from time to time from his food sack the boy would drop a frozen, fist-sized ball of sweet whale fat—what the white man calls "blubber." Each time the boy dropped one of these frozen balls, the bear would stop for a minute to gobble them down before resuming the chase, adding precious time to the little boy's escape. This chase went on throughout the day—with the bear steadily closing the distance between himself and the boy, with the boy continuing to drop the frozen balls of fat in the bear's path until . . . finally, the boy reached into the bag and realized he'd run out of frozen balls with which to tempt the bear.*
>
> *Gripping his small spear all the tighter, the boy stopped and turned back to face the bear . . . and smiled. Far in the distance he saw the*

great beast lying in the snow, unmoving. Small spear at the ready, he approached the—now dead!— bear.

Cautiously, he poked the great bear with his small stone-tipped spear. Peering in close the little warrior smiled once more—but sadly this time—knowing that while fierce spirit no longer filled the once-proud beast's now wide-opened, dead eyes, the great beast's stomach was now filled with the sharpened bone-barbs *the boy had hidden inside the sweet whale fat: compressing them tightly until they were frozen solid inside the blubber, springing loose once the frozen fat was warmed inside the bear's stomach, these "little spears" killing the great beast from within!*

XXIX. Fear spills less blood. A single scare is worth a thousand spears.

In the West they superstitiously warn, "Don't speak the Devil's name lest he appear!"

In China during the Three Kingdoms Period, his foes were so respectful (read: afraid!) of the great general Cao Cao (155–220) that they too warned, "Never speak the Old Dragon's name lest you cause him to appear!"

A bluff is as good as a bullet, so long as it puts your enemy down.

XXX. Bleeding my enemy is the next greatest joy to burying him.

In *A Book of Five Rings*, Miyamoto Musashi teaches us "Cutting-at-the-Edges": When you can't attack an enemy directly, with a single telling thrust, you harass and attack his extremities. This "Cutting-at-the-Edges," classic guerrilla strategy has uses far beyond the battlefield. When Romeo can't reach Juliet's balcony today, he plants the seed that tomorrow becomes the tree with branches strong enough to help him reach his goal.

XXXI. I stagger left and my enemy laughs at the "Drunken Man." Suddenly, I strike right! And all laughter ceases!

I stumble back, my enemy falls headlong onto my sword as he tries clinging to me.

> *Nothing is constant in war save deception and cunning.*
> *Herein lies the true Way.*
> **—Cao Cao**

In China, the great poet Li Po is credited with creating "Drunken Style Kung-fu" (sometimes rendered "Drunken Monkey Kung-fu"), a style of martial arts where the weaving and bobbing deceptive movements of the fighter resemble those of a drunken man. Li Po himself was no stranger to the wine-skin, by the way.

Let's not forget The Trojan Horse. Or, recall how Prince *Hamlet* feigned mental illness in order to appear less of a threat to his evil uncle. In Robert Graves' masterpiece *I Claudius*, to survive into adulthood young future Roman Emperor Claudius uses a similar ploy, exaggerating his infirmities so as to appear "less of a threat" to the more ambitious adults eyeing Caesar's chair. For a more modern reference there's Mohammed Ali's famous "rope-a-dope": deliberately falling back on the ropes in order to draw your over-confident opponent in closer.

When the Romans thought Hannibal was "fleeing" from Spain, he was actually attacking into Italy! This is the same kind of ploy Hannibal used at the battle of Cannae: The center of his army "collapsing" (falling back) under the initial Roman attack, only to unfold on both sides (flanks) to "swallow up" (enfold) and trap the Roman army.

> *Dodge left, strike right. Dodge right, strike left. Fake an attack*
> *forward to cover your retreat. Pretend retreat . . . before springing*
> *forward with ferocity!*
> —Li Chung[172]

XXXII. The patience of sand overtakes all things.
Each thought of man is but a single grain of sand. Yet a single grain of sand can ruin the best bowman's aim, a single grain of sand in the eye can turn the greatest of war-beasts[173] from its task!

First, this Truth warns us to stop a problem before it gets big:

> The Master excels at resolving conflicts before they arise, con-quering his enemies before they become threats. —Tu Mu[174]

Second, Hannibal is assuring us that, strategically, a determined smaller force ("a single grain of sand") can dissuade ("ruin the best bowman's aim") and eventually defeat a much larger army ("turn the greatest of war-beasts from its task").

---

172. 8th century Chinese strategist
173. "Elephants."
174. Chinese strategist, 803–852.

Tactically speaking, by putting the wind at his army's back, Hannibal ensured there would literally be dust in the Romans' eyes at Cannae.

XXXIII. A thousand uses for a rock.

A length of wood, a twirl of string, and a skillful hand and knowing eye crafts a bow.

Gotta use what you got. "Lemons into lemonade." Improvise, don't compromise.

The greatest of Commanders are either born with, or else master, "non-linear thinking," overthrowing the innate tendency of human beings toward what's known as "object fixedness," i.e. seeing only one use for an object (and, by extrapolation, people).

For example: A knife in an assassin's hand cuts throats. That same blade in a surgeon's hand can be used to save life and limb:

> Scipio, we find, entered Spain and by his humane and kindly conduct at once made that country his friend, and won the respect and admiration of its people. We find, on the other hand, that Hannibal entered Italy and by totally different methods, i.e. cruelty, violence, rapine and every sort of perfidy, produced the same effect as Scipio had produced in Spain; for all the Italian cities revolted to him, and all its people became his followers.[175] —Machiavelli[176]

XXXIV. Make the ground fight for you.

Henry V owed his victory that day at Agincourt on St. Crispin's Day in 1415 not only to the bravery of his "Band of Brothers," but also to the sodden ground on that northeastern French plateau—first frustrating, and then trapping, the armor-heavy French knights, making them easy fodder for Henry's eagle-eyed fletchers.

XXXV. Today the enemy has a name for me—Target. Tomorrow I will teach him a new name for me—Master!

> [Rome] never forgave Hannibal, even when his troops were disarmed and disbanded, until they had compassed his death. Owing to Hannibal's reputation for impiety, faithlessness and

---

175. See "Uses of Fear" in *Mind Assassins* by Lung and Prowant (Citadel, 2010).
176. *Discourses* III:21.

cruelty, then, this inconvenience arose; but, on the other hand, he derived from it a very great advantage, of which all writers have spoken of with admiration. For, though his army was composed of men from different races, there never arose any dissention either among the men themselves or between them and him. This can only be due to the terror his person inspired, which was so great that, in conjunction with the reputation he acquired for efficiency, it kept his troops quiet and united.

I conclude, therefore, that it does not matter much in what way a general behaves, provided his efficiency be so great that it flavours the way in which he behaves, whether it be in this way or that. For, as we have said, in both there are defects and dangers unless they be corrected by outstanding virtue. —Machiavelli[177]

THE NATURE OF WAR

XXXVI. War does not feed my sons. But at least it will keep my enemy's sons from eating as well!

Why should my enemy and his family be allowed to dine safe tonight in their ivory tower while me and mine go hungry, huddled in a bombed-out basement? Maybe if I drop a little misery right at his front door,[178] then maybe, just maybe, he'll begin to understand how I feel?

No other of The Ninety-nine Truths so challenges—offends *and frightens!*—modern sensibilities than this and the following Truth, and with good cause.

Hannibal is pointing out what is the most harsh of war realities: You must deny your enemy his "comfort zone"—his succor, a safe place to lay his head, even for a single night. "No rest for the wicked," and our enemies *are* wicked—why else would we be fighting them?

Guerillas (or invaders like Hannibal) cannot operate without the support of the local populace—the little people. Likewise, would we be so willing to go to war for "glory" if we took more time to consider the hardship we are asking our own friends and families at home to endure as well? For every soldier bleeding on the battlefield, there are at least two people crying at home.

---

177. *Discourses* III:21
178. Or on his World Trade Center . . .

XXXVII. "Do not make war on women and children," they cry. Why not? Without his woman's arms to comfort him, his ears filled with the hungry cries of his children, I have twice discomfited my enemy!

XXXVIII. Waste is worse than war.

Never burn a field that may one day feed your own sons.

In a "cutting-at-the-edges" ploy, Hannibal wrecked the Roman economy by plundering and burning as he headed south down the Italian peninsula, causing Roman coinage to be devalued several times.[179]

PEACE

XXXIX. War should be swift, peace swifter still.

XL. Peace is a time for sharpening the plow.

Spy out your neighbor's plow often.

This Truth has a double-meaning. The obvious, first, is that in times of peace war is replaced with planting and thus a farmer sharpens his plow. And, for Westerners, this of course brings to mind the oft quoted Biblical injunction to "Beat your swords into plowshares."[180]

All good and well, we love this verse so much that in front of the United Nations building in NYC the words are carved on the statue of a man doing just that—beating his sword into a plowshare. All well and good. What we conveniently forget is a similar Biblical line—closer to the sensibilities of Hannibal's time—where we're told to:

"Beat your plowshares into swords."[181]

Peace has ever been the best time to prepare for war:

The more you sweat in times of peace, the less you bleed in times of war. —Cao Cao

Hannibal's father Hamilcar used the "peace" following the first Punic War to build a power base in Spain, toward the day when he knew Hannibal and his other sons would again have to fight Rome.

Years later, during the second Punic War, Hannibal's brother Hasdrubal,

---

179. David Soren, *Carthage* (A Touchstone Book, Simon & Schuster, 1990).

180. Isaiah 2:4

181. Joel 3:10

finding his army in Spain surrounded by the superior Roman forces of Claudius Nero, successfully deceived and delayed Nero by making proposals of peace, until he had a chance for his army to slip away to join Hannibal in Italy.

XLI. The peace should never cost more than the war.

War reparations and treaty restrictions were debilitatingly high for Carthage following the first Punic War, setting the stage inevitably for the second Punic War, in the aftermath of which additional reparations were heaped on Carthage, (1) doubling the indemnity Carthage was forced to pay Rome, (2) restricting the Punic fleet to a mere ten ships, (3) depriving Carthage of the right to wage war without Rome's consent, and (4) rewarding Rome's African allies (who had turned against Carthage) with large tracts of land formally controlled by their Carthaginian overlords. As a result of the second Punic War reparations:

> The once proud Carthaginians were reduced to impotence, and the expression "Carthaginian peace" entered the language, denoting a dictated settlement designed to crush an opponent permanently. —Richard L. Greaves[182]

Compare this to the war reparations foisted on Germany's Weimar Republic following WWI, with the same predictable results: simmering hatred for the conquerors which makes it all the more likely a charismatic "Hitler" promising to regain "past glories" will gain the ear of the people.

> When Hannibal, who had enjoyed great glory in Italy for sixteen years, left it on being recalled by the Carthaginians to help his own country,[183] he found Hasdrubal and Syphax routed, the kingdom of Numidia lost, and the Carthaginians cooped up within their own walls, destitute of hope except what he and his army should bring. Realizing that his country was reduced to its last stake, he was determined not to risk that till he had tried all other remedies, and so was not ashamed to sue for peace, since he was convinced that, if there was any hope at all for his country, it lay in this and

---

182. *Civilizations of the World* by Richard L. Greaves. Harper Collins College Pub. 2nd ed. 1993:148

183. As Scipio intended when he invaded into North Africa.

not in war. When peace was refused, he did not decline to fight though bound to lose, since he felt that he could still win, but if he had to lose, he could at least lose gloriously. If then, Hannibal who was so full of virtuosity,[184] and had his army, still intact, preferred peace to war when he saw that, by losing, his country would be enslaved, what should a man do who has neither the experience of Hannibal? Yet there are men who make this mistake, in that to their hopes they set no bound, and are ruined because they rely on such hopes and take no account of other things. —Machiavelli[185]

By the way, Ben Franklin disagrees with Hannibal. According to Franklin, "There never was a good war or a bad peace." But he was still enough of a realist to admit: "One sword keeps another in the scabbard."

XLII. It is hard to show an open hand to an enemy. Harder still to show a firm hand to a friend.

XLIII. So long as my right hand grips the sword and my left hand holds fast to the dagger, both remained closed to grasping friendship.

Two points here: The first, Hannibal is reminding us to keep an open mind when it comes to the possibility of peace. The Carthaginians were, first and foremost, traders. War was just the regrettable cost of doing business. Left to their druthers, they'd have "druther" had peace and trade than war and no trade.

The second point of this Truth is a lesson from Sun Tzu with universal application: "Never fight an army with its back to a mountain or to the sea." In others words, in all endeavors, whether a hostile takeover on Wall Street, or a fist-fight in an alley off Main Street, always leave your enemy a way out—a way to exit with a little of his dignity, or at least some of his teeth, still intact. Trapped men fight twice as hard and to the death. The Alamo. The Spartan 300.

XLIV. If it began with a word, it can be ended with a word. If it began with the sword, the sword will surely end it.

---

184. Machiavelli's "virtuosity" (literally "virtue," from the Latin "*virtu*") means not so much "morality" as it does a combination of such ephemerals as "vital energy," "will," and "determination"; a mix somewhere between Nietzsche's "will to power" and the Asian concept of *chi*, inherent vitalizing energy.

185. *Discourses* II:27

The first part of this Truth is a clear call for de-escalation and negotiation.

The second part, not so much so.

Old wounds may heal over, but there's always scar tissue and sometimes . . . they really, really *itch*. Yugoslavia is the perfect example.

Always a patchwork of hurriedly hammered together, ethnically-diverse, independent-minded warring duchies and would-be kingdoms, the modern state of Yugoslavia emerged for one more hopeless try at unity following WWII under the leadership of WWII "hometown hero" Tito. Things were fine so long as Tito was alive. He died. And in the 1980s the world was shocked by the brutality exhibited when the province of Serbia—on the pretext of holding the country together—invaded into its "fellow province" of Bosnia and began massacring their former fellow "Yugoslavians."

What those not students of history failed to understand was that, back in WWII, the Bosnians had sided with Hitler, helping him exterminate Serbs. Now, fifty years later, it was the Serbs' turn to get revenge for the humiliation and deaths of their parents and grandparents.

Machiavelli calls these "The Sons of Brutus," those elements left over from the old regime that will never stop plotting against the new regime, no matter how much you try to assimilate them into the new order. The logical—safest—solution is simply to kill them. Shocked? Read your Old Testament—*Joshua* and *Judges*.

The modern-day business analogy of this situation would be the arrival of a new boss who must either (1) go to great lengths to win over old workers, or else (2) replace those old workers with new workers. That's why a new president always brings his own people into the White House with him. Or, as the Bible puts it, "Don't put new wine in old wineskins."[186]

XLV. Shame your enemies with your mercy.

Here, at least one other notable strategist parts company with Hannibal:

> May God have mercy upon my enemies, because I sure as
> hell won't! —General George S. Patton

XLVI. Mercy is the most costly of conceits . . . as if life and death were truly yours to give! The power of life and death is but on loan from the gods. Use both wisely.

---

186. Matthew 9:7.

Reward all those wise enough to join you, utterly crush all who dare
oppose you, and do so in so savage a manner as to completely cower
any others who might dream of resisting your will.
—The Conqueror's Dictum

THE GODS

XLVII. The gods favor those who first favor themselves.

Hannibal's time believed in gods we no longer know. Just as it's hard for
modern Westerners to understand what it takes to highjack a plane and crash
it into a building—believing the next face you'll see will be your god greet-
ing you with a hardy handshake and forty-two virgins for a job well done—
so too, it's hard for us in modern times to understand such ancient
superstitions and practices as child sacrifice—or any human sacrifice for that
matter.

Whether one truly believed in the gods or couldn't care less . . . a commander still had to care. The pecking order then decreed that all kings and
princes were put in place by the will of the gods. Thus, to question—let
alone strike down!—a king was to defy the gods themselves. Thus, when a
general went to war—then as now—it was only with the blessing of the
"powers that be," or rather, the "powers that *believe*"—those High priests
and low pundits not only holding the purse-strings, but also holding a solid
grip on the hearts and minds—if not the actual souls—of the people. Then
as now, before kissing his loved ones good-bye and soldiering off to war, all
too often, a general had to first kiss the ass of the politicians!

> For a Carthaginian general each campaign was a holy war.
> A loss was an impiety, and a failed leader might be expected
> to sacrifice himself on a pyre or starve himself to death . . .
> —David Soren

Did Hannibal himself subscribe to any of this?

> Was Hannibal superstitious? It is not easy to say in the case
> of a Carthaginian of his day. Certainly he never claimed
> attributes of divinity like Alexander or the "divine" Caesars of
> later empire. Nor did he claim aid from the unseen gods as
> did Scipio, whether from conviction or policy. Apparently
> Hannibal depended on his own efforts, and his remarks of

record to his army urged only realistic effort for tangible rewards. —Harold Lamb[187]

Chance ever favors the prepared mind. And God—or, in Hannibal's case, *gods* plural—help those who help themselves . . . their vindictive streak aside!

Their legions unbeatable on land, their gods seemingly on vacation, the Romans found themselves at a decided disadvantage at sea against sea-going Carthaginians. So Rome was quick to take advantage of that Punic warship running aground in Roman-controlled territory, quickly sending her best wainwrights to reverse-engineer the warship's construction so that, within a year, Rome had begun building what would soon become a formidable fleet, complete with innovations such as a special dropping drawbridge that could be dropped and locked onto an enemy ship, allowing Legionaries to storm onto Carthaginian ships.

XLVIII. The Gods may feast on faith . . . but they always wash it down with blood!

Someone has to pay the wine bill. Life's arbitrary, at best. Compare with Truth XCI.

XLIX. We all dance for the gods' pleasure. Entertain them well. There's nothing more dangerous than a bored god!

> *As surely as bolts from the blue may fell you, so too there will always be those of your fellows who try to dissuade you from success—your daily progress only making their daily regress all the more apparent. And should you stumble during your quest to ride the lightning, they will instantly shrill about you like a murder of crows, "We told you not to tempt the gods!" Has it ever occurred to them the gods might appreciate a little entertainment from time to time?*
> —Lung and Prowant, *Mind Control*, 2006

Hannibal often told the story of how, at age nine, before leaving Carthage for Iberia (Spain), his father Hamilcar took him to the temple of Zeus (called *Ba'al Hammon* by Carthaginians) where he made the boy swear never to be friends with Rome. Hannibal kept his promise and, at the very least, always kept the gods entertained!

---

187. *Hannibal: One Man Against Rome* (Doubleday, 1958).

L. Trust in the Gods . . . but always carry a spare sail.

Respect the Gods and Buddhas without counting on their help.
—Miyamoto Musashi

Trust in Allah, but tie your camel
—Old Arabic saying

If you want to hear God laugh, just tell him your plans.
—Anonymous

According to Harold Lamb, in his 1958 book *Hannibal: One Man Against Rome*, Hannibal's house in Libyssa, a Bithynian fishing village in the shadow of Mt. Olympus, had no less than *six* doors opening out of it . . . this, in addition to a secret escape passage. Considering that, at that time he was near the end of his life, on the run from Rome, thus the most hunted man on earth, the distinction between "prepared" and "paranoid" is probably moot!

LI. The gods choose whom they will . . . But so too do we choose our gods!

You can tell a lot about a man by his choice of gods—or lack thereof. Compare with Truth XCI.

LII. The pull of the current, will and warriorhood, and the whim of the gods: These three determine a man's fate.

Like many warriors of Hannibal's day, despite the occasional, cursory nod to the gods—to their whims—the Carthaginian believed a man's fate rested in the blade in his hand and the brains in his head. Did you notice there's actually *four* items listed here? Evidently Hannibal considers "will" and "warriorhood" to be, at the very least, two sides of a very valuable coin, or else, one and the same. We would not be amiss in comparing—perhaps even identifying—Hannibal's "will" with Nietzsche's "will to power"—that innate drive in all human beings to daily stretch towards, and eventually reach, their fullest potential. "Warriorhood" speaks for itself.

As a boy Hannibal had undoubtedly listened wide-eyed at the retelling of the tale of when Leonidas and his "300 Spartans" were told they could not rush to Thermopylae to defend against invading Persians because it was a sacred Spartan holiday when warfare was forbidden. Sighing, Leonidas picked up his sword and shield and, with a cursory bow to the priests, he agreed not to offend the gods. When the priests asked what he was going to do in the meantime, Leonidas smilingly informed the priests, "I'm simply going for a walk . . . in the general direction of the Persians." And—for safety's sake—he was taking along his 300 bodyguards!

There is a similar tale told of Hannibal's reaction to the question of divination, normally a matter of great importance back in those days. When told that he could not begin a battle because the entrails of a particular calf were unfavorable—too many blemishes, or was it too few?—Hannibal is said to have retorted: "Do you put more faith in a slice of veal than in an old general!"[188]

VENGEANCE

Do nothing without dedication and when you have acted, do not regret it.
—Jesus, son of Sirach

LIII. The wine of a true friend is fine indeed. But some thirsts can only be satisfied by the blood of a foe!

Fleeing from Carthage with a price on his head following the second Punic War, Hannibal was given asylum by King Prusias of Bithynia, who told his honored guest he was welcome to live out his days in peace in Bithynia if he chose. Reportedly these are the very words Hannibal used when toasting his host, both men knowing the Carthaginian would never rest in his quest to bring down Rome.

In hindsight, Hannibal's words ring ironic, given that Roman bloodlust (and fear) of their aging Carthaginian foe could, likewise, only be sated by blood. Indeed, Hannibal's final words before taking his own life just minutes in advance of the arrival of a Roman hit-team were:

It is time now to end the great anxiety of the Romans who have grown weary of waiting for the death of a hated old man.[189]

---

188. T. W. Potter, *Roman Italy* (University of California Press, 1987), 172.

189. Roman sources record that Hannibal drank poison (as befits a Roman statesman), others that he fell on his sword (as befits a Roman general). Mostly, we have only Roman versions to go by. Given his reputation for efficiency, leaving nothing to chance and little to the benevolence—whim—of the gods, perhaps he did both.

LIV. The nearer the blood, the more it burns.

Blood always tells, but you may not like its tales.

We cannot but help think of the influence on Hannibal of the defeat of his father in the first Punic War, not to mention the death of his brothers Mago and Hasdrubal during the second Punic War.

LV. Revenge should wait until both your sword and your wits have been sharpened.

LVI. Revenge demands a steady hand and a steadier eye.

LVII. Revenge demands a long blade . . . and a longer memory.

If there were a hundredth Truth of Hannibal's, it would undoubtedly be that "Revenge *is a dish best served cold.*" Carthaginians were famed—and rightly feared!—for their long memories.

Consider: The most dangerous Sicilian Greek of all time was Gelon of Gela. The story of his rise to power and the subsequent consequences is a perfect illustration of the uses of both espionage and revenge:

> Gela was a powerful, anti-Punic, Greek city-state on Sicily's south coast, ruled by a man named Gelon who dreamed of a unified Greek Sicily. Gela's economy was growing and needed to expand so Gelon set his sights on Sicily's greatest city, Syracuse. In 485 B.C., Gelon (1) forced an alliance with King Thereon of nearby Akrigas, (2) sent *agents provocateur* to agitate civil war between factions in Syracuse culminating in (3) a popular "democratic" call by the citizens of Syracuse for "Good King Gelon" to save their city by intervening to act as "negotiator"[190] between the warring parties.
>
> Once firmly entrenched in power in Syracuse, within short order Gelon displaced and replaced most of the population of Syracuse with people of his native Gela, in effect, making himself tyrant over not only Syracuse, but also nearby cities to become tyrant of all southeast Sicily!
>
> Gelon went on to make "alliances of convenience," even as he was busy gobbling up more land. Finally he sent his ally King Thereon to attack the much-prized trading center of Himera on Sicily's north coast. Carthage immediately

---

190. By the way, Gelon spelled "negotiation" *No-gotiation*!

sent a fleet to Himera's aid. But Gelon's masterful espionage network succeeded in intercepting a secret commu-
niqué from the captain of the Carthage fleet ordering the
Himeran cavalry to rendezvous with them when they made
landfall. Now privy to where the Carthaginians planned to
establish their beachhead, Gelon dressed his own men in
Himera uniforms, approaching unchallenged to defeat the
Carthaginians in a sneak attack, burning their ships. Gelon
ordered all Carthaginians prisoners sacrificed to the gods on
the spot.

Gelon's victory at Himera—more the result of subterfuge
than swordplay—was an especially tough pill for Carthage to
swallow. Carthage would not regain her power for another
seventy years. But we've already established that Carthaginians
have long memories . . .

Finally, in 409, King Hannibal Gisco returned Carthage to
superpower status by (re)conquering the Sicilian city of
Himera. Ravaging the city with mercenaries, Gisco ordered all
the men of Himera ritually slaughtered on the very spot
where his own grandfather Hamilcar had been killed by
Gelon's "Himerans" seventy years before.

LVIII. Revenge, like fine wine and royal blood, takes time to ferment properly.

The forty-seven Ronin suffered two long years under the black banner of
dishonor before finally getting revenge for the unjust death of their master.
Yugoslavia Serbs waited forty years to avenge the Bosnian atrocities of World
War II. Hannibal Gisco's revenge for the massacre at Himera took seventy
years to come to fruition.

Since Hannibal includes "royal blood" in this equation, this may be a
subtle swipe at the *nuevo riche* of Carthage, constantly hampering his campaigning in Italy by placing politics and profit above provisions for his men.
In the words of renowned critic and social theorist John Ruskin (1819–
1900): "It is better to be nobly remembered than nobly born." Or, as Ben
Franklin observed:

Sudden power is apt to be insolent, sudden liberty saucy—that
behaves best which has grown gradually.

HONOR

LIX. Duty flows out from my breast. Obligation pours into my ear!

Duty is the debt you own yourself. Obligation is what others seek to foist upon you.

LX. He who fights for blood soon finds it dripping from his own heart.[191]

He who fights for glory never lives long enough to hear the victory songs.[192]

He who fights for gold is already blinded by the glitter and glare of his own greed, all too soon led astray by all things shiny.

He who fights for sport seldom finds the gods in a sporting mood.

He who fights for love must leave the one he loves the most behind so he can dance with the one he hates the most.

But he who fights for honor cannot be led astray.[193]

LXI. Skin cut a thousand times eventually heals. Honor wounded but once never heals.

With this follow-up Truth, Hannibal elevates honor above all else.

LXII. War always begins with deceit. This is why war is always the final recourse of an honorable man.

The art of war is the art of deception.
—Sun Tzu

War is deception
—Muhammad

LXIII. War always ends in desperation and death . . . and the death of honor is the most tragic of these.

Again, Hannibal holds honor in the highest regard. Don't let an enemy make you compromise your principles.

---

191. Revenge, like any good blade, cuts both ways.
192. Only a single, thin line separates "glory" from "gory."
193. These are often referred to as "Hannibal's Six Movers": Blood, Glory, Gold, Sport, Love and Honor, i.e., the six motivations of men, e.g., those who will not fight for "honor" might be mercenary enough to risk their lives for "gold."

THE NATURE OF MAN

LXIV. Employ men according to their humors, deploy men according to their fevers.

Having had the benefit of a well-rounded education, thick in Greek studies, Hannibal was undoubtedly familiar with Empedocles' Four Humors. However, as we've learned, Hannibal's psychology for "moving" men was much simpler: Loves, Hates, Needs, and Desires.

LXV. The most treacherous of beasts wears its fur on the inside.

Hannibal is, of course, referring to man.

LXVI. The barking of beasts is a blessed thing . . . it warns of their approach. Do not fear their noise, fear their silence.

Practical advice here against bragging beforehand, saber rattling, and taking note of noise—fear—in the enemy camp.

LXVII. Back-slapping in fat times, back-stabbing in lean. In lean times, one piece of meat is just as good as another. My enemy's heart is just meat!

> *In your presence his mouth is all sweetness, and he admires your*
> *words, but later he will twist his speech, and with your own words*
> *he will give offense.*
> —Jesus, Son of Sirach[194]

> *A man will kiss another's hands until gets a loan, and will lower*
> *his voice when speaking of his neighbor's money, but when the time*
> *comes for repayment he will delay, and will pay in words of*
> *unconcern, and will find fault with the time.*
> —Ibid.[195]

LXVIII. An enemy may blacken your face with blows, but only you can blacken your own heart.

LXIX. Trust the heart before you trust the skin
His skin is white but his heart is black.
His skin is black but his heart is white.
All blood runs red.

---

194. 27:23
195. 29:5

Trust your gut, it evolved earlier. Don't judge a book by its cover. During his life, Hannibal was betrayed by allies—his Numidian[196] cavalry at the Battle of Zama—[197] and defended by his enemies—Scipio argued the Roman Senate unsuccessfully not to arrest Hannibal following the second Punic War. Thus, better a faithful enemy than a false friend.

So long as a cat can catch mice, it is a good cat no matter whether it is white or black.
—Deng Xiaoping

LXX. Failure boasts of few friends. There are no feasts at Failure's table, his sons fallen to the sword and to slavers.

Many princes sin with David; but few repent with him.
—Ben Franklin

Every friend will say, "I too am a friend." But some friends are friends only in name.
—Jesus, son of Sirach[198]

Do not forget a friend in your heart, and be not unmindful of him in your wealth.
—Jesus, son of Sirach[199]

The allies we gain by victory will turn against us upon the bare whisper of our defeat.
—Napoleon

Following the second Punic War Hannibal was forced to flee Carthage after rival Carthaginian leaders gave in to Roman demands for his being turned over to them.

---

196. Fellow North Africans.

197. A surprising reenactment of the Battle of Zama was portrayed in Russell Crowe's 2000 movie *Gladiator.*

198. 37:1.

199. 37:6

LXXI. The emotions of men shift as surely as the wind and are as unsteady as the shifting sands.[200]

My footing is always firm! I walk the shifting sands with ease. I know the direction of the wind before the wind itself decides which way it will blow.

Adapt or die:

> Seizing the chance ahead of time means carefully observing your opponent's mind and making an appropriate move just before he makes up his mind. —Yagu Munenori

LXXII. Beware calling another man "genius." A tree always looks tallest when surrounded by shrub.

Hannibal lost many battles due to the incompetence of others. For example, in 210 the city of Arigentum (a town controlled by Hannibal) was handed back to the Romans by mutinous Carthaginian auxiliaries.[201]

Turnabout's fair play. Machiavelli[202] points out how this worked to Hannibal's advantage when the politician Varro, despite any military experience, "talked" himself into a military command, ultimately leading to Rome's disastrous defeat at Cannae.

And though it can hardly be counted against his otherwise competent record as an able lieutenant commander, Hasdrubal's defeat and death at Metaurus[203] effectively doomed his brother's Italian peninsula campaign.

---

200. A couple thoughts on the subject from Machiavelli: "Nor does it help such a one to have won victories in the past, for the present disaster cancels them all out." (*Discourses* 1:53) and "One sees here how great men remain the same whatever befalls. If fortune changes, sometimes raising them, sometimes casting them down, they do not change, but remain ever resolute in mind and in conduct throughout life that it is easy for anyone to see that fortune holds no sway over them. Not so do weak men behave; for by good fortune they are buoyed up and intoxicated, and ascribe such success as they meet with, to a virtue they never possessed, so that they become insupportable and odious to all who have anything to do with them." (Ibid. 3:31)

201. M. Cary, D.L.H., and H. H. Scullard, F.B.A. *A History of Rome,* 3rd Ed. (Macmillan, 1975), 133.

202. *Discourses* 1:53.

203. The result of a dispatch from Hannibal to his brother (outlining the where and how of their intended rendezvous) being intercepted and acted upon by the Romans.

> *Do not praise a man before you hear him reason,*
> *for this is the test of a man.*
> —Jesus, son of Sirach[204]

And what's that old saying about "a one-eyed man in a blind kingdom"?

STRUGGLE AND STRENGTH

LXXIII. Test yourself with fire and ice, sand and sea, bile and blood, before your enemies do.

A near-identical passage appears in the ancient Norse-Viking Havamaal (Sayings of High Odin):

> "Test yourself with fire and ice before your enemies do."

LXXIV. Pain is ever the best teacher.
Pain is only weakness leaving the body.
Death is only pain leaving the body.

Some thrive on pain. According to Machiavelli, despite their several initial defeats at Hannibal's hands, the closer the Carthaginian approached Rome, the more resolve the Romans showed:

> When Hannibal invaded Italy, one sees how, after three
> defeats and the death of so many generals and soldiers,
> [Rome] was still able, not merely to withstand the enemy, but
> to win the war. All this comes from having fortified well the
> heart, but of the extremities made less account.[205]

LXXV. A first taste of defeat, though bitter, goes far to prepare your palate for future feasts.

The Samurai have a saying, "Nine times down, ten times up!" and so we learn from our mistakes—provided we survive of course. This adage has been taught a thousand ways across as many years. Steel can only be made by fire.

Learning to be a "good loser" really does build character . . . Of course, learning to be a good winner builds a bigger bank account!

---

204. 27:7
205. *Discourses* 11:30.

For those who've never tasted defeat—and thus never had to drag themselves back up, dust themselves off, and jump back into the fray even more determined—that first taste of defeat can, indeed, be bitter. Some never recover. Modern-day example? Boxer Mike Tyson remained undefeated and, indeed, appeared undefeatable, until a relative unknown named Buster Douglas laid him out in the first round. "Iron Mike" went down hard and, in many ways, never got back up (considering the nosedive both his professional and his personal fortunes took after that).

LXXVI. Discipline is ever an iron trap—be sure you are the one to set it in place.

FAMILY AND FRIENDS

LXXVII. The best hearth doubles as a kiln.

Never underestimate the influence of family on your early development—"Mama, drama, and trauma" . . . first comes "Mama."

Hamilcar Barca taught his sons well.

LXXVIII. No one teaches my sons as well as my enemies.

Our enemies make us strong. This harkens back to Truth VI.

It was often the custom in ancient times for a conquering people to "adopt" the sons and daughters of conquered kings, keeping them at the central court. This served not only the purpose of educating future leaders of the conquered in what was expected of them, but also allowed the conquering king, emperor, etc. to have *hostages* to insure the cooperation of the conquered people. For example:

> When the Romanian Christian duchy of Wallachia was conquered by the Turks, as part of the surrender terms, Vladimir, the young son of the Count of Wallachia, was taken to be "safeguarded" and "educated" at the Turkish court. Reportedly the boy saw and suffered all manner of horror and abuse at the hands of his Islamic "hosts," including their forcing him to participate in tortures and executions of fellow Christians firsthand (all valuable skills his Turkish mentors reasoned a ruthless up-and-coming ruler would need).
>
> Upon his father's death, the Turks returned their Christian protégé, now an adult, to rule Wallachia (today the Roman-

ian territory of Transylvania). No sooner was Vladimir enthroned than he turned on his Islamic masters, waging monstrous war on his former mentors to the point where they now began to fear the very creature they had created as one who had become intoxicated by his untold atrocities and tortures—a slow death by impaling being his favorite to watch. His name was Vladimir Tepes, but we know him better as Vlad Dracul—*Dracula*!

Ironically, the Romans likewise credit Hannibal with "training" their sons. Case in point: Both Claudius Nero (the consul commander who trapped and killed Hasdrubal at Metaurus), and Publius Cornelius Scipio (aka Scipio Africanus)[206] had both survived Hannibal's earlier victory at Lake Trasimene (where Scipio lost his father by the way), learning from that disaster, to both later contribute to Hannibal's downfall:

> Publius Cornelius Scipio proved to be one of the greatest soldiers of antiquity, and has even been called by a leading military expert "a greater than Napoleon." He appears to have possessed a genuine belief in his direct communication with the gods, especially Jupiter, as well as a magnetic power of conveying his supreme confidence in himself to others. At the same time he had a keen sense for practical details and a readiness to take lessons in warcraft from his adversaries. He rivaled the victories of Hannibal by adapting Hannibal's methods to the service of Rome.[207] —Cary and Scullard

However, in some things, methodology for instance, experts find grand differences between the Roman and the Carthaginian. For example, when Scipio was campaigning in Spain:

> He did not seek to engage the enemy in pitched battles until he had exercised his troops in new tactical movement derived from Hannibal's school, and rearmed them with the finely an-

---

206. Also listed alongside Hannibal as one of the "100 Greatest Generals" of all time. *Armchair General*, March 2008.

207. 1975:134.

nealed Spanish sword. He also resumed, with notable success, his father's policy of winning over the native chiefs, so that the Punic dominion was widely undermined. —Ibid.

As a result, he succeeded in countering Hasdrubal in Spain, taking the Barca family possessions, leading Hasdrubal to abandon Spain for Italy, where Hannibal's brother ultimately met his fate.

Both Scipio's father and uncle had been killed in battles with Hannibal and he had grown up observing firsthand Hannibal's tactics. Finally, at the age of twenty-six he was given the job of ridding Italy of Hannibal. He decided to do so by first defeating Hasdrubal (causing Hasdrubal to dash headlong to Italy and to his death). Scipio then made a special trip to North Africa to encourage Hannibal's Numidian allies to revolt against Carthage—knowing this would be especially troubling for Hannibal since Numidian calvary made up an important contingent of Hannibal's fighting force in Italy. Scipio had learned well from his "mentor" Hannibal.

LXXIX. All that is required of a father is to teach his sons patience.
Sons, by their very nature, teach their fathers patience.

While history records nothing of any of Hannibal's surviving sons, this Truth succinctly sums up Hannibal's relationship with his own father, perhaps even by way of apology? Jesus, son of Sirach contributes the following, which can also be seen to apply, not just to Hannibal, but to the other sons of Hamilcar Barca:

> The father may die, yet he is not dead, for he has left behind him one like himself; while alive he saw and rejoiced, and when he died he was not grieved; he has left behind him an avenger against his enemies, and one to repay the kindness of his friends.[208]

LXXX. Mirrors tell the cruelest tales.
A good mirror never shows the same reflection twice.
Can you remember your face before we had mirrors?
The face of a friend is the truest mirror.

These first two verses refer not only to the obvious—that mirrors really do tell the cruelest tales, by their unbridled honesty!—but this can also be seen as an admonition to change up our strategy from time to time, as pru-

---

208. 30:4

dent, in order to keep the enemy from developing an effective counter-strategy. Two of the best examples of this are Hannibal's victory at Cannae (where Hannibal won by refusing to fight in the type of formations the Romans excelled in, although he initially tricked the Romans into thinking he was going to give such battle), and at Zama, where Scipio ultimately defeated Hannibal by forcing him to fight—against all his experience and better judgment—the Roman way.

The third verse here is perhaps an injunction against vanity—undesirable in all, deadly to a general.

The final verse? Never were truer words spoken, in Hannibal's time, or in our own.

LXXXI. The enemy of my enemy is my friend.

Whether Hannibal himself originated this succinct strategy, or whether, more likely, it was already well-worn wisdom by the time he first took up the sword—How are we to know for certain? In the absence of its being carved into stone before Hannibal's time, the credit for this Truth must go to the Carthaginian.

It is unclear whether Hannibal is saying this is true out of necessity—strange bedfellows—or because my enemy's enemy is more vulnerable to manipulation? Keep your friends close and your enemies closer. In anticipation of crossing the Alps, Hannibal allied himself with as many of the "barbarian" Celtic tribes as possible, knowing they had common cause to hate Rome.

> *Keep yourself far from your enemies, and*
> *be on guard toward your friends.*
> —Jesus, son of Sirach

Having invaded into Italy, Hannibal attempted to ally himself with King Philip of Macedon as they had common cause: So long as Rome had to fight on two fronts (against Hannibal in Italy and Philip in Greece) the Romans would have only half as many men to throw against either of them fighting alone.[209] You will have of course recognized this as a variation of Sun Tzu's:

> Not knowing where I will attack, my enemy must prepare everywhere. Having to prepare everywhere, he is strong nowhere!

---

209. Cary and Scullard, 1975:132.

WIT AND WISDOM

LXXXII. Men are never as helpless, nor ever as clever as they believe themselves to be.

Times change, people seldom do. Never was this Truth more true than it is today.

Teach people that they are not near as helpless as they believe themselves to be and they will love you because of it and follow you anywhere. Herein lies the secret of Hannibal's charisma in uniting and then leading for near-two decades men from vastly different cultures, men fighting for different reasons,[210] but all united in their respect for their commander.

Conversely, teach your enemy that he's not as clever as he believes himself to be and he will hate *and fear* you because of it.

LXXXIII. Wit is the sharpest of swords but the thinnest of shields.

LXXXIV. The words we weave today bind us to tomorrow.

The truth might set you free, but a lie is the worst of prisons. Tell the truth and, in time, then truth will tell.

LXXXV. Today's lie, tomorrow's test of memory.

Wasn't it Abraham Lincoln who said no man has a good enough memory to be a successful liar?

LXXXVI. Truth makes a fine philter but a meager meal.

Hannibal is saying here that he would rather hear the harsh truth than a soothing lie.

There is a line in the Biblical book of the apocalpse[211] where John is told to eat the scroll of truth, being told by the angel, "It will be sweet in the mouth, but bitter in the belly." So, too, the English word "philter" comes to us from *philein* by way of *philtron*, meaning both "medicine" and "to love." One might therefore argue that we can both "love" the truth while not being at all enthusiastic about taking our well-deserved "medicine."

LXXXVII. Tradition makes a fine footstool but a poor ladder.

For some, "tradition" is a tool for focusing their energies; for others "tradition" is a weapon for "guilting" (i.e. manipulating) others. Miyamoto Musashi time and again warned against favoring one weapon or one combat technique over another, to the point where an enemy has you "pegged." Your

---

210. See Truth LX.
211. Nowadays more sensitively called "The Book of Revelation."

safest bet? Adopt "a tradition of breaking tradition" by doing the last thing your enemy expects you to do.

LXXXVIII. A single thrust to the heart saves a thousand cuts to the limbs.

There's something to be said for efficiency . . . and Hannibal just said it!

Cut off the head and the body dies. Threaten his homefires and your enemy forgets about the brush fires. In other words, hit 'em where they live.

Following the first Punic War, Rome was slowly bleeding Carthage by post-war restrictions and demands for outrageous reparations. Time and again Carthage and Rome bumped heads. Realizing that it was only a matter of time before full-blown warfare erupted, Hannibal, wisely, decided that, rather than snipe at Rome out in the boondocks, he would attack into Italy directly, threatening Rome itself.

Ironically, sixteen years later, having learned his lesson from "The Master,"[212] Scipio Africanus used the same ploy, attacking Carthage directly in order to convince Hannibal to abandon his Italy campaign.

Compare this with the 1968 Tet Offensive in Vietnam. This coordinated attack on southern cities, including Hue and Saigon, while a *military disaster* for the Viet Cong, accomplished more than years fighting in the jungle, proving to be a *media victory* for the Communists, turning many Americans against the war.

LXXXIX. In for a sip, in for a sea.

Commitment. Put up or shut up and then stay the course. Like Caesar crossing the Rubicon, once Hannibal stepped that first step into the Ebro River in Spain—marking the northernmost boundary set by Rome—he knew there was no turning back.

XC. Mercenaries at least fight for pay . . . Fanatics fight for any-thing . . . and for nothing!

Psychologist Carl Rogers (1902–1987) concluded that all human beings naturally judge all their actions and experiences in terms of their value for facilitating or hampering our actualization growth—in other words we want to know "What's in it for me?" Far from being a cynical view of mankind, this is a vital survival mechanism that evolution has programmed into us. Therefore, when approaching someone with a proposition, asking them for a favor, etc., always come armed with the intention of telling them—up front—what's in it for them.[213]

---

212. See Truth LXXVIII.

213. Review Truth LX.

Mercenaries are at least predictable. Fanatics less so. Like all com-manders, Hannibal loves a predictable enemy.

Around 550, B.C. Mago, Carthage's first known king, introduced the use of mercenaries into the Carthaginian army. A practice—unfortunately for the Carthaginians—continued down to Hannibal's time. The end of the first Punic War saw the aptly-named "Revolt of the Mercenaries" (241–238), resulting from Carthage's inability/refusal to pay her mercenaries.[214]

XCI. Victors sing the victory songs. Dirges to the defeated. Which sounds sweetest of all to the gods? War cries!

This is simply Hannibal's variation of "The winners write the history books," with a possible sarcastic stab at the gods thrown in. Compare with Truth XLVIII.

XCII. No true gift comes with tax, toil, or tail attached.

Beware of Greeks bearing gifts! The tale of the Trojan Horse would have been well-known in Hannibal's time. Or, as Don Corleone warned Michael, "Whichever one of your own lieutenants brings you the offer of peace from your enemy, he will be the traitor."

Gifts wrapped in too many ribbons soon become bothersome.

XCIII. No shadow walks without some light.

No light that doesn't carry its dark brother. So with shadows, so with men.

Too much light blinds as surely as too little.

The light of truth never casts a false shadow.

Two sides to every coin. Yin-yang, as they say in the East. Strategy-wise, you must learn to put yourself in your enemy's shoes. What is he thinking? What does he want? What is he willing to give up to obtain what he wants? Is compromising with him possible, or is crushing him completely your best—safest—option?

XCIV. To be thankful for what you have been given, remember what was given up.

The light of truth never casts a false shadow.

Sacrifice always bears fruit. Ask yourself: how hungry are you?

XCV. No spire higher than fire, no ocean deeper than fate.

Did Hannibal believe in fate? Perhaps destiny? If so, why look askance at "the whim of the gods"?[215] It's been said "There are no atheists in fox-

---

214. This bloody revolt was finally crushed by Hannibal's father, Hamilcar
215. Truth LII.

holes." Perhaps, but for a warrior there's still some distance between "bleeding" and "believing."

> *An educated man knows many things, and one with much*
> *experience may speak with understanding. He that is inexperienced*
> *knows few things, but he that has traveled acquires much cleverness.*
> *I have seen many things in my travels, and I understand more than*
> *I can express. I have often been in danger of death, but have*
> *escaped because of those experiences.*
> *—Jesus, son of Sirach*[216]

Oft repeated "Chance favors the prepared mind." In the end, "Luck" often lives to tell the tale "experience" writes in blood.

DEATH

XCVI. My son will die today. My son will die a hundred years hence. My tears will taste the same. Grief does not take notice of the sun's passing.

XCVII. Death is death no matter from what direction she comes to embrace you.

According to Greek mythology,[217] when the gods first created mankind, they were androgynous, strange hybrid creatures possessing both sexes. Realizing this ungainly creature just wouldn't do, the gods separated the sexes— and we've all been searching for our "better half" ever since.

For Hannibal, as for many warriors in many lands, death comes as a welcome lover. The Carthaginian's thoughts—beliefs?—on this may have been similar to those of the Norse Vikings, who either saw themselves carried aloft after death by High-God Odin's *Valkyries*—often portrayed as beautiful maidens, or else ushered down an underworld ruled by the Goddess Hel—that's right, from which we get our modern word "Hell".

The "Samurai creed," perhaps the creed of all warriors in all times: The inevitability of Death is what gives life its sweetness.

XCVIII. Better an early death than a late trial.

At the conclusion of the second Punic War, Hannibal briefly dabbled in politics, returning to Carthage as an elected *suffete* (one of the two co-leaders of a city, similar to Roman consuls). But Hannibal's long-time Carthaginian

---

216. 39:4
217. Why is it the other guy's religion is always "mythology" but ours is "historical"?

rivals kept reporting to Rome that he was hatching new war plans until, finally (ironically over the protests of Scipio Africanus) the Senate in Rome ordered Hannibal arrested. Well aware of the forces moving against him, Hannibal escaped Carthage to the court of Roman-hating King Antiochus of Syria, where he led naval operations against pro-Roman Rhodians of South Turkey, until Antiochus was defeated by the Romans in 189.

Forced to flee again, first to Crete where he lived as a pirate, and then to Bithynia (south coast of Black Sea east of Constantinople), where he offered his expertise to King Prusias—then busy at war with neighboring Pergamum. Rome eventually sided with Pergamum, ordering Prusias to give back lands he had seized from Pergamun and, as an additional slap in the face, ordering the king to turn over Hannibal.

Betrayed by Prusias, the hounds literally at his door, Hannibal committed suicide by falling on his sword. He was sixty-four.

By taking his own life "Samurai" fashion, Hannibal joined a long line of notables who, realizing the game was up, defiantly denied their enemies the satisfaction of capturing them alive, thus also sparing themselves—and their loved ones—the bitterness and humiliation of a "show trial" or, horror of horrors, the fate of a Mussolini.[218]

Another take on this Truth could be the old argument that a man can live a good life but if in the end he shows corruption or cowardice, that's all that people will remember of him. Case in point: O.J. Simpson. On the other hand, even a man who has led a less than exemplary life who, at the end of his life, dies in service to others—that's all people remember. He died well. What we call "redemption" in these parts.

Or, how about "the James Dean" (or, if you prefer a more Eastern reference, Yukio Mishima),"Live fast, die young, and leave a beautiful-looking corpse!"

Death is nothing, but to live defeated and inglorious is to die daily.
—Napoleon

XCIX. Love and death are the only things of value that come looking for us.

---

218. After being shot, the bodies of Benito Mussolini and his mistress were dragged through the streets, their corpses mightily abused, before then being hoisted by their ankles and left to hang upside down in the city square for days. When word of Mussolini's humiliation reached an already besieged Hitler in Berlin, *Der Fuehrer* immediately made elaborate plans to insure that he did not suffer a similar fate. Not taking any chances, once capture was imminent, he took poison *and* shot himself in the head, after which, per his instructions, his body was cremated.

15.

The Machiavelli Method

I hear all sorts of things, and observe the various tastes and ideas
of men.
—**Machiavelli, in a letter to his friend Vettori**

THOUGH THEY LIVED 2,000 miles and as many years apart, Niccolò Machiavelli (1469–1527) shares much in common with China's Sun Tzu. Both men thrived in turbulent, uncertain times—times made all the more turbulent by the whimsical ambitions and constant shifting alliances of petty princes. Uncertainty flourished, compounded by the ineptness and corruptness of the day's military minds—there were the very forces that might have succeeded in helping the age stand and fight and perhaps claw its way up out of chaos, had those generals not been more eager to serve shadows than to dispel them.

Both Sun Tzu and Machiavelli were self-made men, purposely hurling themselves into their respective seas of outrageous fortune, determined to better their fortunes by showing their respective princes how to more easily attain and then better safeguard their own fortunes.

Ultimately having achieved fame (if not fortune) through their brilliant *appreciation* of rational thought and, more importantly, the *application* of same, both masters wrote down their winning strategies to the benefit of subsequent generations—strategies that warring factions have since struggled hopelessly to understand, before then stumbling helplessly in their sophomoric attempts to apply these grandest of strategies to their pettiest of squabbles.

And while the modern world has nothing but praise for both Machiavelli and his ancient Chinese counterpart, were either alive today they undoubtedly would show only *scorn* for us.

Five hundred years removed from Machiavelli's fractured peninsula, 2000 years the other side of Sun Tzu's Warring States China, we find our human lot so little improved, still finding ourselves awash in a sea of troubled times eerily similar to those of Sun Tzu and Machiavelli. And so Machiavelli shares one more thing in common with Sun Tzu: Many have been the translations and (mis)interpretations of Machiavelli, both of the man and his mutterings. Seems everybody talks about Machiavelli, but nobody does anything about him. Our old problem of appreciation versus application.

THE DOCTOR OF THE DAMNED?

His philosophical simplicity saved him from a lot of irrelevant nonsense.
—Leslie J. Walker[219]

Though they bear many disturbing similarities, Machiavelli's times were not our times. He did not have to contend every four years, with a dog-and-pony show designed to pick which candidate can play the saxophone better. In Machiavelli's land and time, the decision as to who ultimately ruled was decided not by rapier wit, but, all too often, by the actual rapier itself!

Back in Machiavelli's day, the enemy you defeated seldom called to congratulate you on "a campaign well-run." No, enemies in Machiavelli's day—if you were foolish enough to leave any alive!—patiently plotted your future immolation, not your eventual impeachment.

So we must not be so quick to judge Niccolò by the oh-so-politically correct sensibilities of today. He was a man well-suited to his times, and, through study of his methods, we may just be able to prevent his times from becoming *our* times!

Often referred to simply as "the Florentine," Machiavelli was called a lot worse in his day, up to our day: The Englishman Felix Raab, in the

---

219. Leslie J. Walker, *Niccolò Machiavelli: The Discourses.* 1929.

sixteenth-century *English Face of Machiavelli* helped lionize (or is that demonize?) Machiavelli in rhyme and pun: "*Hatchevil, or not to be matched in evil!*" Conversely, Sir Francis Bacon (1561–1626) held the Florentine in higher regard, once calling him "the Supreme Realist."

The Jesuit Leslie Walker, in his original 1929 translation of Machiavelli's *Discourses*, variously refers to him as "*a cold technician,*" "*an extremely free, original and honest mind,*" and "*the Doctor of the Damned*".

Given the times and the all-encompassing power of the Vatican, Machiavelli was wisely a "convenient" Christian, albeit an often outspoken critic of the Church's dabbling in politics, at least once characterizing the religion as "effeminate".[220]

Not surprisingly then that, on more than one occasion, Machiavelli was accused of being both a pagan and an atheist who, despite penning treatises telling ruthless Princes how to enjoy being even more ruthless, how to wield "Ultimate Control," he was sometimes condemned by that self-same plume as a democratic-minded satirist—an earlier incarnation of Voltaire. And while on the subject of lives past and future, the Jesuit Walker accuses (or praises?) Machiavelli for being the "*pre*-incarnation" of Lenin.

One modern-day reinterpretation (or is that reincarnation?) of Machiavelli credits him with being the first Madison Avenue "Image Maker":

> He knows that brute force is not enough; the people must also be entranced. —Michael A. Ledeen[221]

Likewise, avant-garde sociologists Stanford Lyman and Marvin Scott hail Machiavelli as one of the precursors of their 1989 book *A Sociology of the Absurd*.[222]

In a Hamlet nutshell, the "Sociology of the absurd" attempts to understand social interaction by beginning with the premise that (1) the world has no intrinsic meaning, only that meaning which (2) human beings impose upon it. To accomplish this (and in order to keep us from going mad and slaughtering one another wholesale) we (3) establish a "consensus

---

220. Walker, 1929.

221. *Machiavelli on Modern Leadership* (Truman Talley Books/St. Martins, 1999), 119.

222. 2nd Ed. (General Hall, 1989).

reality" (agreed-upon social structures, mutually-validated social identities, etc.) we can literally all live with:

> Nothing in the social world has an inherent meaning. Meaning consists only of that which is imputed by people to the persons and objects as they go about their daily lives trying to make sense of the world. —Lyman and Scott (1989:19)

How's Machiavelli fit into all this?

> For Machiavelli . . . all such ideas about the structure of the world are as illusionary as the fortresses with which fearful princes deluded themselves into a false sense of security. Machiavelli, we believe, is the father of the Sociology of the Absurd because of his insistence on the essential meaninglessness of the world and his perception of how most people impute a meaning to their illusions, that is, constant social realities out of the shreds and patches of their experiences and memories. —Ibid:12

To the average person, Machiavelli's name is synonymous with ruthless politics, a diabolical mastermind giving his blessing to all manner of totalitarian terror. A monster and a madman. Well, they got the "mastermind" part right at least.

Webster defines "Machiavellianism" as "The doctrine of Machiavelli that denies the relevance of morality in political affairs."[223]

But Niccolo was no immoral sycophant to the powers-that-be, nor should he be dismissed as being "unprincipled" just because he understood it was sometimes necessary to rule with an iron fist. In all things, Niccolò's first choice was the velvet glove.

The first thing for us in the modern world to understand is that Machiavelli didn't hold the anti-Nature ideal that "All men are created equal" up as the "can-do-no-wrong" sacred cow we do today. In his time everyone understood: "*Quad licet jovi licet bovi*" ("What is allowed for the gods is not allowed for the cattle").

Machiavelli wasn't writing for the common man. His advice was

---

223. *Webster's II New Riverside Dictionary*, 1996.

intended for Princes, to help them gain, maintain, and freely exercise "Ultimate Control."

According to Machiavelli, the position of Prince not only brought with it certain rewards, but also certain responsibilities—if you wanted to hold on to your princedom that is:

> One of Machiavelli's contributions to the Sociology of the Absurd is his understanding that, as with love, all human relations have the qualities of a game. Although ordinary people might not perceive this ubiquitous quality, the prince has to do so in order to persevere.[224]

Like Nietzsche and Marx, and other *utilitarian* philosophers who came in his wake, Machiavelli's words not only deserved to be appreciated, they also *demanded* to be applied. These were not some dried musing on what "might" have been or what "might" be; Machiavelli's writings were a training manual— a guidebook on how to acquire, maintain, and exercise "Ultimate Control."

Machiavelli's one myopic failing (since he concentrated on writing for the appreciation of potential and practicing *princes*) was that his "instruction manuals" would one day fall into the hands of lesser mortals, who might discover ways to apply his principles Ol' Saint Niccolò never imagined.

"Lesser mortals" . . . That would be *us!*

Machiavelli penned his philosophy in *The Discourses* (1517), and *The Art of War* (1520). But by far his best known work is his earlier *The Prince* (1513):

> [*The Prince*] may be (and has been) read as a handbook on how to fool friends and influence people, a sort of Dale Carnegie for rogues. Public life, Machiavelli argues, consists largely of deceptions, lies and broken promises. Since ordinary people tend not to think in terms of multiple realities, they can be made to believe in illusions which are mere chimeras and calculated performances. —Ibid.

However, by all accounts, *The Prince* was written in haste, shortly after Machiavelli had been released from torture and prison (for backing a failed regime). Most serious scholars would agree that *The Discourses* (based on the

---

224. Ibid. 1989:10.

first ten books of Titus Livy's *History of Rome)* is Machiavelli's crowning work. Unlike *The Prince*:

> [*The Discourses*] was not written in the white heat of despair, and many think, it contains a more considered politico-philosophic outlook than *The Prince*, closer to what Machiavelli actually thought. It also differs from *The Prince* in being more plausible, mature, and moderate—unsensational qualities which assured its eclipse by *The Prince*. —Paul Stratern[225]

In fact, there is no essential argument in *The Prince* which is not repeated in *The Discourses*.[226]

Likewise, *The Art of War*, while a worthy read for historical purposes alone, can't stand up to *Discourses*:

> *The Art of War* repeats or assumes every essential proposition of both *The Prince* and *The Discourses*—for the art of war is an extension of the whole social condition of a society.
> —Ibid.

Unlike many philosophers, Machiavelli never had a problem making the evolution from appreciation to application. He studied well all of those "Masters" who came before him, particularly the Greek and the Roman.

And then he applied what he learned, advising the ambitious aristocrat, tutoring the prince-in-training. All the while he was tempering his personal strategy of "the Pyramid of Power," those three *"external forces"*: *Virtù, Necessity*, and *Fortune* that motivate men towards their destiny. Further honing his observations, Machiavelli then isolates four *internal forces*, or "elements" he felt influence all man's interactions: *Bread, Gold, Meat* and *Steel*.

Before examining Machiavelli's particular strategies and tactics in depth, we need to look at the leitmotif running through the whole of Machiavelli's philosophy—three salient points that, at first glance, might seem cynical, even amoral—in keeping with his reputation for ruthlessness but, upon closer inspection, we'll see them for the succinct observations on human nature they are. Machiavelli was convinced that (1) people are basically stupid, unable and unwilling to govern themselves, and (2) they need strong

---

225. *Machiavelli in 90 Minutes* (1989), 70.
226. Walker, 1929.

leaders who will do whatever is necessary to maintain order and promote prosperity. You might recall Katilya of India made pretty much the same argument a couple thousand years earlier.

- **People are inherently stupid** and can't be trusted to organize their lives so as to take care of themselves, stay out of trouble, and keep the world out of trouble.

In *Discourses*, Machiavelli warns us that "Men are more prone to evil than to good" as he shakes his head against, "the malignant-humors to which men are prone." Finally, after "sighing" in disappointment and frustration he explains that men don't know how to be wholly good or wholly bad, "magnificently bad" or "perfectly good," because they are, by nature "both ambitious and suspicious, and know not how to use moderation where their fortunes are concerned"!

We detect a trace of Buddhist realism (some argue "cynicism") to much of Machiavelli's thought. Is it possible the Florentine could have brushed up against the Enlightened One's philosophy, given the increasing trade between East and West flourishing in Machiavelli's day? Or could it simply be that both Niccolò and Siddhartha were keen and kindred judges of the human condition? Both agreed that men are slaves to their desires. For example, Machiavelli argues in *Discourses*:

> Furthermore, human appetites are insatiable, for by nature we cannot long for, but by fortune we are such that of these things we can attain but a few. The result is that the human mind is perpetually discontented, and of its possessions is apt to grow weary. This makes it find fault with the present, praise the past, and long for the future; though for its doing so no rational cause can be assigned.

According to both Buddha and Machiavelli, man suffers because he makes unrealistic demands of himself and his environment. When Machiavelli warns us in the *Discourses* that "inherent in everything is its own particular malady," we hear a definite echo of the Buddha's teaching that everything man touches, every thought he thinks, contains the seed of his future suffering.

But Machiavelli is only agreeing with Titus Livy that, individually, human beings are cowardly and feeble.[227] This is why men are so easily led astray. Says *Discourses*:

> Men in general are as much affected by what a thing appears to be as by what it is, indeed they are frequently influenced more by appearances than by the reality.

At times, Machiavelli follows Buddha's calm condemnation—while simultaneously foreshadowing Nietzsche's rants against the despicable "herd"—when declaring his dismal disappointment and dismissal of mankind in general:

> Nothing is more futile and more inconsistent than are the masses. —*Discourses*

- *Strong leaders are needed* **to maintain order.**

In Machiavelli's time there was this thing called "The Great Chain of Being," a universal pecking order with the All Mighty planted firmly at the top followed, in descending order, by the Heavenly Hosts, then the pope and his crew, next royalty, and finally the lower masses. In other words, despite romance novels to the contrary, people back in Machiavelli's day were pretty much stuck where they were born.

Peasants were stuck being peasants, while princes—aristocrats and royalty—were pretty much free to battle and back-stab for position within the exclusive blue-blood food chain. Too many princes, not enough kingdoms to go around—always trouble waiting to happen.

Machiavelli's writings were well-intentioned, meant to help separate the wheat from the chaff, *prince-wise*.

Machiavelli accepted the need for strong leadership—a monarchy—what other choice did he have? "Democracy" was just another word for "*mob rule*" back then.[228] When a church "theocracy" ran things, it got even worse. The best Machiavelli could hope for was that an iron fist—albeit one encased in a velvet glove—would succeed in uniting the land.

---

227. See Walker, 1929.
228. Yeah, like so much has changed!

Machiavelli left the option open that, ideally, there would be some sort of "popular will" that would be able to oust such a tyrant should he prove more bellicose than benevolent.

That Machiavelli would accept the need for such a ruler is understandable given all the examples since time immemorial that, given the choice between security (a tyrant) or freedom (chaos), the masses will give themselves over to a tyrant every time.[229]

Keep in mind that, in Machiavelli's time, there was one set of rules for the masses, a separate set of rules for princes. "*Quad licet jovi licet bovi.*"

In his time, princes were better educated and, to Machiavelli's thinking, better also to make decisions, less likely to make gross and mean decisions as might an uneducated, unworldly peasant. The prince must do what has to be done—more on this in a minute.

Ideally the prince would be loved by the people but, in what is Machiavelli's best known maxim: *It is better to be feared than loved*. Fear is constant— once you put 'the fear of the Lord' (or at least the fear of the all-mighty stun-gun!) into them, they never waver. Love, on the other hand, can change to hate in an instant. What Machiavelli actually said is that it's preferable to have both but, push come to shove, bank on fear! And, that push having come to shove, the prince—ruler—is given *carte blanche* to push back, to do whatever is necessary to keep the peace. *Ergo*:

- ***The end justifies the means.***

One more time: "*Quad licet jovi licet bovi.*" Resources and recourses forbidden to the rest of us, —things like secrecy and deceit— are "the means" forgiven to a prince when he is motivated by a worthy "end." Thus:

> In Machiavelli's world—the real world as described in the truthful history books—treason and deceit are commonplace, as are conspiracies against constituted authority, all undertaken for personal satisfaction. . . . —Michael A. Ledeen[230]

---

229. Noted psychologist Erich Fromm, in his *Escape from Freedom* (1941) agrees with this sad observation.

230. 1999:61.

Not surprising then, secrecy and deceit are permitted to princes:

> For one should not declare one's intentions, but should seek
> to get what one desires anyhow. There is, for instance, no
> need in asking someone for a weapon to say "I propose to kill
> you with it," since you can satisfy your appetite once you have
> the weapon in your hands. . . . Although to use fraud[231] in any
> action is detestable, yet in the conduct of war it is praise-
> worthy and glorious. And a man who uses fraud to overcome
> his enemy is praised, just as much as he who overcomes his
> enemy by force. —*Discourses*

No surprise then that sometimes a prince must do *bad things* for what he
considers *good reasons*:

> It is a sound maxim that reprehensible actions may be justi-
> fied by their effects, and that when the effect is good, as it
> was in the case of Romulus,[232] it always justifies the action.
> For it is the man who uses it to mend them, that is blame-
> worthy. —Walker, 1929

The prince must not resort to such methods haphazardly, neither must
he ever make light of or gloss over a bad action he's been forced to do, and
under no condition should he take pleasure in such harsh—albeit
necessary—action.

We did what we had to do—a bad thing—but for a good reason. If you
thought it right enough at the time to do the thing—all its possible repercussions accepted in advance—then you can now stand firm in reaping
either your reward or your punishment. Any wavering now on your behalf
only belies your claim to having carefully considered the consequences to
yourself, others, and to our cause before you set foot on such an infirm
path.

Machiavelli was a lot of things, but naïve wasn't one of them. He clearly
understood the dangers of an individual stepping outside "normal" bounds

---

231. "Fraud" here is translated from "astuzia," lit. "to be astute," also known (somewhat
admirably) in Machiavelli's time as "sharp practice."

232. Romulus was forced to kill his own brother, Remus, in order to secure the founding
of Rome.

of conduct—how much more dangerous it was when a powerful prince did it:

> When no such normal means are available, recourse is had to abnormal means, which unquestionably have a worse effect than does the normal method. —*Discourses*

When we must employ treachery, or any other foul method against a fouler enemy, we must do so with determination to see it through to the end—and over quickly. Classic Sun Tzu: "Victory has never been associated with long delays." Common sense.

Therefore, that decidedly uncommon thinker Machiavelli tells us that when we must embark on such a harsh—but necessary—task, we must use "*the Roman Method*": Either leave your enemy be . . . or else utterly crush him! This includes killing "the sons of Brutus," any elements surviving within the enemy camp that might someday conceivably return to reap vengeance.

Never leave an enemy for your own sons to have to deal with.

Japanese history and folklore are filled with tales of wronged heroes, thought dead or disgraced, who one day return to wreak vengeance on their past persecutors: the Miyamoto clan, Ito Ogami (aka "Lone Wolf and Cub"), and the forty-seven Ronin.

Any time you hear someone spouting off about how "ruthless" Machiavelli was, the thing to remember is that Machiavelli always weighed in on the side of order. Whatever a prince had to do to establish order and maintain it was justified since, ultimately, the people would benefit.

More than a prince creating his times, a prince had to be astute enough to respond to his times.

It's always necessary—and prudent—to adjust to the times, to shapeshift to better accommodate shifting realities. The trick isn't in not compromising your principles, it's having principles that don't need to be compromised—*realistic* principles that fit the time and place.

If an army finds its conventional tactics ineffective against a terrorist force that refuses to "play by the rules," then adjustments must be made accordingly in that army's way of fighting if they are to have any hope of victory. Yet, by the same token, we must always keep in mind Nietzsche's warning that "those who contend with dragons must beware lest they become dragons themselves."

The line between praise and prison depends on whose head you bring back.

So was Machiavelli a reflection of his time, ahead of his time, or a man for all seasons?

And how does Machiavelli's philosophy ring true for us today?

> The fragmentation of the peninsular principalities rendered Italy little more than a concept in Machiavelli's fertile brain; similarly, the fractionalization of modern societies into races, classes, and sub-cultures makes consensus unlikely and order problematic . . . The modern Machiavellian—that is, each of us—is more on his or her own mettle than ever before to remain poised under the pressure of everyday affairs.
>
> —Lyman and Scott[233]

MACHIAVELLI'S PYRAMID OF POWER

Between blunder and brilliance lies dumb luck.

Machiavelli saw life as a struggle between three external factors: *Virtù* (often simplistically translated "Virtue"), *Necessità* ("Necessity"), and *Fortuna* ("Fortune").

These three bear an uncanny resemblance to our "Three Knows":

1. Know yourself: Virtù.
2. Know your environment: Necessity.
3. Know your enemy: Fortune. Of course, should you succeed in making Fortune your friend—or at least an ally of convenience— your chances of success will always be assured.

According to Machiavelli, these three forces animate the world and the degree to which they are present in our fields of endeavor determines our monumental success or our abysmal failure—and all degrees of intolerable tepidity in between.

But we have no choice but to deal with these three prime movers—to "play the game"—because they not only control the world around us, but the world *within* us as well!

Inside our psyche swirl three subjective energies, reflecting—and fueled by—the similar play of their objective, worldly counterparts. In order to

---

233. 1989:198.

MACHIAVELLI'S PYRAMID OF POWER

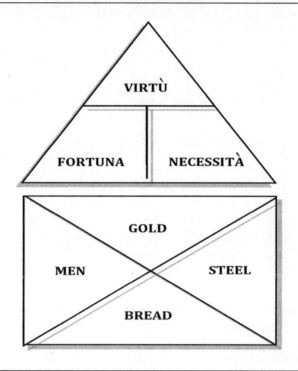

Figure 19.

balance these three within, we must consider—and learn to control—the influence and effect the world at large has on us.

Mastering this first phase, having gained Ultimate Control over our inner landscape, we can then extend our own reserve of the three outwards—to effect Ultimate Control on the world around us.

And while we all possess each of these three energies to varying degrees, some of us are dominated and motivated by virtù, other catapulted—or constrained—by necessity. Still others seem to be either consistently elevated or else constantly thwarted by the whims of fortune—whom Machiavelli likened to "a fickle whore"!

It is the degree to which each of these three prime movers is current and cultivated within us that determine our personality—how we (1) react,

(2) interact and/or (3) refuse to act with the world at large. Our personality, in turn, so often determines our fate. The masters of the mind, who have gone before, like Machiavelli, might clarify: Your personality *is* your fate!

Virtù

For all writers are of the opinion that virtue is praised and admired even in one's enemies.
—Discourses

Michael A. Ledeen, in his *Machiavelli on Modern Leadership* (1999) renders Machiavelli's "virtue" (*virtù*) as synonymous with "virtuous." This somewhat "limiting" definition works if one is trying to "inspire" modern business-men to be moral in their dealings with one another—as seems to be Ledeen's admirable intent. However, "virtù" had a much more subtle—sometimes even deadly!—meaning in Machiavelli's day.

While it's true one modern "virtue" comes from the same root, Machia-velli's "virtù" more closely reflects the personality and attitude of the warrior than that of any office yes-man. Neither should Machiavelli's virtù be confused—or watered down—to meet any modern day use of feigned "moral-ity."

Indeed, Machiavelli sees virtù and the Christian doctrines of "humility" as diametrically opposed. Usually the word "virtù" is far more morally neutral.

For Machiavelli, "life-force," "guts" (as in intestinal fortitude), "will" and "will power" (and perhaps a little of Nietzsche's "will to power"), "valor" and "enthusiasm", all contribute to "virtù," yet all are still insufficient—both individually and collectively—to act as a synonym for "virtù."

Certainly there are occasions when Machiavelli uses the word simply to mean "technique" and "efficient."[234] Indeed, the word "*vutuose*" from the same root, means "efficient."

Machiavelli's time inherited the word *virtù* from the Roman "*vir*" (man) and "*virtus*" ("what is proper for a man"). What was thought of as proper for a man during Roman times included such traits as courage, fortitude, audacity, skill, and civic spirit. Thus, virtù has been used as a synonym for all of these.

---

234. Walker, 1929.

Virtù is also akin to the early Greek *arte*, the antonym of which is *ozio*, meaning "indolence" and "corruption."

Another close cousin is the Sanskrit "*dharma*," translated as "duty," but with all the inherent personal and social responsibilities. According to the Hindus, with each station in life comes specific duties—rights and responsibilities—yet each man's *dharma* is uniquely his own. Says the Hindu *Bhagavad-Gita*: "Better to do your own dharma (duty) half-performed, than to do another's perfectly performed."

Japanese Samurai have a similar concept: "*giri*,", likewise meaning "duty," but carrying with it all the responsibilities, duties and deportment expected of a Samurai in his relationship to his family, clan, *Daimyo* and Emperor.

In Japan, a man performing his giri impeccably, flawlessly without unnecessary flourish or fault, was said to be a man of "*shibumi*"—a term reminiscent of the T'ai Kung's *Chün-tzu*, "Men of Worth."

Thus, even in the best of times, "virtù" is a hard word to define. For example, in the war cry "*Oper fortune o per virtu!*" ("By fortune or by prowess!"), virtù becomes "prowess."

From Machiavelli's time the root virtù passed down to us in our word "valiantly"—from "*virtuosamente*," and "*virtuosity*." Indeed, "virtuosity" comes perhaps closest to the mark for a modern word we understand that encompasses all the meanings inherent in virtù, as used by Machiavelli. A "virtuoso" is, after all, "one with outstanding, recognized talent in a specific field."

In *Discourses*, "virtuosity" is the word Machiavelli uses when describing Hannibal the conqueror.

Machiavelli observes that, all things being equal, when two forces comparable in strength and virtù clash, the one with the greatest *determination* carries the day. Machiavelli then adds "vigor" and "expeditiousness" to the list of synonyms for virtù:

> And when a young man is of such virtue that some noteworthy deed of his has become a matter of public knowledge, it would be most harmful if the state could not then avail itself of him, but should have to wait till he had grown old and had lost that vigour of mind and that expeditiousness of which his country at the time could have made good use.
>
> —*Discourses*

Virtù carries within it the elements of "valor," "integrity," "worth," "accumulated merit," "moral perfection," and "personal power," i.e., charisma and presence.

Virtù is ultimately *the character of a man*, the calm, composed face he maintains against the outrageous onslaught the world throws at him, the most important aspect of which is "respect." This concept carries with it an inherent valor, strength, and manliness.[235]

But virtù isn't just a "macho" thing. In fact, in *Discourses*, Machiavelli praises a certain Countess Catherine Girolamo for *her* virtù:

> Her husband murdered and her children being held hostage by conspirators, she uses her wile to first escape her captors and then, from a safe distance, taunt them—and convinces them she didn't care if her children were killed. She raised her skirt, exposing her private parts, declaring loudly how she would just produce more sons who would someday come for the heads of the conspirators!

Discussing *virtù* is the closest Machiavelli comes to being a "mystic".

> So men, to Machiavelli, are free to choose—men with virtu, at least. But they must know the price of their choices. And sometime the price of achieving one set of values is, in terms of another set of values, almost unbearable. —Walker, 1929

Necessity

> *Since, however, all human affairs are ever in a state of flux and cannot stand still, either there will be improvement or decline, and necessity will lead you to do many things which reason does not recommend.*
> *—Discourses*

In *Discourses*, Machiavelli says of the Roman Senate:

> It was never ashamed to adopt a course which was contrary to its usual procedure and to do other decisions it had made, when necessity required it.

---

235. Lyman and Scott, 1989:14.

Machiavelli goes on to attribute this to the fact that the Roman method of decision making successfully took into account (1) the measure of a man (*virtù*), (2) the whims of fortune (*Fortuna*), and (3) necessity (*necessità*), sometimes called "prudence."

Titus Livy called necessity "the last and best of all weapons."

You do what you can do . . . and then you do what you gotta do to accomplish the mission.

This is why Sun Tzu admonished us to always leave a man a way out, because a man—or a whole army for that matter—will do anything and everything to survive.

The necessità requires not only doing what is necessary, but also carries with it all the subsequent "necessity" arising out of our choice to do what we thought necessary in the first place.

> It would appear that in human affairs, as we have remarked in other discourses, there is, in addition to others, this difficulty: that when one wants to bring things to the pitch of perfection, one always finds that, bound with what is good, there is some evil which is so easily brought about in doing good that it would seem to be impossible to have one without the other. This is the case in everything that man does. And it is because of it that good is with difficulty attained unless you are so aided by fortune that fortune itself eliminates this normal and natural inconvenience. —*Discourses*

This is Machiavelli's way of telling us that "no good deed goes unpunished."

There are always hidden necessities inherent in any choice we make— the consequences of the thing—a new necessity born of the choice(s) we made to act on the previous necessity. In the East they call this "karma"— the collective weight of our past actions that so often limit our present-day decision making which, in turn, affects how wide open the future holds her arms for us:

> Necessity narrows the range of alternatives, but choices have to be made. Further, it is possible by reason applied to experience to make meaningful generalizations (at some level of abstraction) about how likely certain types of action are to

succeed in certain types of circumstance (but even then, there
is always Fortuna. —Walker, 1929

Did you catch Walker's "reason applied to experience" formula?

A man is driven to do an action (*necessità*) by two factors: circumstance
and personality.

- **The necessity of circumstances.** Things are what they are. We respond
  to our times. A few of us contribute positively to them:

  Those owing to bad judgment or to their natural inclinations
  are out of touch with the times are in most cases unfortu-
  nate in their life and unsuccessful in their undertakings. But
  it is otherwise with those who are in accord with the times.

  —*Discourses*

Circumstances change. What brings you praise today might get you
indicted tomorrow. What works in one place and time doesn't work in all
places and all times—no matter how similar your wily enemy makes it *appear*
to you. He's only trying to suck you into an ambush.

"Circumstances" also means taking into account the tools and other
resources—especially people—you have at your disposal.

For example, the "necessity" of war requires the little army to behave
differently than the big army, since a guerilla force doesn't have at its beck
and call the unlimited resources of the big—conventional—army. Failing to
factor in such circumstance dooms the "little" army.

- **The necessity of personality.** You are who you are. Sigmund Freud
  didn't really have much good to say about mankind as a whole:

  Among those instinctual wishes [of man] are those of incest,
  cannibalism and lust for killing.

  —*The Future of an Illusion,* 1927

Machiavelli likewise had a pretty dismal view of mankind overall:

  Men never do good unless necessity drives them to it; but
  when they are too free to choose and can do just as they
  please, confusion and disorder become everywhere rampant.

  —*Discourses*

And recall that even Buddha warned us against making unrealistic demands on our environment—including ourselves and others.

Here then is the one golden key to understanding your own personality—its assets and liabilities—as well as your enemy's personality:

Does your personality (and your enemy's personality) allow for making *realistic assessments* of what will be demanded of you should you embark on, or continue on, your present choice of action that—right now—you're so all-fire certain is "necessary"?

Every thing isn't for everybody. Some people just don't have what it takes to make the tough decisions—simple things . . . like *Who lives? Who dies?*

> If you wish to achieve X, you must do Y and Z. It is "necessary for a prince to know how to act like a beast as well as a man"—that is if he is to maintain position. —Walker, 1929

If you can't stand the heat, stay out of the kitchen. Don't take the job if you can't handle it. And don't start something unless you're willing to see it through to the end . . . willing to do *what* needs to be done—and WHO needs to be done—in order to finish the job.

Killing the "sons of Brutus" is both necessary—and prudent. Broken arms, left to mend, come back stronger than before. Machiavelli thus speaks of "the necessity for deceit" and elsewhere of "the ruthlessness of necessity." After the Roman fashion he preferred wars to be "short and crushing" and, in order to accomplish these two martial ideals, a commander was justified in doing whatever "necessary" to achieve swift, telling—and final—victory.

Are you a self-starter? What about your enemy? Just as objects in motion tend to stay in motion, objects at rest tend to sit on their fat arse until something important enough, or ugly enough or hot enough!—comes along to make them move.

Necessity is not only the mother of invention; it's also the best fire to light under somebody's ass!

On the positive side, such things as justice, honor, duty, *virtù*, can act to motivate a man to get up and get moving. On the flip side, any and all of The Five Warning F.L.A.G.S.[236] are also prime movers.

Other times our "bad karma" simply catches up with us enough to get

---

236. Fear, Lust, Anger, Greed, and Sympathy.

our blood pumpin' and our feets a-movin'. At such times it does no good to kick against the bricks. Instead go with the flow:

> [The Prince] has need of a mind ready to turn as the winds of
> fortune and changes in situation dictate. —Walker, 1929

If you took notes during your required Black Science Institute class of "How to Lie Successfully," then you know that lying to *yourself* is grounds for an automatic "F".

"To thine own self be true" was as valid in Hamlet's time as it is today. Therefore, if "necessity" demands you do . . . *ugly* things, never—ever!—try to convince yourself you're not doing . . . ugly things. Call the Devil by his name. Gird up your loins and do what has to be done to take care of you and yours.

Trust me to see to me and mine.

Sometimes you have to do ugly things to save the beautiful things in your life:

> [Machiavelli] seems to say, for God and man's sake, recog-
> nize that what for the moment you are doing is evil, and do
> not fall into calling it good. —Ibid.

Fortune

Chapter twenty-five of *The Prince* likens "fortune" (*Fortuna*) to a river that, once we find ourselves caught up in, we're helpless to resist or escape. Our only hope lies in our making preparations against the inevitable flooding of fortune. It seems fortune, like chance, favors the prepared mind.

And while in this instance Machiavelli chooses to compare fortune to an unpredictable, raging torrent, his most often used metaphor for describing fortune is to femininize "her," in keeping with the Roman worship of Fortune as a goddess.

The thought that fortune has turned her back on us is debilitating to many. It means the Universe no longer loves us.

For the religious minded, ill-fortune is seen as "A sign!" Someone's sinned. This is where your local cult leader or psychic steps in, offering to "cleanse" all the evil in your life, suffering that coincidentally appeared right about the time you got that big inheritance from your recently dearly-departed Uncle Guido.

* * *

Surely you've heard of "the old handkerchief switcheroo?"[237]

> During the course of your talks with your new Gypsy psychic you tell her all about your troubles and casually happen to mention the recent stress caused by your rich uncle dying—and his leaving you a wad of cash big enough to choke Linda Lovelace!
>
> Immediately the gifted psychic intuits that the money is "tainted"—cursed!—because of some shadiness on the part of Uncle. To be free of your suffering you must bring the money to her for ritual "cleansing." Fearful of ill-fortune, you produce the money (or expensive ring, etc.).
>
> While you watch, the psychic ties the money up in a hand-kerchief—or briefcase if your uncle Guido was a serious Soprano! Then the psychic tells you that—without untying the handkerchief!—you must bury the money in the ground—someplace only you know about—for three days, after which you can dig up the now "clean" money. Of course, somewhere along the way, the psychic has switched your handkerchief bundle for one filled with newspaper, but you won't discover the switcheroo for three days, plenty time for the psychic to abscond with your bundle. Poor Uncle Guido, rolling over in his watery grave!

Thus, we can undermine our enemy's confidence by convincing him kindly fortune has turned her back on him; secretly making little things to go wrong in his life, until his self-worth (not to mention his actual financial worth!) stumbles, falls, and shatters into a million pieces.

Using misfortune to attack our foes pays homage to Musashi's "cutting-at-the-edges" approach: making our enemy sweat the small stuff. Guerrilla tactics, little distractions designed to drain his resources and make him more vulnerable to our final "push."

Some people just seem to be victims of wildly vacillating capricious fortune, highs and lows, feast and famine, events they seemingly have no

---

237. Aka "The Pigeon Drop."

control over. We always seem to find such people either tripping over the proverbial pot of gold, or else not having a pot to piss in.

According to Titus Livy, *Fortune blinds the minds of men so they cannot oppose her*. Still, even she must appreciate a good challenge from time to time. That's right, "she." Whether reflecting some personal misogyny (based on first hand frustrating experiences both in the bedroom and on the battlefield!), or merely writing to the level of his audiences, there's nothing remotely politically correct about Machiavelli's penning Fortune as a "fickle whore."

As Machiavelli alerts us in *The Prince*:

> Fortune is a woman, and if you wish to master her, you must strike and beat her, and you will see that she allows herself to be more easily vanquished by the rash and the violent than those who proceed more slowly and coldly.

But, for Machiavelli, it's a love/hate relationship:

> The esoteric relations of man and woman are the paradigm of all social relations. For Machiavelli, man is in a potential relationship between the world's fortuna and his own virtù.
>
> —Lyman and Scott[238]

So if fortune is indeed a "fickle whore," what kind of lover is *she* looking for? What Casanova or Don Juan can succeed in swaying, swooning, and ultimately seducing her?

We seduce fortune by first recognizing her for what she really is.

Admit it: All too often you see a fine looking piece of tail and think, "There's no way I could even get close to that!" Thus, you defeat yourself before you've even begun.

Fortune is no different. What's that old motivational saying, "Think you can. Think you can't. Either way, you're right!"

If you presently subscribe to a philosophy or religion that tells you that you don't have any say in what goes on in your world . . . this is *not* the book for you. You've boarded the wrong ship. If, on the other hand, you're ready to captain your own vessel . . . then hoist the Jolly Roger and full speed ahead!

---

238. 1989:10.

Despite your past omissions and transgressions, that "bad karma" that keeps catching up with you, "the unexpected" happens every day, your fortune—your fate—*isn't carved in stone*:

> Machiavelli's Fortune is not simply accident, nor is it a kind of deterministic sociology, nor yet the preordained "Doom" of the northern myths or even the fatalism of the inactive cynic: it is the sudden, awful and challenging piling up of social factors and contingent political events in an unexpected way. —Walker, 1929

Most people don't do "unexpected" well. Change is hard. Sudden change harder still. And frightening. To successfully challenge fortune—or at least catch her attention and keep her entertained long enough to get her into the sack—we must adopt the attitude and the personality of what Jesuit Walker calls "the really extraordinary leader":

> Tendencies work in a particular direction, but it is always possible for fortune to change or for the really extraordinary leader to reshape things. —Ibid.

And of what exactly does this "personality" consist of that's capable of remaining erect under the intense scrutiny and potential scorn of fortune? What traits must we possess, what deeds must we do?

1. *We must possess virtù*—"super-abundant" virtù:

> Fortune is not necessity. It can, in theory and occasionally in practice, be resisted by men of super-abundant virtu. —Walker, 1929

2. *We must be heroic.* Though fortune purposely—perhaps vindictively—stacks the odds against us, we know from personal experience and from the study of history that she at least respects perseverance, expects nothing less, and accepts nothing less:

> It is prudent to accept Fortune as she comes; but it is heroic, and sometimes successful, to resist. Something of the god-like is attributed to the man who can rape Fortune. And this need not be a mere literary imagery in Machiavelli: it is a touch of Classical paganism, that man and gods are (unlike in

Christianity) of one substance, so that a man who has super-abundant skill, force, manliness and all that can possibly go to make up virtu, becomes a demi-god. —Walker, 1929

3. **We must be constant and consistent** in all things in life, but especially if we ever hope to impress Fortune enough to get her to invest in our schemes.

Success is not always a given, but consistency is a must. From consistency comes credibility. Credibility, in turn, opens the door to future opportunity. Therefore, consistency is the best investment in your future you can make.

Once others—like fortune—see you investing in yourself, they will be impressed enough to follow suit:

One sees here how great men remain the same whatever befalls. If fortune changes sometimes raising them, sometimes casting them down, they do not change, but remain ever resolute, so resolute in mind and in conduct throughout life that it is easy for anyone to see that fortune holds sway over them. Not so do weak men behave; for by good fortune they are buoyed up and intoxicated, and ascribe such success as they meet with, to a virtue they never possessed, so that they become insupportable and odious to all who have anything to do with them. This then brings about a sudden change in their lot, the prospect of which causes them to go to the other extreme and to become base and abject. —*Discourses*

4. **We must pay attention to fortune's whims**, adapting ourselves to circumstance and flux:

There are two reasons why we cannot change our ways. First, it is impossible to go against what nature inclines us to. Secondly, having got on well by adopting a certain line of conduct, it is impossible to persuade men that they can get on well by acting otherwise. It comes about that a man's fortune changes his circumstances but he does not change his ways.
—Ibid.

Don't wonder and worry whether your enemy has good fortune . . . become his *mis*-fortune!

> As the world reveals its arbitrariness, as fortune unfolds before man, he increases his commitment to its challenge, his intense interest in its investigation, his desire for action.
> —Lyman and Scott[239]

Rock, Paper, Scissors

Machiavelli invented the popular game "Rock—paper—scissors" only he called it "Virtù—Necessity—Fortune."

The interplay—struggle!—of these three make up a man's life, his personality, in turn determining his wealth, his happiness, and his ultimate fate.

Of the three, only virtù is something a man can truly control. This is because necessity is sometimes an objective reality, all too often a subjective perception. And fortune does what she will.

Its old sage advice (reincarnated as "The Serenity Prayer") that we should "Change the things we can, accept the things we can't, and hope we're smart enough to know the difference."

But whereas a man—via his virtù—must constantly respond to the demands of necessity, while at the same time, learning to bob-n-weave and occasionally recoil from the blows of fortune, Machiavelli's pyramid of power isn't a simple pecking order—with fortune as capstone, necessity filling out the middle, and man's virtù—perhaps predictably—at rock bottom.

Depending on circumstance and flux:

* Necessity sometimes conspires with fortune to tempt a man into taking short-cuts, compromising his virtù.
* Other times, a man's virtu will make him stand defiantly naked against the raging onslaught of bother, necessity and fortune.
* Occasionally such heroics so impress fortune that virtu succeeds in seducing her away from the side of necessity.

---

239. 1989:12.

Vettius Messius maintained that, when two forces (individuals or armies) equal in valor (virtù) meet, necessity—which he called "the last and best weapon of all"—carries the day.

Thus, necessity sometimes trumps virtù.

Remember virtù is *subjective*; it is in the man himself. Therefore, unlike *objective* fortune, virtù shouldn't be subject to arbitrary change or compromise.

Necessity is a wild card, since it possesses both an objective "It is what it is" aspect, along with a "It is what *we think* it is" aspect. In other words, what you think of as a "necessity," I might think of as a luxury.

Thus: Your honor and duty (virtù) should remain a constant. Necessity changes with *perceived* need. Fortune changes her mind whenever she feels like it.

Fortune (both the abstract kind and the kind you keep in your off-shore bank account!) is often dependent on necessity—i.e. correctly reading the times:

> I have often thought that the reason why men are sometimes unfortunate, sometimes fortunate, depends upon whether their behavior is in conformity with the times. For one sees that in what they do some men are impetuous, others look about them and are cautious; and that, since in both cases they go to extremes and are unable to go about things in the right way, in both cases they make mistakes. On the other hand, he is likely to make fewer mistakes and to prosper in his fortune when circumstances accord with his conduct, as I have said, and one always proceeds as the force of nature compels one. —*Discourses*

In *Discourses*, Machiavelli lamented that where men have little virtue, fortune (aka *mis*-fortune) makes a great display of her power. He repeats this same opinion in *The Prince*:

> Fortune . . . displays her power where there is no organized valor [*virtù*] to resist her, and where she knows that there are no dikes or walls to control her.

Yet we've already shown how virtù (armed with its sword and buckler of *foresight* and *determination*) can stand against fortune and, with a "super-abundant" virtue, can bend her to his will . . . or at least give her a good run for her money!

Sometimes virtù can make an alliance of convenience, teaming with necessity to defeat fortune, or so says Jesuit Walker: "This Virtu, if it studies necessity, can combat fortune."

But virtù must beware lest *seeming* necessity cause him to compromise his honor or neglect his duty. Virtù constantly must balance circumstance (necessity) and flux (fortune). As daunting as this prospect might at first appear, we have many heroic historical example of men (and women) successfully doing so.

In what could be seen as a positive note, in *Discourses*, Machiavelli proposes that necessity sometimes helps create virtù. Could he be telling us that dire consequence (i.e., hard times) sometimes brings out the best in people? Hardly sounds "Machiavellian."

MACHIAVELLI'S FOUR ELEMENTS OF SUCCESS

The nation making the best use of sword will always subjugate that having more gold and less courage.
—Voltaire

In his *The Art of War*, Machiavelli gives us his formula for success in life: "Men and steel will always find gold and bread, but bread and gold do not find men and steel."

Whereas virtù, necessity, and fortune form an *external* triangle of influence on our fate, these four elements actually form the *internal* base, completing Machiavelli's Pyramid of Power (Figure 19, p. 271).

These four elements (see Figure 20, p. 286) are both tools of the trade and the rewards of wielding same. They interact—and in some instances, contradict—virtù, necessity, and fortune.

- "Gold" (physical money as well as the promise of power) and "bread" (hunger, poverty) can make a man compromise his virtù.
- A steel blade held to your throat can make you think twice on whether or not something is really a "necessity."

MACHIAVELLI'S FOUR ELEMENTS OF SUCCESS

ELEMENT/ CONCERN	ABSTRACT	CONCRETE	APPROACH STRATEGY
BREAD ("needs")	Security and safety needs. Basics. Actual needs.	Sustenance. Enough food to eat. Shelter.	Increase his poverty before then offering him a way out of that poverty. Convince him the world is a cold place but you'll show him how to dress accordingly.
GOLD ("greeds")	Self-actualization. Feelings of self-worth. Success.	Money. Promise of power. Worldly success.	Wave opportunities in front of his face. Send him off down that yellow (gold) brick road sans courage, heart, or brains!
MEN ("seeds and feeds")	Support network.	Sources and resources. Helpers and hindrances. Soldiers and angels. Friends and family.	Attack from oblique angles, taking away his support network. If you can't put the knife in his back, put it in his tires. Either way, he turns up "late."
STEEL ("bleeds")	Strength. "Face" (i.e., standing in the community, etc.)	Material resources. Influence (i.e., power at your disposal in the form of men and material).	Make him betray his honor for a "higher" good. Get him to break the law or compromise his principles to save a friend. Trap him with a "sympathy" ploy.

"Men and steel will always find gold and bread, but bread and gold do not find men and steel."
—Machiavelli, *The Art of War*

Figure 20.

- Fortune, properly seduced—or at least distracted long enough—can literally put a gold fortune in your hands!

Few people suspect, let alone understand, the interconnectedness of these four elements—elements that bind us, elements our enemies can use to manipulate us:

Bread

Sustenance, (i.e. food to eat, shelter from the storm, Maslow's bottom-rung "Safety Needs"). At the very basis, these are your wants and needs. Some people have greater "needs" than others. Some want a little butter with their bread. Remember Hannibal's warning:

> What a man loves, what he hates, what he needs, what he desires: These are the four pillars that support his house.
>
> —Truth IV

Steel

In Machiavelli's day "steel" meant just that, sword steel, implying the attitude and (hopefully) ability to protect yourself and your loved ones. Of course, this didn't mean you actually had to go blade-to-blade with the enemy. Perhaps your "steel" was the strong prince you supported who, in turn, protected the realm.

> It is easy for force to acquire a title, but not, for a title to acquire force . . . the prince who has an abundance of men, but lacks soldiers, should bewail not the cowardice of his men, but merely his own laziness and folly. —*Discourses*

Machiavelli apparently agrees with Sun Tzu (and any commander worth his salt) that it is the general who bears responsibility if the men aren't up to snuff.

Men

A prince needs men—advisors and soldiers. But, from a broader perspective, we all need people. Man is a social animal and we need our support network, "our crew," "our posse"—those who likewise advise us and, if need be, go to war with us.

A man can use a rock when no hammer is to be found. But the man himself cannot be replaced.

"Men" in this instance refers overall to all our sources and resources; where we get our information, the information itself, and those who aid us—or hinder us—in acting on that information in a timely fashion.

Gold

This not only refers to having enough financial (and other) resources available to accomplish the task at hand but, on a more metaphorical level, "gold" refers to Maslow's "Self-actualization needs," the human *need* for feeling self-worth and accomplishment—literally, a desire to win the "gold" star. Call these "success needs."

In Machiavelli's time they lived by "The Golden Rule" . . . those who had the gold, ruled!

Have times really changed all that much?

Of course "gold" also has an abstract meaning in Machiavelli's time—as it does in our own—as the ultimate symbol of worldly success.

But "gold," in this instance, is a synonym for any kind of success the individual can achieve.

One man's trash is another man's treasure. Likewise, one man's pinnacle, his "success" in life, might merely be another man's starting point.

Times haven't really changed all that much. Gold still rules.

With enough money you can buy "bread" (sustenance) and "steel" (relative safety—at the very least a good stun-gun and a Doberman!).

Gold can also buy "men"—employees, not friends. But still the right people to get the job done.

> For war is made with steel, not with gold . . . for gold does
> not find good soldiers, but good soldiers are quite capable of
> finding gold. —*Discourses*

Machiavelli's argument of "gold not finding men and steel" refers specifically to *finding* good men versus *buying* them. For, as we all know, as Machiavelli well knew, men *can* be bought.

As previously mentioned, Rome had a standing army. Its perpetual foe, Carthage, did not, preferring instead to take the profits from their lucrative sea-trading and hire mercenaries when needed. The bill came due when, immediately following the first Punic War, left unpaid, Carthage's mercenary army revolted, besieging and almost overtaking the city-state. Like his father before him, Hannibal warned the leaders of Carthage against this practice since mercenaries were (are) notoriously unreliable, especially when the gold runs out.

Later, it was Hannibal's forced reliance on mercenary troops that ultimately doomed his invasion of Italy.

Good money can buy good help. But it can never buy you loyalty. In other words, gold can't buy *virtù* . . . but it has a long history of compromising it.

It's no secret men will risk their lives for gold, and for the prestige and power that gold can buy. But once that gold is in their pocket, their attention all too often wanes. In addition, there comes a point where the scale tips in favor of pure survival—What good is gold if you can't stay alive long enough to enjoy it?

As you can see, beyond their obvious—concrete—physical meanings, each of Machiavelli's four elements has abstract psychological/sociological meanings and applications. In addition, we can spot distinct *personality types* arising out of these four elements.

To differing degrees all four of these elements—"concerns" we'll call them—influence our lives. We all need sustenance, food, and shelter. We all want to feel safe—and having "men" and "steel" at our disposal usually helps.

Beyond this, we all have varying degrees of need for "success" ("gold")—whether that "success" is correctly guessing fantasy football winners or conquering a small nation nobody was really using at the time.

You may find yourself comparing these four elements to Abraham Maslow's "Hierarchy of Needs" pyramid; with sustenance and safety needs closer to the base, self-actualization (i.e., success needs) at the apex (see Figure 2 above, p. 17).

However, it's reasonable that one person might have more concern or anxiety concerning one of these elements than another—for example, it's too hard to plan world conquest (a "gold" success need) on an empty stomach (a "bread" sustenance need). Likewise, a success need like attending college might have to play second fiddle to lack of money (in this case, lack of money qualifies as a "bread" sustenance need), and/or "steel" safety needs (e.g. living in a bad neighborhood where punks keep trying to stick you with real steel!).

Once we discover which of these four elements most influences our enemy, which concern dominates his thoughts, our strategy will then simply be either (1) preventing him from achieving his need, or else (2) using his "need" to tempt him into a line of thought and action detrimental to his health—bodywise, financialwise, and otherwise.

> Preparing for war makes you tough, and reminds you of the qualities necessary for victory: cold, prudent judgment, alertness to changing conditions, bravery under fire, courage when challenged, solidarity with your comrades-at-arms, and total commitment to mission. —Michael A. Ledeen[240]

Finally, Machiavelli has something in common with the Marquis de Sade[241]—and believe it or not, it has nothing to do with whips and stiletto heels. These two astute observers of the human condition not only share the distinction of having had their philosophies so misunderstood and so misapplied by so many, they both have also inadvertently lent their names to *psychological disorders*.

"Sadism" we are of course familiar with—some, it seems more so than others . . . But did you know there is a disorder—or, at the very least, a distinctive character trait—known as "Machiavellianism"?

"Machiavellianism" is defined—and diagnosed—as "an interpersonal style that embodies a cool, calculating manipulativeness."[242] Though they usually can find a cerebral solution to most problems, those "suffering" from Machiavellianism are not above resorting to force to achieve what they consider a worthwhile goal.

Guilty as charged, Machiavelli clearly accepted that "an economy of violence" was sometimes necessary to accomplish one's goals (1) speedily and (2) with the *least* amount of disturbance and bloodshed. Thus, in *The Prince*

---

240. Ibid. 91
241. Another of Lyman and Scott's *A Sociology of the Absurd* (1989) "pioneers."
242. Kelly G. Shaver & Roger M. Trarpy. *Psychology*. 1993:547.

Machiavelli advises we must play the fox—a schemer—as well as the lion—using force when necessary.

Psychologists have even developed a "Machiavellianism scale"[243] that can be used to determine just how infected you might be with the "Niccolo Virus" of ruthlessness:

> Research using this questionnaire shows that people who are high in Machiavellianism ("high Machs") are cool, cerebral individuals who view interactions as opportunities to manipulate others. They initiate and control the structure of the interaction, concentrate on the rules of the game rather than the people involved, and resist social pressure. From the standpoint of high Mach individuals, the most favorable situation involves face-to-face interaction in which there is latitude for improvisation; under these conditions they can create irrelevant emotions in the other participants. When all others are responding emotionally, the high Mach has the greatest opportunity to manipulate them. Thus, interpersonal styles can enhance social influence. —Shaver and Tarpy[244]

So if you think you might be suffering from Machiavellianism, if this sounds like you, you can either (1) contact a shrink immediately or, (2), thank your lucky stars you're destined to be a *success* in life!

We'll leave Niccolo to his own benediction:

> Although owing to the envy inherent in man's nature it has always been no less dangerous to discover new ways and methods than to set off in search of new seas and unknown lands because most men are much more ready to belittle than praise another's actions, none the less, impelled by the natural desire I have always had to labour, regardless of anything, on that which I believe to be for the common benefit of all, I have decided to enter upon a new way, as yet untrodden by anyone else. And, even if it entails a tiresome and difficult

---

243. See Christie and Geis, *Studies in Machiavelliansm*, 1970.
244. Ibid. 548

task, it may yet reward me in that there are those who will look kindly on the purpose of these my labours. And if my poor ability, my limited experience of current affairs, my feeble knowledge of antiquity, should render my efforts imperfect and of little worth, they may none the less point the way for another of greater ability, capacity for analysis, and judgment, who will achieve my ambition; which, if it does not earn me praise, should not earn me reproaches.

—*Discourses*, preface

16.

Rogers' Nineteen Rules of War

WE HEAR A LOT about Eastern masters like Sun Tzu, Cao Cao, and Musashi, and deservedly so. But the West has also produced its share of strategic and tactical geniuses—Hannibal, Scipio, Napoleon, Clausewitz, T.E. Lawrence, Rommel and Patton, and H. Norman Schwarzkopf.

During "The Seven Years War" (also known around these parts as "The French and Indian War"), circa 1769, Major Robert Rogers commanded a 600-man force of American Colonial Irregulars fighting for the British. But in less than a decade those same colonists—those that survived—would be rebelling against the same "lobsterbacks" they had previously broke bread—and bone—with. Even more ironic, when fighting for their freedom from Mother England, they'd use the same "marching orders" drawn up by Major Rogers ten years earlier.

At first glance "Rogers' Nineteen Rules of War" may seem simplistic—just common sense. What we have to remember is that what we today might take as "common sense" problem solving wasn't all that common back in Rogers' day.

The French had Native American (Indian) allies on their side—*guerilla* fighters all. And while a phalanx of British regulars was a fearsome thing to have to face across an open field, Iroquois and Mohawk weren't about to be so stupid.

Where British commanders remained resistant to change, Rogers recognized the need to adapt to this new type of warfare, adopting the Indian's way of moving and fighting, in effect creating America's first "special forces" unit.

In traditional martial arts, students are encouraged to kick to the opponent's head during practice—although seldom do they actually do so in a real fight. The idea behind mastering kicks to the head being that, if you can skillfully deliver a solid—knockout!—kick to head level, anything below that level "belongs to you." In the same way, if these "old school," "ancient," and antediluvian tactics and techniques have proven themselves time and again for other fighters on a hundred unforgiving battlefields, might not those same tactics and techniques also come through for us?

Just as any battle plan must be adapted to differing terrain—we fight different in the desert than we do in the snow—so too Rogers' Rules—and other teachings in the same vein—must be adapted to fit our current needs. Thus don't allow yourself to be confused by any insignificant *particulars* such as the fact Rogers carried a musket and a tomahawk while you carry a cell phone and a Palm Pilot.

Once you master the *principles* inherent in Rogers' Rules, your enemies will learn to fear you just the same as they did Rogers' Rangers!

However, while we today may have *appreciation* for Rogers' adaptability, we may still run into that same old hurdle of finding practical *application* for his rules. You say you just can't seem to find any application for this kind of "outdated" thinking in today's world? That's the test, isn't it: To seek out those strategies, tactics, and techniques that will better help us keep our head *above* water while ruthlessly holding our enemy's head *under* water until we stop seeing bubbles!

That's the test. There's always a test. Pass, and prosper. Fail, and be forgotten . . . with only your discarded, marrow-sucked bones left over after your enemy's feast!

Adapt or die. Major Robert Rogers adapted.

According to author and former Navy SEAL Richard Marchinko, the nineteen rules laid down by Rogers in 1759 still form "the tactical backbone" of all Spec War[245] operations.[246]

In nearly every one of his popular *Rogue Warrior* series of books, Marchinko, no stranger to combat himself, gives Major Rogers his due:

---

245. *SPEC*ial unconventional *WAR*fare.
246. Richard Marchinko, with John Wiseman, *Rogue Warrior: Task Force Blue* (1996), 110.

Major Robert Rogers was the first American Spec Warrior. He led a band of buckskin-clad, flintlock-and-hatchet-carrying commandos during what's come to be known as the French and Indian War, and he tore the French and Indians some new assholes with his unconventional tactics.[247]

Rogers' Rules

1. Don't forget nothing.

Musashi admonished us to "Pay attention even to trifles" and that sounds a lot like "Don't forget nothing." All too often it's the little thing we miss, that we don't take notice of or keep track of, that spell our doom.

The media loves stories of *"America's Dumbest Criminals"*: the way criminals forget that their name and address are on the back of that "stick-up" note, forget to put gas in the getaway car, stupid.

It's a good thing we learned to use our senses fully in the last section, because that's exactly what we need now.

Memory is king. 99.9 percent of who we are is based on our memories. The good news is memory is trainable, you improve your memory—which is basically just paying closer attention and giving the brain enough time to fully "process" incoming information. The bad news is, as we've already learned, memory can all too easily be manipulated.

On a purely physical level, "Don't forget nothing" means checking your equipment twice, and then one more time, just to be sure. It means checking the fine print on a contract, kicking the tires, and memorizing your ATM pin-number instead of writing it on the back of your credit card.

On a more cerebral level, "Don't forget nothing" is another way of telling us that "Forgive and forget" is highly overrated . . . costly, and even potentially deadly, especially when it comes to giving our enemy a "second chance" to screw us over. Oh, but doesn't everyone deserve a second chance? No.

2. Have your musket clean as a whistle, hatchet scoured, sixty rounds of powder and ball, and be ready to march at a minute's warning.

Rogers' second rule isn't just telling us to check and then double-check our equipment, our plans, and our mind-set before the fecal matter collides with the oscillating rotor. "Have your musket clean as a whistle" is another

---

247. Ibid. (2000), 167 (fn. 55).

way of telling us to have our house in order—whether being prepared for an impromptu IRS audit, or the next 9/11.

The time for training is not when the wolves are already at the door. You have to prepare beforehand. More training now, less *paining* later.

This same attitude served the rebelling colonists well when it came time to tear down the Union Jack and raise the Stars and Stripes. They didn't call them "Minute Men" for nothing.

There's also the fact that you can tell a lot about a man by how well he takes care of his tools—metaphorically, as well as literally. You can also tell a lot about a man by how well he takes care of his enemies too!

3. When you're on the march, act the way you would if you are sneaking up on a deer. See the enemy first.

One of Musashi's maxims tells us "Make your everyday stance your combat stance, and your combat stance your everyday stance." In this same way, here Rogers compares moving on a march to the way one would sneak up on a deer.

All Rogers' men were veteran woodsmen to begin with, men who hunted for game out of necessity, men well acquainted with the ways of the wild wood. Therefore instead of teaching his Rangers a new way of moving through the woods, Rogers wisely built upon knowledge and experience he knew each man already possessed.

In any realistic martial art, take for instance *Zendokan-ryu Taijutsu*, rather than teach beginning students complex movements alien to their natural movements, knowledgeable instructors take into account the student's body type (e.g., long-legged students have an advantage kicking, etc.), in order to teach their students realistic combat skills built on natural movements of the body.

For example, faced with an overhead clubbing attack, a person's *natural instinct* is to cower lower (instinctively making themselves a smaller target). Simultaneously they throw both arms up to protect themselves from the descending club. Rather than teaching a student a complicated, hard to learn, hard to remember, stepping-blocking-counterstrike, Kan-Ryu stylists build on those natural reactions already "hard-wired" into the student. After correct instruction, that instinctive cowering is transformed into a spring-loaded "Tiger's Squat" (from which the defender can shift into any attacking or defending position), while the instinctive raising of the arms is turned into an overhead "Whipping Branch" that both blocks and strikes into the arm holding the club. This is paired with a simultaneous cross-body palm-strike from the other rising hand.

You couldn't ask for a better example of "adapting," taking something that already exists (in this case, a natural reaction) and turning it to your advantage.[248]

Thus the same way we stalk a deer, we can use to stalk a man.

To extrapolate this further, the skills we learn in the woods can easily help us in the "wilds" of the city.[249]

We are reminded yet again of Musashi's advice to *"Learn the ways of all professions"* since you never know what particular skill might come in handy. In other words, what piece of trivial knowledge do you possess that your enemy doesn't know you possess—that one piece of information he couldn't possibly have dug up, and therefore couldn't possibly have factored into his plans for moving against you.

The *"see the enemy first"* part of Rogers' third rule is built on the first part of the rule, "sneaking up on a deer."

It'll come as no surprise to you that the more your plans come as a surprise to your enemy, the better your chances of success. Keeping your secrets well-hidden comes from (a) limiting access to those secrets and (b) by spreading disinformation in places you're sure the enemy will find it.

Philosophically speaking, "See the enemy first" can also be seen as a serious suggestion to really "see" the enemy, that is, accurately assess his threat level, spy out his plans before he does the same to you. First pig to the trough gets his snout the wettest.

4. Tell the truth about what you see and what you do. There is an army depending on us for correct information. You can lie all you please when you tell other folks about the rangers, but don't never lie to a ranger or officer.

Nothing is more important for a general planning a campaign than to obtain good intelligence.

As already established, "intelligence" comes in two varieties: *innate intelligence* we're born with (and hopefully develop further as we grow), and

---

248. For a complete training course in such realistic martial arts see: *Lost Fighting Arts of Vietnam* by Dr. Haha Lung and Christopher B. Prowant (Citadel, 2006).

249. Dirk Skinner, *Street Ninja: Ancient Secrets for Surviving Today's Mean Streets* (Barricade Books 1995).

gathered intelligence—information we glean from our surroundings, environment, and the incessant cackling of others.

An endless stream of facts isn't enough; what we need is accurate and timely information.

In dire need of information about the land of Canaan which he was preparing to take from the Canaanites (i.e., Phoenicians), Moses sent twelve spies into the land to gather intelligence on such things as whether or not the people lived in easily over-run camps or in impossible-to-breech strongholds; whether the land was rich or poor; whether there were forests with fruit trees—all the stuff a wily commander needs to plan a successful conquest. However, when his twelve spies returned, they gave vastly differing assessments.

While agreeing that the land "flows with milk and honey," ten of Moses' spies warned him that the Canaanites were too united and too strong for the Israelites to conquer, even going so far as to claim the people in Canaan were giants, so huge that the Israelites spies "were like grasshoppers in their sight."[250] But the two remaining spies, Caleb and Joshua son of Nun, believed the Israelites had a chance of overcoming the Canaanites and advised Moses to invade immediately.

Due in part from the lack of solid intelligence consensus, Moses decided to take the cautious, roundabout route into the "Holy Land" . . . forty years worth.

And, while accurate intelligence is vital to the commander in the field, did you notice that Rogers tells his men it's all right to lie (i.e., brag) when talking to others about the Rangers? (1) This is good PR, good propaganda. (2) It's an excellent recruiting tool. (3) If any French or Indian spy happened to overhear some of this bragging, they would only be taking *distorted* intelligence (i.e. "misinformation") back to their commander.

A report illustrating the value of spreading disinformation comes to us from China, yet another exploit of master strategist Cao Cao:

> Cao Cao found himself campaigning against a wily foe, a brilliant young general, albeit one working for a petty king. Time and again this wunderkind had successfully countered Cao Cao *cheng* (conventional) maneuvers with cheng maneuvers of his own. Clearly some sort of *ch'i* (unconventional) strategy

---

250. Numbers 13:33.

would be necessary to teach this youngster to respect his elder . . .

During a respite in the campaign, seemingly for no apparent reason, Cao Cao suddenly decided to pardon a condemned soldier who had been found guilty of stealing from a local farmer—a violation of one of Cao Cao's strictest rules.

Calling the soldier into the command tent, Cao Cao handed him a small ball of wax. "If you were indeed telling the truth about not being a thief, you should have no trouble swallowing this ball of wax. If you're lying, it will surely stick in your throat." With a smile of triumph (and relief) the man quickly gobbled down the small ball of wax. On the spot, Cao Cao pardoned him.

However, Cao Cao explained to the man that, it would not be good if the rest of his soldiers thought their general was getting soft. Therefore, Cao Cao told the pardoned man he must secretly leave camp and, to accomplish this, Cao Cao had the man disguise himself as a Buddhist monk. The thief—now dressed as a monk—was sent on his way . . . in the direction of the enemy pickets.

Predictably, in short order the fake monk was captured. Presumed to be a spy, he was immediately taken before the enemy king.

Interrogated, the "monk" quickly told his improbable tale about the "truth test" with the ball of wax, how Cao Cao had then pardoned him, dressing him as a monk, before sending him on his way.

Already convinced the "monk" was a spy, upon hearing about the mysterious ball of wax, the king drew his sword and immediately gutted the monk up the middle (!), spilling the thief's entrails, along with the ball of wax.

Inside the ball of wax the king found a letter from Cao Cao to the king's brilliant young general. The letter not only outlined Cao Cao's plan of attack, but also praised the king's general for having decided to betray his king at Cao Cao's signal. Once the king was dead, Cao Cao and the young general would split the kingdom between them.

Enraged, the king commanded the immediate execution of the—innocent!—young general, thus, proving that sometimes "The pen really is mightier than the sword." With a single stroke, Cao Cao not only rid himself of a thief, but also proved himself a master thief by stealing away the enemy king's best general!

This particular *Cao Cao* ploy is a perfect example of using an "expendable agent," one who is given false information in the certainty that when captured, one way or another, he'll give up that information to the enemy.

In addition to "expendable" agents, Sun Tzu listed four other types of agents: "Native" agents (those guides and spies recruited from within an enemy's own territory), "Inside" (disaffected enemy officers and officials), "Double" agents (captured or compromised enemy operatives who are "turned"), and "Living" spies—especially when they possess true intelligence about our operations that, should it—they—fall into enemy hands, could prove disastrous to our cause.[251]

5. *Don't never take a chance you don't have to.*

Bravado endangers not only yourself, but also your comrades.

Before committing ourselves to any potentially costly undertaking, we have to consider what affect failure—or even success—will have, not only on ourselves, but our family, friends, and business partners as well.

Billionaire J. Paul Getty always took into consideration what the affect of any business deal, merger, etc. might have, not just on his personal finances, but also on the people who worked for him—would workers lose their jobs, would their families have to go hungry?[252]

If you recall, from both *Black Science* (2001) and *Mind Manipulation* (2002), ploys such as "Six Degrees of Separation" and Musashi's "Cutting-at-the-Edges" rely on attacking an enemy (who can easily defend himself against a head-on attack) through those near and dear to him, in effect, undermining his support network.

Likewise, we must guard ourselves and our loved ones against this oblique angle of attack.

No man stands alone. Each of our actions affects others. Every foolish chance you take (those who are foolish enough to love you) takes it with you.

---

251. Sun Tzu's *Ping-Fa*, chapter XIII.
252. See "Getty's Five" in *Mind Control*, 2006.

6. When we're on the march we march single file, far enough apart so one shot can't go through two men.

Ever heard of "Don't put all your eggs in one basket"? Same thing.

Large ships and submarines are "compartmentalized." This means they have doors and bulkheads that can quickly be slammed shut, sealing off a flooding compartment section in order to keep the entire ship from sinking. Speaking of the ship going down: Don't take others down with you.

Spread out your investments, diversify your interests. Hedge your bets.

This same "compartmentalizing" strategy should be used with any complicated, multi-faceted operation. We should be organized in such a way that should one part of our operation suffer a loss or setback, we can immediately shore up that section, reinforcing it until it can stand on its own again.

The same holds true when fielding teams of operatives—or running any group for that matter.

It's the old adage: "The chain's only as strong as its weakest link."

In any team operation, you need to have redundancies—with each person's area of expertise overlapping another's. This is sometimes accomplished by having your team members "apprentice" under one another during the training phase in order for each to pick up the basic skill(s) of their fellows, in case called upon in an emergency to stand-in for a wounded or missing comrade.

This is also a good way for a squad leader to judge how well his team will work together before taking them out onto the killing field.

We must also use this attitude when doing our realistic self-assessment—Sun Tzu's "Know yourself." We should take a true accounting of our strengths and weaknesses—before our enemy does! Having discovered any "weak areas," we then put effort into bolstering those areas and/or we compensate for our weaknesses by magnifying our strengths. Of course, we take the exact opposite approach when undermining our enemy—pruning down any strengths he might have, already in his garden, while planting as many sinister seedlings of ours as possible.

7. If we strike swamps, or soft ground, we spread out abreast, so it's hard to track us.

Before launching your attack, "leak" false information about your attack plans (i.e. leave confusing "footprints"), and order diversionary attacks designed to confuse, distract, and draw off enemy defenders from your true objective. What is it Sun Tzu says? "Not knowing where I truly intend to attack, having to prepare for me everywhere, my enemy is strong nowhere!" This is especially important in "soft ground," i.e., areas and operations that can all too easily come under outsider scrutiny.

It's the old politician's ploy: Meet the press at the front door with jokes and a big smile, distracting them with double-talk, while the hooker skips out the back door.

Taken literally, this rule tells us a man being tracked through the woods—across "soft ground"—has two chances to throw his pursuers off:

> Leave no tracks, or
> Leave too many tracks, so many that searchers will be dissuaded—
> or at least slowed down—trying to figure out which direction
> you actually ran and/or how many of you there are.

This same strategy applies for getting away with a crime. For police the only thing worse than having no suspect, is having too many suspects.

While actively seeking information on the enemy, we must always be sure to jealously guard our own intel, and not leave "footprints" of our intentions and actions in "soft ground."

Figuratively, "soft ground" refers to those little things, those lapses in attention span, that give us away. (Isn't that why there's presently about a gazillion shows on TV called "CSI-this or that"?)

Remember Cousin Vinny's brilliant idea to do a little creative hydroponic gardening in his basement? He covered all his tracks, leaving no footprints for the police to follow . . . so how'd John Law know where to come looking for his magic garden? Seems somebody down at the electric company noticed 'cause he had suddenly started using up a lot more electricity than usual and alerted the local tin-stars. You know, all that extra electricity for all those high-powered lamps Vinny needed to keep his little plants happy.

Remember the old Zen ideal: "Seek passage without traces."

8. When we march, we keep moving till dark, so as to give the enemy the least possible chance at us.

It's harder to hit a moving target.

Guard the development of your mission—whether personal, financial, or military in nature—until ready to deploy, then:

In knowing, strike. In striking, strike well. In striking well, accomplish all things!

Once on the move, don't hesitate, don't look back. Always follow the form of your drawn-up plan, while at the same time, reserving for yourself (as leader) the right to revise and improvise in order to accommodate shifting circumstance and flux.

Form + speed = power. Power that has gained momentum can gain the world.

9. When we camp, half the party stays awake while the other half sleeps.

One sentry can be silently removed. It's twice as hard to take out two sentries.

Develop redundant systems of operation and command. The "B" in "Plan B" stands for "back-up," and a good back-up plan can be the one thing that finally makes your enemy back up.

Always keep a spare key, while trying to spy out where your enemy hides his.

Downtime is dangerous time. Men grow lax in between bloodletting—figuratively and literally. There's a big difference between the bush and the bivouac. Some people are just not cut out to handle waiting. Other personality types can be too patient. Too much patience equals hesitation and procrastination.

I think we already know Dr. Lung's opinion on "hesitation."[253]

Always keep yourself and your soldiers busy in between operations, and between phases of an operation. Don't break momentum.

If you've already done everything you can possibly do to succeed in your mission . . . check your stats again, check your equipment again. Stay focused on the job at hand.

As much as possible, eliminate *waiting* from your life. There's a reason they call it DOWNtime.

There's this politically incorrect term older African-Americans once used among themselves, "CPT," or "Colored People Time." A disenfranchised majority, one way slaves and later freed Blacks maintained a modicum of control over their own lives was to do things "in their own good time," deliberately taking twice as long to do a task, deliberately making "Whitey" wait. The current slang for this is *slow-walkin'*—a treasured tradition now being maintained by every DMV clerk on the planet.

As for better managing your own time: Begin by noticing how much time you waste every day—stuck in traffic, waiting in the checkout line,

---

253. Hesitation = death.

waiting for your boss or the doctor to "find time" to see you. Spend that time constructively. Read a book. When the boss finally comes out, let him "catch you" studying the latest operations manual instead of just sitting there twiddling your thumbs.

When trapped in that slow-walkin' check-out line at the supermarket 'cause the checkout broad's trying to show you who's boss), don't give in to boredom and start reading those tabloid headlines (that's why they put them in the checkout isle!). Instead, take the time to practice your senses training: Notice the people around you. Is that trembling, sniffling, anorexic dude in line in front of you so bored too he's playing "pocket pool" . . . or is that a gun in his pocket he's nervously fingering!

Increase your own efficient use of time while slow-walkin' your enemy as much as possible.

10. If we take prisoners, keep 'em separate till we have had time to examine them, so they can't cook up a story between them.

Question and double-check all enemy intel, even when it comes from trusted sources. Your source may be reliable but his information may not be—anyone can be misleading. Disinformation is a two-way street.

In the same vein, don't offhandedly discard information that comes from sources outside your normal circle. The one bringing you the information might have an axe to grind against your enemy. "The enemy of my enemy is my friend"—sound vaguely familiar?

In fact, we should seek out those who either (a) hate our enemy for some real or imagined slight, and/or (b) have something to gain by his fall.

Sometimes we can nurture already gestating hate, or plant such hate ourselves, turning one of our enemy's allies against him.

Major Rogers would have made a great cop since he practically invented "Good Cop/Bad Cop," the time honored technique of driving a wedge between two suspects, between two friends, or between lovers (paging *Othello!*).

When forced to decide between conflicting stories, choose the one told by the man *with the most to lose*, since his fear of loss will help keep him honest. The man who has *the most to gain* will exaggerate his case, tell almost any lie, in order to attain his goal.

Remember the tale of King Solomon deciding the case of the two women who were both claiming the same baby? Which one had the most to lose? *Voilà!*

11. Don't ever march home the same way. Take a different route so you won't be ambushed.

Taken literally, this rule cautions us against falling into a routine—a routine an observant enemy can spy out and use to his advantage. Remember: There is no greater blessing than a predictable enemy.

Ninja burglars are taught you never come out of a broken-into building the same way you went in.[254]

Philosophically speaking, this rule of "not marching home the same way" is telling us to take the lessons we've learned the hard way "out in the field" and internalize them, for use in our everyday life. In other words, our actions lead to new life experiences. Those life experiences—provided they don't become death experiences!—in turn lead us to reevaluate our previous actions, while urging us towards new—perhaps better thought-out—actions.

Nietzsche sneered that a person's "philosophy" isn't worth a plug nickel unless that philosophy causes that person to act. In fact, it has oft been observed that "Before Nietzsche philosophy was just philosophy. After Nietzsche, philosophy became *dangerous!*"

Your philosophy of life isn't written in a book, it's written in your footsteps.

12. No matter whether we travel in big parties or little ones, each party has to keep a scout twenty yards ahead, twenty yards on each flank and twenty yards in the rear, so the main body can't be surprised and wiped out.

We operate on a need to know basis. This is part of what Cao Cao meant when he said his "soldiers could share in his victories, but they could never know the travail that went into their general's crafting of those victories."

In any team operation, each member must do his part. You—as leader—always pick your team members—assigning them individual and collective duties—with this in mind. It's not necessary—nor is it prudent—for all team members to know everything about the operation. Thus "need to know." That way, if captured or otherwise compromised, one team member cannot betray the whole of our operation to the enemy.

This is why guerrilla and terrorist organizations "compartmentalize" by organizing themselves into "cells," small semi-autonomous groups. Should one cell be compromised (discovered, infiltrated, or captured), individual members will only have detailed knowledge of their cell and cannot betray the larger organization.

---

254. *Knights of Darkness* (Citadel, 2004).

Each link in our chain must be tempered, each cog in our mission machine well-greased.

The "center" must hold, no matter the beating we take on our flanks. Eyes ever on the prize, focus full-speed ahead.

President Lyndon Johnson once said:

> When you find yourself up to your ass in alligators, don't
> forget that your job is to drain the swamp!

In Medieval Europe, when disputes broke out between two neighbors there was always a conciliatory third voice reminding the warring factions to "Keep the church in the middle of the village"; a reminder how most medieval villages were built up around their spiritual center and that, no matter what disputes or difficulties arose, so long as the "center" remained sacrosanct, the village would survive.

13. Every night you'll be told where to meet if surrounded by a superior force.

This is more "need to know." It also harkens back to us always having a "Plan B" . . . and maybe even a "Plan C" ("C" for "You can never be too *Careful!*").

Notice Rogers says "every night you'll be told"? Again, a good commander needs to control information flow. First the obvious, so vital information doesn't fall into enemy hands and, second, because nothing undermines the confidence of your men as do faulty rumors, grievous gossip, and incessant naysaying.

This is one of the reasons we beam propaganda into our enemy camp—and into his mind! And why we infiltrate agents provocateur into his territory to spread doubt and despair and to encourage defection and desertion.

It's important your men know where to "regroup" in case of emergency. Should unforeseen circumstance rear its ugly head, you don't want your team wandering about, wondering what to do.

You can't risk a breakdown in the chain of command as panicking—or even well wishing—team members run around like chickens with their heads cut off trying to "fix" what might not truly be "broken." It could all just be a piece of disinformation cake your team's just bitten into.

This is the type of confusion and chaos we send our enemy for his birthday, not the present we want to receive from him.

Remember Secretary of State Alexander Haig's reaction when word reached the White House that President Reagan had been shot? What's that? You don't remember Alexander Haig . . . exactly!

14. Don't sit down to eat without posting sentries.

Just because the battle seems to be won, don't relax too soon. Likewise, the closer to the end of the battle we get, the more confident we are of successfully "closing the deal," the nearer we get to your front door, the *more* we need to be alert.

In his *A Book of Five Rings*, Musashi gives us ploys for causing our opponent to relax prematurely, to get him to literally and figuratively drop his guard, techniques collectively known as "Passing it on." The Sword Saint even observes that by faking a yawn, we can induce our enemy to yawn as well—striking suddenly as he does!

15. Don't sleep beyond dawn. Dawn's when the French and Indians attack. [255]

Know yourself. Know your enemy. Test yourself before your enemy does.

16. Don't cross a river by a regular ford.

Robert Frost penned, "I took the road less traveled and that has made all the difference . . ." It sure did, because our enemy is sure enough waiting down that "road *more* traveled," to ambush us!

We're all creatures of habit—that is, until those habits get us killed. Even the mangiest of lions knows to lie in wait for the naïve young deer to dip his head at the watering hole. They wait along the path leading to, and away from, the life-sustaining water that deer must, sooner or later, have. Even the densest of crocodiles knows that if he waits patiently, buried in the mud and silt at the waterline, sooner or later his prey will come to him.

Metaphorically, Rogers' sixteenth rule invites us to be more innovative, to be our own man, to stop following the herd—literally, stop following them to that same damned watering hole!

17. If someone's trailing you, make a circle, come back into your own tracks and ambush the folks that aim to ambush you.

As a safeguard against computer hackers, modern databases install a "backfire byte" that, in effect, follows the hacker home. In the same vein, when an intelligence agency realizes it's been compromised, that someone

---

255. Hannibal's Truth VI reads in part: "I give thanks for my enemy. Were it not for my enemy I would sleep past dawn, I would eat too much, I would become loud and over-proud, and both my arm and eye would grow lax."

within the agency is deliberately (or sometimes inadvertently) leaking information to the other side, several slightly altered versions of sensitive information, for example a report, will be circulated through the various departments. That way, when one of the reports shows up in enemy hands, agency trackers can tell by specific markers encoded into the writing, paragraphing, or syntax exactly what department is responsible for the leak.

On a simpler level, this works when you don't know who's spreading rumors about you when you tell different people slightly differing stories and then sit back, waiting to see which version of the story "surfaces." Other times, you can use this ploy by deliberately leaving "bread crumbs" for your enemy to "follow," false bits of information you allow him to "discover" on his own, disinformation that will act as a diversion, leading him off in the wrong direction.

18. Don't stand up when the enemy's coming against you. Kneel down, lie down, hide behind a tree.

Don't get cocky. Bravado can prove costly. Overestimating yourself and underestimating your foe are the twin blades on the executioner's axe that's already aimed at your neck!

Never let the cat outta the bag too soon. Don't expose yourself or your plan prematurely no matter how certainly you *think* you smell victory. Keep your own counsel. And remember to operate on a "Need to Know" basis—Rules twelve and thirteen.

19. Let the enemy come till he's almost close enough for you to touch him. Then let him have it and jump out and finish him up with your hatchet.

At first glance, this final rule sounds a little harsh: Basically, shoot your enemy down and then jump out and finish him off with a hatchet to the head just to make sure he stays down.

You have to remember that Major Rogers' war took place long before that pesky Geneva Convention.

First of all, Rogers' kind of warfare required that his Rangers move fast. There was no time to take prisoners, nor was there anywhere to keep them if you did. In other words, there was no way to take care of them . . . except to "take care of them."

In Japan, there's a thousand Samurai tales about "the one that got away"—the grievously wronged hero, his family slaughtered, himself left for dead . . . only to return one day, stronger than before, to harvest his vengeance from the fields of all who dared raise a sword against him and his.

There's Yoshitsune Miyamoto who, after his clan was nearly annihilated by a rival Samurai clan, is saved and trained by Tengu (Ninja) and returns years later to lead his clan to victory over his enemies.

And then there's Ito Ogami, "The Lone Wolf" who, after his family is slaughtered, is forced to go on the run, taking his infant son "the Cub" in tow. After years of harrowing ordeals and hairbreadth escapes, both father and now-grown son return to reap their revenge.

The Samurai have a saying, "Nine times down, ten times up!" testifying to their determination to keep trying, no matter how bad things get.

Faced with such an intractable foe, it's usually a good idea to:

- **Kill him**
- **Kill anything that looks like him**
- **Kill anything that might grow up to look like him!**[256]

Recall that the Romans called such men "*the sons of Brutus*," the sons (and sometimes daughters) of a wronged man—blood relations you imprudently leave alive who will one day rise up to seek revenge for what you did to their kin.

The survivors of the fall of Troy went on to found Rome. How might history have differed had the Greeks been more efficiently ruthless in their conquest?

From the Old Testament: God Almighty, through his human mouthpiece the prophet Samuel, ordered King Saul of Israel to kill everything that moved in the city of Amalek:

> Now go and attack Amalek, and utterly destroy all that they have, and do not spare them. But kill both man and woman, infant and nursing child, ox and sheep, camel and donkey. —I Samuel 15:3

But Saul, for whatever reason, spares the life of Agag, King of Amalek. Upon finding this out, Samuel not only castigates Saul for not following through, but takes up a sword himself and hacks Agag to pieces!

Who are we to question the obviously effective methods of God

---

256. Of course, if anyone handing out international indictments for "war crimes" should ever ask, Dr. Lung is only speaking "metaphorically" . . .

Almighty and His prophets? Evidently God and Samuel knew enough not to leave an enemy alive who might one day rise up against you again.

The world was appalled at the slaughter taking place when Serbia invaded Bosnia and Croatia, especially after stories of mass rape and torture started filtering out.[257] Not that anything in the world could justify such horrors, however, as the modern saying goes: *"Payback's a bitch!"*

Lest we forget: Five decades earlier, during WWII, the Bosnians and Croats had sided with invading Germans, helping Nazis rape and torture, and slaughter Serbs. Fifty years later, the sons of those wronged Serbians—and even some old Serb WWII survivors—finally got their revenge.

And, speaking of *der* "Little Corporal," Hitler first attempted to take over Germany by force with his ill-fated "Beer Hall Putsch." For this failed coup, he served only a few months in prison—just enough time to write *Mein Kampf*, his blueprint for conquest once released. Had the Germans imposed harsher punishment on Herr Hitler—at the very least longer imprisonment, or perhaps even execution . . . a moot point.

And yes, we should have killed Osama Bin Laden when we had the chance, long before 9/11. Woulda, shoulda, coulda.

Ever wonder why that crazy guy with the green hair and the white clown face doesn't just put a bullet in the head of that bat-eared dark knight, the same caped crusader he somehow manages to capture at least once every comic book? Let's be logical, instead of strapping the masked man to some complex, convoluted clown contraption that you just know he's gonna find a way to escape from using some really cool device from his trusty utility belt—instead of that happening again and again and again, why not just put a few cents worth of lead in his brain-pan? So why does the crazy clown keep making the same mistake over and over again—letting his arch-enemy live?

Hello! Because he's *crazy!*

Try not to be crazy. Don't joke around when it comes to bashing your enemy's balls in. That's what bats were made for!

In wildness is the preservation of the world.
—Henry David Thoreau

---

257. See *Theatre of Hell: Dr. Lung's Complete Guide to Torture* (Loompanics Unlimited, 2003).

17.

Steel Lessons:
What Would Stalin Do?

One does not become an emperor, one does not subjugate all one's
rivals, without having reasoned clearly.
—**Voltaire**

IN THE BOOK *A Ranking of the Most Influential Persons in History* (1985), Joseph Stalin is ranked lowly #63, with the following comment

> The outstanding characteristic of Stalin's personality was his total ruthlessness. No consideration of sentiment or pity seems to have influenced him in the slightest. He was also an intensely suspicious person, verging on paranoia. He was, however, an immensely capable man: energetic, persistent, and shrewd, with an unusually powerful mind.

This is hardly fitting, considering that Joseph Stalin is arguably the single most influential figure of the twentieth century. Yet even when they compile a list of the most influential persons of just the twentieth century, Stalin still doesn't get the respect—and fear!—he deserves. That's because we'd like to think the most influential person of the twentieth century was one of the "nice guys": Gandhi, Martin Luther King, John F. Kennedy, or at least Bill Gates.

But even if we narrow it down to a list of only the "bad guys" in history, or the twentieth century alone, Stalin still always gets eclipsed by Hitler.

Historians conveniently forget:

- Stalin took power long before Hitler.
- Stalin outlived Hitler, surviving him by eight years.
- Whereas Hitler died by his own hand, after the collapse of the Third Reich, Stalin died in his bed, still ruling half the world.
- In the end Stalin had a higher body count than Hitler—and that means a lot when they're passing out the "Dictator of the Century" plaque.

Here was a man who not only survived, but also prospered through World War I, the Russian Revolution, and subsequent Russian civil war, World War II, and the Korean War—which only came to an end with his death in 1953.

Today the North Korean "threat" looms large, but few remember that Stalin was the one who put the North Korean Communist regime in power at the end of WWII.

THE MAN

Stalin had little personal charm, and could be brutal to even his closest friends. He seemed unable to feel pity. He could not take criticism, and he never forgave an opponent.
—Albert Marrin[258]

You don't have to embrace Stalin's politics—or even like the man—but give credit where credit is due. There are many lessons to be learned from the man, from studying his life, his survival skills, his political acumen— hard lessons . . . "Steel Lessons."

Stalin was always looking for an edge. For example, at one point he tested psychic Wolf Messing to see if Messing's "powers" could somehow be harnessed as a weapon.[259] In fact it was during Stalin's rule that the Soviet

---

258. World Book, 2005

259. See *Black Science* (Paladin Press, 2001) and *Mind Manipulation* (Citadel, 2002).

Union began seriously investigating the potential of adapting psychic powers (ESP) for military use.[260]

Despite his constant searching for new ways to extend his reach and exercise Ultimate Control over his enemies, all agree that the two weapons that Stalin already had in his arsenal—weapons he was a master at wielding—were violence and terror.

He has accurately been accused of committing, and later authorizing, wholesale atrocities. However, similar accusations of his resorting to "random violence" against his foes simply aren't true.

Any violence on Stalin's part was *deliberate, and directed,* toward a specific target.

There's a misperception that using violence willy-nilly will make a dictator (or your office boss) greatly feared.

While true that unexpected acts—especially violent ones—make people fearful, "random" acts of violence can backfire on the perpetrator since now *everyone* feels they're in the crosshairs. As a result, former, even long-time enemies begin to bond together against you because you have given them a common identity ("We have to stick together 'cause we're all targets!"), uniting them in "common cause"—against *you!*

If, on the other dictatorial hand, specific acts of violence—"surgical strikes"—are directed towards specific individuals or against specific groups, then individuals will (1) naturally—consciously or subconsciously—divorce themselves from a targeted person or populations ("They *must* have done something to deserve it!"). Thus you keep potential enemies separated.

And (2), individuals and groups will curry your favor by informing ("ratting") on one another and/or acting as your bludgeon with which to beat their fellows just to keep their own head off the chopping block. Divide and conquer.

The man we know as Stalin seems to have known this intuitively from a young age.

Born Iosif Vissarionovich Djgashvili, in the Russian state of Georgia, Stalin's peasant father was a failure and a drunk, but the son was literally a born survivor—three of his siblings died shortly after birth. He himself survived potentially deadly smallpox at age six. Not content with the hand

---

260. Ostrander and Schroeder, *Psychic Discoveries Behind the Iron Curtain* (1970).

fortune dealt him at birth, as he grew, Stalin reveled in physical labor, making himself strong, constantly training himself against pain.

Entering his teen years, he began studying for the priesthood in Tbilis, capital of Georgia—the only way someone of his lowly social status could afford an education. It's a myth and a propaganda prejudice that Stalin was stupid and slow. By all accounts he was a bright student.

Caught up in the revolutionary fervor spreading across Europe in general and Mother Russia in particular, he left the seminary and began writing articles for a Georgian Marxist journal called *Brdzola* ("The Struggle"). Years later he would serve as editor for the Marxist newspaper *Pravda* ("Truth") writing under the nom-de-guerre "Stalin," literally "Man of Steel." Later, in 1923, he would tell his fellow Bolsheviks: "Print is the sharpest and the strongest weapon of our party."

That hardly sounds like the resume of an illiterate peasant.

The game of radical politics always exacts a heavy price from its players. All told, Stalin spent seven years in prison between 1907 and 1917, escaping many times, including a daring 1904 escape from Siberia.

Unwilling to give Stalin credit for outwitting the *Cheka*, the Czar's police, time and again, some have speculated and suspected young Stalin of having been a double agent.

It is possible Stalin could have given up information—or even acted as an informant—for the Cheka. If so, given his later (mis)deeds, let us give him the benefit of the doubt that, far from being a turncoat, he may have been a triple agent—a false convert, funneling disinformation to the Cheka about his Marxist comrades while simultaneously infiltrating and giving accurate intelligence to the secret police on his political enemies. Thus:

Steel Lesson #1: **The enemy of my enemy is my friend.**

Steel Lesson #2: **Get a dog to eat a dog.** Nobody knows what a skunk's ass smells like better than another skunk.

Coincidentally, following WWI, Adolf Hitler had a similar job for German military intelligence investigating potentially bothersome political groups. This is how he first investigated, joined, and soon came to dominate the fledgling *German Worker's Party* . . . Later to become—under his dictatorship—The *National Socialist German Worker's Party*—the Nazis!

When Stalin first officially joined the Communist Party (Lenin's Bolsheviks), the snobby urban intellectuals running the show looked down their noses at this country bumpkin.

Steel Lesson #3: **It's a blessing when your enemies underestimate you.**

Sizing him up as a "street thug," they put him to work robbing banks, intimidating rival political parties, and committing the occasional assassination.

For his part, Stalin did a "Dale Carnegie," spending his time—in between terrorist acts—winning friends and influencing people in the street; using his time in the streets to toughen himself further, and to earn the respect—and fear—of other "country bumpkins" also relegated to the barricades and back-alleys.

It was around this time Stalin made friends, or at least allies, with Feliks Dzerjinsky, future Godfather of the KGB—as loyal and lethal a Polish pit-bull as ever there was.

Steel Lesson #4: **"You cannot make revolution with silk gloves."**

After suffering a series of strokes, Lenin increasingly came to depend more and more on Stalin's intelligence network to bring him "the word on the street." By then Stalin had what they nowadays call "street cred," meaning he'd literally bled at the barricades alongside other revolutionaries still fighting for control of Moscow streets.

Steel Lesson #5: Blood seeks blood. Men will bleed for you only when they see you're willing to bleed for them.

While others in Lenin's circle were spending all their time squabbling over who got what office in the recently-vacated Royal Palace, Stalin was busy building his power base.

Having come from peasant stock himself, he was accepted by the common people. He spoke their language and they respected—and feared—him, seeing he wasn't afraid to get his hands dirty—or bloody, figuratively and literally.

Steel Lesson #6: **The sharpest axe-blade isn't worth a damn without a hardy handle.** In other words, all the brains in the world doesn't mean squat unless you got some brawn to back it up.

Stalin had both the brains and the brawn. More important, he had patience.

Lenin's Bolsheviks finally clawed their way to power in 1920 after winning the civil war that had broken out following the 1917 Russian Revolution.

All this time, Stalin remained loyal to Lenin, doing his dirty work:

political opponents intimidated, bothersome people disappeared. Stalin honed his craft. Stalin bided his time.

Steel Lesson #7: Only patience can properly whet a blade.

For all his ballyhooed genius, Lenin was slow to realize that Stalin was so much more than a simple street thug until it was far too late in the game. Stalin's game.

Lenin survived several assassination attempts, only to succumb to a fatal stroke in 1924.

Word has it that, on his deathbed, Lenin wrote a letter *warning* the other members of the party about Stalin. A little too little, a *lot* too late.

Stalin intercepted the letter.

*Steel Lesson #*8: **Control the flow of information and your enemies will die of thirst!**

Having prudently positioned himself for the power struggle within the Communist Party he knew would be inevitable when Lenin died, before Lenin was even in the ground, Stalin had formed a "Troika" (Triumvirate) with two powerful Communist allies, Kanenev and Zinoviev.

*Steel Lesson #*9: **Make a show of sharing what little you have to get more of what you want.**

Together this Troika succeeded in beating out the faction of Lenin's *presumed* successor Leon Trotsky (1879–1940) for control of the Communist Party.

Trotsky was smart enough to read the writing on the wall—and his name on the list in Dzerjinsky's black gloved fist! Trotsky fled Russia. No sooner had Trotsky fled, than Stalin turned on the Troika—before they could turn on him.

*Steel Lesson #*10: **Dogs that bit their old master will not hesitate to bite their new one.**

By December 1929, the day the smoke cleared, Stalin was the uncontested ruler of the USSR.

*Steel Lesson #*11: **Practice patience on yourself, before practicing war on your enemies.**

Stalin knew all about those "sons of Brutus"—perhaps from reading Machiavelli?—and so sent agents to hound Trotsky to the ends of the earth. The ends of the earth turned out being Mexico sixteen years later where a Stalinist agent was able to lic his way into Trotsky's confidence long enough to cleave the expatriate's skull in two with an axe.

Steel Lesson #12: **"Sleep is never so sweet as when you have settled a score with an enemy!"** Stalin's words upon being informed of Trotsky's death.

Steel Lesson #13: **"No man . . . no problem!"** —Stalin

THE MASTER

During his life, Stalin made many alliances—some of which he broke even before the ink was dry. Like his deal with Hitler.

Steel Lesson #14: **Marriages of convenience make for strange bedfellows . . . and for very messy divorces.**

Politics indeed sometimes make for strange bedfellows. But somehow Stalin always ended up with all the covers, his "allies of convenience" left with but a sheet over their faces!

Upon taking power—in fact, throughout his reign—Stalin had to purge inner enemies, even when doing so made him more vulnerable to external foes.

In 1935, Stalin gutted the leadership of the Soviet Communist Party, purging anyone he suspected of not being one hundred percent loyal in a series of "show trials."

These show trials served two purposes, (1) terrorizing anyone even dreaming about moving against Stalin, and (2) showing the world that the Soviet Union had nothing to hide.

Of course, there's also the underlying threat: if this is how we treat Russians . . . imagine what we do to outsiders!

Stalin saw the looming WWII as an opportunity for the Soviet Union to seize more territory.

He signed a non-aggression pact with Hitler—both knowing the treaty wasn't worth the paper it was written on.

Stalin knew, sooner or later, Germany would invade Russia. Unlike so many "Huta"[261] politicos at the time, he'd actually taken time to read Hitler's Mein Kampf. Stalin's plan was to meet and beat Hitler's advancing army in Poland.

Steel Lesson #15: **Always fight in enemy territory.** If you win, you're

---

261. "Head up their ass"

already close to his women. Heh-heh-heh. If you lose, and have to with-draw, you leave *his* lands in ruin.

Once Poland was "saved" from the invading Hun, Poland would be "invited" to join the Soviet empire. By the end of WWII, a lot of other people would be "invited" to join the Soviet empire: Latvia, Lithuania, Estonia, Poland, East Germany . . . *ad nauseum*.

Stalin, an avid outdoorsman, was only following hunter's etiquette:

Steel Lesson #16: If you kill it, eat it! (Or, at the very least, drag it home as a trophy!)

Throughout WWII, Stalin was often criticized for taking credit for "win-ning" battles he had nothing to do with.

Steel Lesson #17: Always give credit where credit is due . . . and if you happen to see some credit just lying around, credit no one's using at the time, take *that* credit for yourself.

When Moscow was most in danger of being captured during WWII, Stalin ordered the government moved to Kuynyshev. But Stalin stayed in Moscow. We can draw two Steel Lessons from this example:

Steel Lesson #18: Always take time out to inspire the troops.

Steel Lesson #19: Don't leave a boiling pot unattended.

Stalin's power continued to grow after WWII. In fact, he came out of WWII one of the three most powerful men on the planet. Some would argue he was the most powerful, since those other two guys—Truman and Churchill—had to worry about being re-elected.

Feeling his oats, Stalin embarked on a campaign that amounted to world conquest: swallowing up Eastern Europe, while "adventuring" in Africa, Asia, and Central and South America. As already mentioned: Stalin enthroned the North Korean Communists regime. In fact, had the Russians not backed Mao's Communists in China, Mao may never have gotten the upper hand to seize power in 1949.

Also in '49, NATO was created to counter Stalin's aggressive policies.

Until his death—in bed—in 1953, he remained, if not the most pow-erful man on the planet, then at least the most feared.

THE MONSTER?

Ruthless or realist? Bloodthirsty or just power-hungry? Man or monster? To this day no one's certain how many deaths Stalin is "responsible" for:

- Personal enemies (He was a man who knew how to hold a grudge.)
- Political enemies (Just the cost of doing business.)
- War enemies—massacres carried out under Stalin's direct orders (e.g. the Katryn Forest Massacre of the entire Polish officer corp)
- Untold millions . . . And that's only inside the Soviet Union.

If we factor in Stalin's influence on conflicts in China, North Korea, and Communist insurgencies worldwide, repercussions still being felt . . .

Steel Lesson #20: **"A single death is a tragedy, a million deaths is a statistic."**

18.

Looking Out for Number One: Bring in the Ringer!

Forget foundationless traditions, forget the "moral" standards others
may have tried to cram down your throat, forget the beliefs people
may have tried to intimidate you into accepting as "right."
—Robert J. Ringer, 1977

ROBERT J. RINGER HAS BEEN HERALDED as "the modern Machiavelli." Strong praise indeed. Big shoes to fill—*ruthless* shoes. In both his 1975 best-seller *Winning Through Intimidation*, and his 1977 follow-up *Looking Out for Number One*, Ringer teaches us his practical "looking out for number one" philosophy, the backbone of which is that we can't help others unless we first put our own house in order. Yeah, I know. It says pretty much the same thing somewhere in the Bible, that part about not worrying about "the speck in your brother's eye until you get that beam out of your own"?

Ringer's version of this is just a whole lot more entertaining—and, oh yeah, unlike the Bible, *guilt-free!*

Ringer freely borrows from past masters, adopting and adapting age-old methods of mind control and manipulation, adding modern insights and his own unique twists-n-turns and switchbacks to these tried-and-true tactics and techniques. Ringer's overall philosophy:

Looking out for Number One is the conscious, rational effort to spend as much time as possible doing things which bring you the greatest amount of pleasure and less time on those which cause pain. Everyone automatically makes the effort to be happy, so the key word is "rational. . . ." To act rationally, and thus to experience pleasure and avoid pain on a consistent basis, you have to be aware of what you're doing and why you're doing it. If you are not aware, you're not living life; you're merely passing through. . . . Remember, looking out for Number One carries a heavy price: *conscious, rational effort*."[262]

This sounds a lot like the "Utilitarianism" of Jeremy Bentham (1748–1832), quote:

Nature has placed mankind under the governance of two sovereign masters, pain and pleasure. It is for them alone to point out what we ought to do, as well as to determine what we shall do . . . every effort we can make to throw off our subjection, will serve but to demonstrate and confirm it. In other words, a man may pretend to adjure their empire: but in reality he will remain subject to it all the while.

Just for the record, Bentham didn't judge the context of utility. Instead he considered pleasure to be a good thing whether derived from vice or from virtue.[263]

Maximize pleasure, avoid pain. Duh, doesn't take a genius to understand that equation. But it just might take a genius to pull it off. And, in his own way, Ringer is a genius.

This smacks of the "egoism" school of thought: "What is good for one's survival and personal happiness is moral." But in Ringer's world we have permission to be selfish:

From this day forward, no more cringing at the words *selfishness and self-interest*. —Ringer, 1977

---

262. *Looking Out for Number One*, 1977.
263. See Joycelyn M. Pollock, *Ethics in Crime and Justice* (1993).

At this point Ringer throws in a little Ayn Rand (*Atlas Shrugged*) assertion that "happiness is possible only to a rational man." Recall Ringer himself told us that the key word is "rational." So what we end up with is what Ringer calls "Rational Selfishness":

> If you're not basing your actions on rational choice, you're out of control, and anything out of control is dangerous to both itself and its surroundings. . . . Every person subjectively draws his own lines concerning what *is* and is not proper action, based either on his own moral standards, the moral standards of others, or what is convenient for him at the time of his action. —Ibid.

To accomplish our goal of complete world domination . . . Ultimate Control, uh, I mean "happiness," Ringer teaches us how to think rationally, how to control ourselves leading inevitably to the ability (and temptation?) to control the other guy. To accomplish this, Ringer's not afraid to take on—or at least caustically comment on—religion, government-too-big-for-its-britches, and society as a whole. And neither should we, any time we think one or more of them stand in the way of our "pursuit of happiness." Catchy phrase, "pursuit of happiness," seems like we've heard that somewhere before . . .

In a nutshell, Ringer is reinforcing what we've already come to recognize as "The Three Knows": Know yourself (strengths and weaknesses, wants and needs), Know your enemy (others), and Know the environment you're going to be operating in (society).

Sun Tzu and Ringer would have gotten along just fine . . . until Ringer tried selling him the Great Wall of China!

RE-EVALUATING EVERYTHING!

Using "The Ringer Method" we:

- **RE-evaluate** our lives, our modus operandi, looking for those flaws in ourselves and gaps in our battle plan; then we
- **RE-vamp** ourselves and our goal, to better reflect the realities of our current environment; and finally we

- **RE-turn** to the field of battle—or scene of the crime, as the case may be.

That's three "R"s and three "E"s, in case you were keeping count. Ringer cautions:

> Most people carry more baggage than necessary on their journey through life. And, like the airlines, Nature charges for excess baggage.

This is Ringer's way of telling us to "travel light," dragging behind us only those items necessary for success. But whatever our field of endeavor—wherever our battlefield, along with our toothbrush there are three essentials we must bring along: a grip on *reality*, *respect*, and our ever-developing taste for *ruthlessness*.

Ringer's Three "R"s

Reality (vs. Really-like-it-to-be)

By now you realize that our perception of reality isn't always to be trusted. Or, as Ringer observed, "Reality is a given; perception is the variable." He goes onto warn us:

> Avoid the pitfall of confusing the way you think things ought to be and the way they really are. Never be so afraid of the truth that you refuse to acknowledge it. How are you to deal effectively with facts if you deny their existence. . . . Proper assessment of reality can be *as* crucial to life as oxygen. To try to make it through this world without a reasonable understanding of reality is like stumbling around in a dark room laden with land mines.

This is the difference between objective "reality" and our sometimes skewed, always subjective "Really-like-it-to-be":

> Reality isn't the way you wish things to be, nor the way they appear to be, but the way they actually are. Either you

acknowledge reality and use it to your benefit or it will automatically work against you. . . . What will *always* be irrelevant
to reality are your wishes. When you allow your desires to
become confused with the fact, you're heading for trouble.

You get the idea that Ringer's "reality" and Machiavelli's "Fortuna" (fortune) went to the same high-brow finishing school?

Ringer recognized that "most people have a tendency to believe their
own bullshit." This harkens back to "Don't get high off your own supply."
Major Rogers' Rule #4.

Lie to everyone else but don't lie to yourself? Where have we heard *that*
before . . . Oh yeah, Sun Tzu, Musashi, Machiavelli, Rogers, Stalin . . .

Vacation anywhere you want. *Live* in reality. The better your grip on reality, the better your grip on your enemy's short-hairs!

Respect

> Respect is contagious. If you have self-respect, it's likely
> that you'll maintain the respect of others too. But if you
> lack it, certainly no one will be able to contract it from you.
> —Ringer, 1977

Living in reality will give you a clear assessment of yourself, leading to
self-respect. (Or else leading to obvious flaws in your personality and your
reasoning, causing you to improve yourself which, in turn raises your self-
esteem and self-respect.) True, realistic self-respect forces others to respect
you. I'm not seeing a downside here?

Respect your opponents . . . if only their ability to make you miserable.

A word of clarification on the difference between "respect" and "fear."
There's the thinnest of lines between the two:

Fear can have an element of respect in it. But respect can never be based
on fear.

Respect is based on *admiration* for another's actions and abilities.

You can respect the most inoffensive of men, but still not fear him. You
can fear the most belligerent of bullies, yet have no respect for him.

Learn from and treasure those things—and people—you respect.

Kill those things you fear.

Ruthlessness

> We sometimes lose sight of the fact that our primary objective is really to be happy as possible and that all our other objectives, great and small, are only a means to that end. To the degree we achieve our subobjectives, and to the extent these subobjectives are rational, we feel good. . . . Every man has the natural right to pursue his own happiness in any way he chooses and to retain ownership over all the fruits of his labor, so long as he does not forcibly interfere with the same rights of others. —Ibid.

Did you notice that word "rational" again?

We don't want to screw over the other guy . . . if you don't have to. But when the Machiavellian "necessity" arises that the only way to accomplish our goal is to use . . . pressure, to turn up the heat, instead of crying havoc and loosing the dogs of war, sometimes a little barking—backed by the promise of biting if it becomes necessary!—is enough to intimidate our enemy into complying.

Remember, Ringer literally wrote the book on *Winning through Intimidation*:

> Intimidation—motivation through fear—is an ever-present headgame played in a myriad of ways. If you give it some thought, you might be shocked to find that a large percentage of your actions are motivated by fear. You may be motivated by fear of physical harm, the fear of losing someone's love, or the fear of being embarrassed, to name a few. Some of these fears are valid, but most are not. It's the preponderance of unfounded fears which unnecessarily disrupts your life . . . All too often, we react like Pavlov's dogs and obey the commands of others at the mere sound of their voices. It can be a miserable existence; motivation through subtle intimidation can become such an accepted mode of life that an individual doesn't even realize he's a perpetual victim.

Ringer's Three "E"s

If you ever want to gain "Ultimate Control" there are three "E"s you have *no choice* but to first get control of in your own life—three *weaknesses* your enemies can use against you. On second thought, you do have a "choice" . . . if you consider *slavery* a choice!

- **Emotions:** Don't tell me you've already forgotten our old friends "The Five Warning F.L.A.G.S.?" *Fear, Lust, Anger, Greed,* and *Sympathy* ring a bell? Learn to control these emotions—yours and then your enemy's—and you control the game:

  > Be strong enough not to let emotion *sway* you. However, just because you're able to reason, don't make the mistake of assuming that the other guy will be logical too. The path to a happy life is jammed with irrational people who are ready, willing and able to do numbers on your head if you can't spot them. Don't assume that all those with whom you come in contact will act rationally; they won't. —Ringer, 1977

- **Excuses and Obstacles:** A fish in a bowl empty of objects will just float there. Put a rock in the bowl and the fish will swim around it all day. Sometimes the rocks in our lives turn out to be diamonds.

There's the old analogy of what one man calls a stumbling block, another man calls a stepping stone. One will perceive that "stumbling block" as an insurmountable obstacle and use it as an excuse to turn around and go home. The road of life *is* paved with many such stumbling blocks:

> Nothing *is* as easy to dwell on as an excuse, and nothing complicates life more easily. An excuse may be justified, but it has nothing to do with improving your life in the future. Directly or indirectly, an excuse represents something of the past. —Ibid.

So we've plenty of excuses for giving up, just as many as there are for not starting in the first place. Those who hold out hope for mankind would say this is a sad commentary on the human race.

But those diligently practicing ruthlessness, well on the road less travelled to Ultimate Control, will see the glass half full, since quitters and whiners, those with a ready-made excuse for every fart and failing in their lives are merely *less competition!*

And obstacles? Those are just fortune's way of spelling "challenge" and "opportunity." As Ringer reminds us, ". . . there's a big difference between hard and impossible." Success isn't for everyone, otherwise there wouldn't be something called "mediocrity."

In *Winning through Intimidation*, Ringer lets us in on his "Iceball Theory": Basically, in a few billion years the sun will burn out and Earth become an iceball. Encouraging, huh? But that's just Ringer's way of telling us (1) everything we sweat and stress-out about is ultimately futile, and (2) get your priorities in order. So why sweat the small stuff?

> Don't let your mistakes be your excuse for quitting. Everybody makes mistakes—you're allowed a few . . . just not the same ones: The bottom line is to keep moving forward toward the solution of your problems. If others make mistakes in judging you, that's their problem. It's also not unusual; people make mistakes every day. —Ibid.

Likewise, don't let fear of change hold you back.

No matter how "stuck in the mud" you are, no matter how much you seem to be spinning your wheels, tomorrow really is another day. Sure, it could be an even *worse* day—Dr. Lung and the Universe never make promises!

But, by the same token, tomorrow could be "The Day" you've waited for all your life, the day fortune lifts her skirt for you. (This would be a good time to review Machiavelli's tips for seducing—and surviving *relatively* unscathed—his "fickle whore" of a girlfriend!)

Change is scary, but change brings with it possibilities, opportunities . . . and yes, *dangers*. Ringer's got one for that too:

> The one absolutely predictable thing in life is that circumstances will always change. You can positively count on it.
> What is not known is *when* they will change.

In the end, life is all about family and friends. Yeah, I know: All that "Get rich and conquer the world!" stuff *is* fun, but that's just what we do in between home visits.

So do a Joseph Campbell and "follow your bliss."

- *Ego:* Ringer coined the term *"Egoruptcy"* to explain what happens when we invest too much time and capital in our own ego:

  > The biggest burden of all can be your ego, particularly if it controls you rather than the other way-around. In fact, it can be the most dangerous traitor in your camp.

Remember, before you feast on your own bullshit, be kind enough to offer your enemies a steaming plate full!

From appreciation to application, we have to make Ringer's three "E"s work for us by:

1. **Controlling our emotions**
2. **Discarding our excuses** and fearlessly forging ahead—over, and around, and, if need be, digging under obstacles
3. **Embracing our ego**—without squeezing it to death.

The bad news is there's a fourth "E" . . . *Enemy.* The good news: He's just as susceptible to The three "E"s as we *used to be.*

  > If calling them your "enemy" offends your sensibilities, call them "competitors" instead. For in truth, we are all in competition, each of us with our fellows. Oft times it is to our advantage to work together for the common good. Sometimes there really is safety in numbers. Other times, you're on your own. Root hog or die. Hell take the hindmost!
  > —Lung and Prowant, *Mind Control,* 2006

WATCHING OUT FOR NUMBER TWO(S)

As a general rule, a person's chances for success will tend to increase the more he's out of step with "society."
—Ringer, 1977

So if you're "Number One" in your life, who's "Number Two"? Everybody else. Especially your enemies.

Of course, you help your family and friends—once you get your own self together, of course. Beyond friends and family there's only competition. So you need to learn to do number two on the Number Twos in your life before they do likewise on you!

Other people seldom live up to our expectations. The best we can hope is that they'll remain so damn predictable as to make our job a whole lot easier. Ringer put it a little more diplomatically: "What man isn't is what you want him to be?" Or, as someone once said, "Hell is other people!"

When it comes to getting ahead, getting over, getting rich—and staying that way, there's "brothers" and there's "others." Most times it turns out your own best brother.

The shell is *not* the ready-to-be-born little chick's friend. What started out as a shelter—a safe, nurturing place for the embryo to grow— now threatens to become its tomb if the little chick doesn't peck its way free in time.

Likewise, we grow up in society, with society nurturing us, molding us to fit its template.[264] But, as we come into our own, what was once a nurturing womb—giving us room to grow, providing us protection from the elements—now begins to restrict us, confine us, both physically and emotionally. Suddenly our thoughts, our urges—our *need* to test ourselves against those elements—must be subjugated and repressed for the "good" of society. All the things we want—all the things society flaunts in front of our pimply face—are now either forbidden, or else come with puppeteer's strings attached.

What once nurtured us, now threatens to prune us before our flower fully opens.

Society has become the enemy, preventing the natural unfolding of our unique brilliance. (Cue Metallica's *"Unforgiven!"*)

"Society" is made up of: our noisy neighbor, our boss, religion, government, and those sinister special interest groups who will say anything, do anything (or anybody!) just to get their way. This is the all-powerful, all-knowing "They." The "They" everybody's always either cussing or else whispering about. "They"—pretty much lumped together as "the other guys"—are Nietzsche's "herd," and the "mob" Machiavelli distrusted.

Society—"They"—try to hold us back and hold us down—convinced in their collective mind that "They" are doing so for our own good. You know, the same attitude that slapped bras on all them native women. Same attitude (and bras), different day.

---

264. Except for those few of Dr. Arron Roy's students who were *raised by wolves!*

Never underestimate them. "They" are masters at using covert tactics and underhanded tricks, *subliminal suggestion* and *trigger words* to stifle us. And, when that doesn't work, they resort to good old-fashioned intimidation.

If your long-dormant "paranoia-gene" just kicked in . . . good! "They" have the power to take the money you worked so hard for—it's called "taxes" and "fines."

Piss them off and "They" leave you homeless, powerless, and scared shitless. Or "They" can just kill you—all legal and proper.

Yeah, "They" run something. But you don't gotta let 'em run *you*.

MYTHS "THEY" USE TO HOLD YOU DOWN

According to Joseph Campbell in his *A Hero's Journey* (1999), myths are a motivating force on this planet—perhaps *the* motivating force, affecting us both consciously and subconsciously: myths that sustain us when the harvest fails, myths that give us a good excuse to take the other guy's harvest. Myths that bind us together. And myths that breed nothing but conflict.

The definition of a "myth"?

> A traditional story that deals with supernatural beings, ancestors, or heroes that serve as primordial types in a primitive view of the world.
> —*Webster's II New Riverside Dictionary*, 1996

So there's nothing really wrong with myths . . . except for that "primitive view of the world" part.

Nothing wrong with myths, and legends, and traditions, even with beliefs[265] . . . until these "abstracts" threaten the real world—you know, preventing us from feeding *real* babies, stopping *real* wars.

Closer to home, we have to be aware (*beware!*) of the myths "They" use to stifle us:

The Myth of "Altruism"

---

265. Remember: You can't write "belief" or "believe" without sticking a "lie" smack dab in the middle.

Recall our agreement that "There's no such thing as altruism." One way or another, everybody gets paid, even if it's just that warm, huggy feeling that "I'm a nice guy."

Ringer doesn't seem to be very worried about being confused for "a nice guy":

> I have no desire to hand out love, friendship, money or any other valuable commodity indiscriminately to anyone who happens to cross my path. To do so would cheapen what I have to offer. Special things are for special people—those who really mean a lot to me. Remember in whose home charity begins. —Ringer, 1977

Something about not casting your pearls before swine?

Have you ever actually read "The Golden Rule"? It's a very selfish statement: I'm going to treat you like I *want* to be treated. It's an ideal predicated upon (1) what I *want* and, (2) what I *fear*—i.e. that you'll deliberately screw me over unless I treat you right.

The Myth of "Equality"

> "All men are created equal": Equal how? I won't insult your intelligence by explaining the obvious absurdity of this statement. —Ibid.

Somewhere between Sherlock Holmes and John Holmes, it dawns on you all men are *not* created equal.

The Myth of "Enemies"

Robert J. Ringer, one of the great minds of the twentieth and twenty-first centuries, informs us that one of the great minds of the seventeenth century, philosopher and mathematician Blaise Pascal (1623–1662) insisted that *all men by nature hate each other*.

This could be true. After all, we are all in competition with one another—it's just not as apparent and obvious as it was back in Og the caveman's primordial day.

Sometimes we invite people into our circle (and confidence) when it suits our purpose, e.g. makes us stronger and/or increases our chances of winning.

And you still can't figure out why someone would be your enemy?

> Why should someone have a desire to hurt you? There could be any number of reasons. He may envy you because of your achievements; he may be frustrated over his own low station in life: or he may be unfortunate enough to possess the traits of hatred, sadism or cruelty to an excessive degree.
>
> —Ringer, 1977

So, any way you look at it, you really *do* have enemies. It's just probably not the enemies you think. It's just more of "those other guys." So don't let some of "those other guys"—"They" again!—tell you a different faction of "those other guys" are your enemy. They're *all* "the other guys." The only thing different is the color of their flags.

Your friends pick you. Never let anybody pick your enemies for you.

The Myth of "Tradition"

> If past ideas contradict reality, logic or current circumstances, they must be abandoned without ceremony. —Ibid.

The Myth(s) of Religion

> If someone says that a particular belief is based solely on faith, then it's not a matter of tipping his hand, but an *admission* that he is not employing his reasoning power. Faith is the antithesis of logic. To base your behavior on faith can be sui-cidal, much like the drunk who, having faith that he will not be harmed, attempts to cross a busy freeway. On the other hand, "faith" supported by fact is not faith at all; it's confi-dence. It's blind faith that poses a danger.

Ringer wrote this 23 years before 9/11.

The biggest "myth" associated with religion is that we'd all kill each other if it wasn't for religion (e.g. threat of God's wrath, eternal damnation, that sort of thing) keeping us off each others' throats.

Sorry. There have been plenty of peaceful and productive societies down through history who haven't lived under an oppressive Inquisition-crazed theocracy, or under the condemning constant eye of "religious police." The truth of the matter is the threat of a policeman's nightstick and a prison cell is enough to keep most of us walking the straight-n-narrow.

As for "*The Separation of Church and State*": That's written on paper and not in most people's minds.

The Myth of Government

Way back in the Dark Ages, 1977, Ringer made this prophetic announcement:

> In this day and age, the government's mystique and sanctity
> are slowly disappearing.

As goes religion, so goes government. The claim that we need government (like we "need" religion) to take care of us, and to keep us from killing one another is cynical at best.

In this case "They" may be right however . . . but only because "They" are the ones who created—and maintained—the status quo in the first place:

> The plain truth is that Big Government is the most ominous
> obstacle in the path of the person seeking to look out for
> Number One. . . . To think of the government as some sort of
> sacred entity, then, is to believe that the human beings who
> actually comprise it are sacred. —Ibid.

The Myth of Getting Paid

> Winning awards can be a pat on the head for not having suc-
> ceeded commercially. What you must decide is whether you'd
> rather get patted or get paid. —Ringer, 1977

A check in your hand, let alone a promise, is *not* money in the bank. The only thing that's "money in the bank" is *money in the bank*! In *Winning Through Intimidation* this is the one thing Ringer emphasizes more than anything else: *Get paid!*

Remember, most accidents happen within a few miles of home, usually when you're on the way home. A check in your hand is not the same thing as money in the bank. A politician's promise, a confidence man's hearty handshake . . . both non-redeemable.

Sorry, by now we've all pretty much realized not even Social Security's going to be there when the time comes—when *our* time comes. Trust only cold hard cash in your hand . . . Better yet, go *gold!*

YOUR EDGE: MURPHY'S LAW REPEALED

This all sounds pretty dismal and discouraging, doesn't it? By now you're thinkin' the odds are stacked against you? Nobody gets out alive . . .

I'm sorry to say, that's a pretty fair assessment. But we do have someone in our corner: Murphy, of "Murphy's Law."

You remember Murphy's Law? Nature tattooed it on all your asses in indelible neon DNA:

NOTHING IS AS EASY AS IT LOOKS.

EVERYTHING TAKES LONGER THAN YOU EXPECT.

AND ANYTHING THAT CAN GO WRONG—DOES GO WRONG . . .

AND AT THE WORST POSSIBLE MOMENT!

That's the bad news. The good news, at least according to Ringer:

All Murphy really wants is a little respect. . . . Murphy doesn't play favorites, he treats us all sadistically.

Murphy is fortune's recently-paroled brother. It's nothing personal. Murphy's not that bad a guy. In fact, Murphy teaches us to think on our feet, to be flexible, to always keep a "Plan B" in our back pocket.

Murphy reminds us that "shit happens." But just because you slip and fall in it doesn't mean you should just lie there wallowing in it.

Didn't you get the latest Black Science Institute school memo:

There really *isn't* room for everybody. Nature's only passing the top ten percentage on to the next grade. *Complain less. Study harder!*

CONCLUSION

"Nature, and Nurture, and Nietzsche, too."

The sad truth is that most evil is done by people who never make up their minds to be either good or evil.
—Hannah Arendt

SOMEWHERE BETWEEN NATURE AND NURTURE and Nietzsche we all eventually find our way.

There's what you were born with—Nature.

There's what's taught and twisted into you in early life—Nurture.

And then there's Nietzsche—who says we needn't remain prisoners nor become perpetual victims of either of those first two.

For Nietzsche, we all start out with the same basic stuff of life—clean slate. It's what you choose to write on that clean slate that makes you—and ultimately marks you—for who you truly are.

Ah, but without "Mama, Drama, and Trauma" to blame for all my moaning, groaning, and shortcomings, I'm left with no one but myself to blame—or to pat on the back?—for what I've become.

And, according to Nietzsche, what I ultimately become is what I *choose* to become. Can it really be that *that* easy? Or is Mr. Nietzsche just really *that* naïve?

He calls it "will to power." He claims we're all born with it, but that society—out of fear—does its best to breed it out of us. And, when that fails, to *beat* it out of us.

This "will to power" trumps both nature and nurture, or so Nietzsche claims.

But how are we to "turn on" this "will to power" gene? And what will we do with it when—if—we do?

"Will to Power" ultimately either makes you love yourself or else hate yourself.

You end up *loving yourself* for having embraced "will to power" fully, for having fully chased after and achieved "Ultimate Control" over your life. A pipe dream, you scoff? No one can ever have "Ultimate Control" over their life. Perhaps that's true . . . But it's definitely true for *you*, if you never try.

And if you never try or, worse yet, try only half-heartedly, then you only end up *hating yourself*, hating the world you've been born into (nature), hating the parents who did or didn't raise you (nurture), and hating uppity philosophers like Nietzsche for reminding you just how little you really matter to the world.

But "not to try" was your choice. You can always, any day, at any juncture of your life, choose the other path. You can choose to boldly lay claim to your Nietzschean birthright—your will to power and that promise of Ultimate Control.

Frightening? Yes! But fear has always stirred the blood more than anger and greed and even love. Fear is your friend. It'll get you up off your ass—fast!—where other emotions falter and fail.

So choose. For what is "choosing" but a single thought. With a single thought, a single trembling of some under-used portion of your brain, you can choose to change, choose to become what you were meant to become, and to exercise the amount of control over your life you were meant to control—*Ultimate Control*!

Ah, to truly exercise the mind. Sweet sweat of synapse! But before the *exercising* of the mind comes the *exorcism* of the soul—casting off the demons of both nature and nurture in order to embrace your inner Nietzsche.

> *Man is ultimately self-determining. What he becomes—within the limits of endowment and environment—he has made out of himself.*
> —Victor E. Frankl, *Man's Search for Meaning*, 1973

GLOSSARY

Amettori-jutsu: (Jp.) "a man of straw." Encompasses all tactics and techniques of deception. The name comes from the ploy of dressing up a scarecrow to make an enemy think it is a real sentry or soldier.

ASP: "Additional Sensory Perception." The full use of our five senses that give the impression to others we possess a "sixth sense," i.e., "ESP."

Assassins: Medieval Muslim secret society noted for its terror, treachery, and mind-manipulation techniques.

Atari-kokoro: Japanese mind-mastery techniques. (See Kiai-shin-jutsu)

Autogenic: Self-generated therapies (e.g. biofeedback, self-hypnosis, meditation, autosuggestion), coined by Zafutto and Zafutto, 1974.

Banking: Holding back valuable and/or damaging information (indiscretions, faux pas, etc.) you've discovered about a person for use in blackmailing and/or disgracing them at a later, more opportune time.

Big Brother: Oppressive government, always watching. Coined by George Orwell in his 1948 novel: *1984*. (See "Orwellian.")

Biometrics: System of scientific measurement of body parts and actions designed to give insight into intent (*See Tells.*)

Bio-resources: People whose talents you can utilize to accomplish your goals.

Black curtain, the: (Jp. *Kuromaku*, lit. "string-puller") Generic, the veil of secrecy and skullduggery a sinister cadre hides behind. Synonym for "smoke screen." Specific, the head of a Japanese Yakuza crime family. (See *Iluminati, Synarchy.*)

Black science, the: Generic, any strategy, tactic, or technique used to undermine a person's ability to reason and respond for themselves. Generic: Synonym for mind control and manipulation. First coined by researcher C. B. Black.

Bloodties: Dangerous and damaging information we hold over another. (See "The Killer B's.")

C.H.A.O.S. principle, the: "*C*reate *Ha*zards (Hurdles, Hardships, etc.) *A*nd *O*ffer *S*olutions," i.e. profiting from difficulties and "crises" you have secretly created.

Cheng and chi: (Ch.) "direct" and "indirect" (i.e., sneaky) actions. Also spelled Zhing and Qi.

Cognitive dissonance: Mental anxiety created when a person must reconcile their contradictory ideas and/or actions.

Cult-speak: Special passwords and coded phrases cults and cliques use to identify one another while marginalizing "outsiders."

"Cutting-at-the-edges": Coined by Miyamoto Musashi (1594–1645). When a powerful enemy cannot be attacked directly, undermine his confidence and ability to fight by attacking and otherwise eroding his "comfortzone" and support network (e.g. family, friends, and financial resources).

Dim-mak: (Ch.) Death touch.

"Dropping lugs" (aka "Lyin' by Implyin'"): Using innuendo and rumor to plant doubt and seed suspicion, especially intended to undermine another's credibility.

Dyshemism: Words used as weapons. (See "Word Slavery.")

Ekkyo: (Jp.) Divination methods that allow us to determine a victim's birth order and examine their interactions with others, especially close relatives.

ESP-ionage: Research and/or application of "Extra Sensory Perception" to gather intelligence, e.g., when spying. (aka *Psi*-War, not to be confused with *PSYWAR*, synonym for psychological warfare in general.)

Finders: *The International Finders*, European freemason-esque secret society, linked to the *Illuminati*.

Five Warning F.L.A.G.S., the: The five Gojo-goyoku weaknesses: Fear, Lust, Anger, Greed, and Sympathy.

Gojo-goyoku: (Jp.) "Five Element Theory." Derived from the Chinese pseudo-science of wu-hsing, which teaches that all reality (including actions and attitudes) is composed of five basic forces: earth, air, fire, water, and void. In all things and all times, one of these elements is dominant. Each element has a corresponding element in opposition to it. See "The Five Warning F.L.A.G.S."

Gray talk: Words and phrases deliberately crafted to confuse the listener.

Hyori: (Jp.) "Deception."

Illuminati, the: Generic, the ultimate secret society bugaboo and boogeyman. Whispered about for centuries, the Illuminati reportedly controls the world economy and pulls the "strings" of world politics from behind the "Black Curtain." Specific, secret society in Bavaria circa 1776.

In-yo-jutsu: (Jp.) Tactics designed to "unbalance" an opponent, to sow doubt and distrust in his mind.

Jodomon: (Jp.) "The way of the cat." Individuals who take this approach depend on tariki ("another's power"). (See *Shodomon*.)

Jomon-jutsu: (Jp.) Use of special words and phrases designed to affect an individual's emotional stability, for example words evoking fear, lust, or patriotism.

Jujushin: (Jp.) Identifies "ten Minds," or ten levels of understanding and functioning into which human beings can be categorized.

Junishi-do-jutsu: (Jp.) Employing the ancient art of Chinese astrology to determine a person's overall temperament as well as his weakest time of the day, when he is most susceptible to physical attack and mental manipulation.

Kami: (Jp.) Spirits, ghosts.

Kiai-shin-jutsu: (Jp.) Tactics and techniques that directly attack the intended victim psychologically by "shouting" into his mind. (See *Atari-kokoro*.)

Ki-dol: (Jp.) The ability to wield *ki* (Ch. *Chi*) force to influence and overpower another, e.g. especially through hypnosis.

Killer B's, the: Techniques for infiltrating an enemy's mind: Blind; Bribery and Blackmail; Bloodties; Brainwashing; Bully; and Bury.

Kuniochi: (Jp.) A female ninja.

Kuroi-kiri: (Jp.) "The Black Mist," confusion in general.

Kuro-kakure: (Jp.) Skullduggery in general, a dark and hidden agenda.

Kuromaku: (Jp.) lit. "a string-puller," originally from Kabuki. 1.) A Yakuza chief. 2.) See *the Black Curtain*.

Kyonin-no-jutsu: (Jp.) using an enemy's superstitions against him.

Makoto: (Jp.) "The stainless mind." Makoto is a balanced state of mind allowing us to remain calm even in the most trying of circumstances. The development of makoto consists of the active cultivation and practice of two skills: *haragei* (awareness), and *rinkioken* (adaptability).

"Mama, drama, and trauma": Slang term for the "nurture" influences in a person's life (as opposed to the "nature" influences).

Masakatsu: (Jp.) "By any means necessary." Strategy that allows for the use of any tactic or technique in order to achieve your goal, i.e., the end justifies the means.

Mekura: (Jp.) The "inner eye," i.e., insight and intuition.

MindWar: Preemptive measures (propaganda, etc.) used to attack an enemy's mind, intended to sap his will to fight *before* physical war becomes necessary. Sun Tzu's ideal.

MK: Spook-speak for "mind control." Coincidentally, these same initials are used to identify the MERCK pharmaceutical company rumored responsible for helping government agencies develop cogniceuticals. (See "Spook-speak.")

Mushroom treatment, the: Overall strategy for dealing with enemies (i.e., "Keep 'em in the dark and feed 'em plenty of bullshit!"), that is (1) deny them access to true information, while you (2) feed them disinformation.

Ninja: (Jp.) "to steal in." Assassin-spies (aka Shinobi) originating in medieval Japan, known for their stealth and skullduggery. Generic, anyone who employs stealth and secrecy to accomplish their ends.

One-eyed-snake: This strategy was comprised of tactics and techniques intended to give outsiders the illusion the ninja possessed true magical powers, e.g. the power to strike down a foe from afar using ESP, kill with a single touch without so much as a mark left on the victim (*Dim mak*), and control others with mystical hypnosis. (See: Yugen-shin-jutsu.)

Pakua: (Ch.) The "Eight Trigrams." Pakua are eight symbols, consisting of three lines each. Each symbol represents one of eight basic relationships and interactions of life. Sometimes spelled *Baqua.*

Plausible deniability: Spook-speak for being somewhere else when the fecal matter collides with the oscillating rotor. (See "Spook-speak.")

Propaganda: Rumor's big brother, or Big Brother's rumor.

Propheteering: The Cult Game. Generic, hiding behind religion for deceitful and devious purposes.

Psychotronics: Any electronic device used to enhance or entrance the mind. In the 1970s Czechoslovakia "psychotronics" was used as a synonym for "parapsychology." (Ostrander and Schroeder, 1970)

Ronin: (Jp.) A masterless samurai. Generic: a rogue

Satsujin: (1) Jp. "insight" (See *Tells*), (2) one of four divisions of Yakuza crime strategy, meting out "murder."

Satsujin-jutsu: (Jp.) insights into the minds or natures of men.

Seishinshugi: (Jp.) literally "mind over matter."

Sennin: (Jp.) master mind manipulators, "Mind Assassins."

Shadow-talk: Akin to Freudian slips. See "Tells."

Shadow-walk: See "Tells."

Shinjiraren!: (Jp.) "It boggles the mind!" Exclamation used when amazed and/or confused by something. Generically, techniques designed to amaze and confuse.

Shodomon: (Jp.) "The way of the monkey," depends on jiriki ("one's own strength"). Individuals with this approach to life are independent; journeying alone, finding their own way; keeping their own counsel; and binding their own wounds—both physically and psychically. On the one extreme, these kinds of people are rugged individualists. At the opposite extreme, they are stubborn isolationists and control freaks, unable to take another's counsel. (See *Jodomon*.)

Siddhas: (Skt.) Enhanced powers of mind and body claimed by Hindu yoga mystics and fakirs. Sometimes used as the name for such masters themselves.

Sons of Brutus, the: Those elements (primarily people) left over after an operation (e.g. palace coup, hostile corporate takeover) that may prove "troubling" (i.e. seek revenge!) at some future date. According to the Romans (and Machiavelli) prudence calls for this element to be completely eliminated.

Spook-speak: Euphemism and code words used by intelligence agencies.

Suggestology: The science/art of suggestion. Includes and/or touches on hypnotism, the power of persuasion, propaganda, etc. Coined by Dr. Gregori Lozanov, Bulgaria. (See: Ostrander and Schroeder, 1970.)

Tantric: (Skt.) "Forbidden." Taboo mystical practices (drugs, sex, nigromancy, etc.) used by Hindu mystics as a shortcut to enlightenment and siddhas. Also spelled Tantrik.

Tells: Twitchin', itchin', and bitchin' body language and speech faux pas that inadvertently reveal what a person is *really* thinking and/or may reveal a person's unconscious desires and fears. Also known as "shadow-talk" and "shadow-walk."

Ten Minds, the: Buddhists use each of the "ten Minds" (jujushin) as stepping stones to enlightenment. For ninja, on the other hand, the jujushin was just another stumbling block to place in the path of a foe. These Ten

Minds are: Goat's Mind, Fool's Mind, Child's Mind, Dead Man's Mind, No-Karma Mind, Compassionate Mind, Unborn Mind, Single-Truth Mind, No-Self Mind, and Secret Mind. Each of the ten Minds contains the seed of the others.

Thought Reform: Brainwashing by any other name.

Wa: (Jp.) Your spirit, presence, or intention.

Warning Flags, the: The five weaknesses: Fear, Lust, Anger, Greed, and Sympathy.

Word slavery: The deliberate use of words and language to control and/or otherwise influence another human being. Includes the use of subliminals, culturally taboo words, slur-words (insults) and purr-words (lulling and soothing words).

Wu-hsing: (Ch.) "The Five Movers." This concept maintains that all reality is made up of five basic elements: earth (chi); air (fu); fire (la); water (sui); and void (ku).

Yakuza: Japanese "Mafia."

Yugen-shin-jutsu: (Jp.) Literally "mysterious mind," uses various methods of hypnotism and subliminal suggestion to influence and control the minds of others.

Zen-zone: That level of functioning where stainless mental awareness (see *Makoto*) and physical awareness merge, allowing us to instantly and effortlessly adapt to rapidly shifting circumstance.

Zetsutjin: (Jp.) "offspring of a talkative tongue." An accomplished talker and manipulator, a mastermind.

Zhing and Qi: See *Cheng and Chi*.